THE**DUCATI**STORY

THE**DUCATI**STORY

Racing and production models from 1945 to the present day

IAN FALLOON

FOREWORD BY ING. FABIO TAGLIONI

3RD EDITION

Haynes Publishing

First published by Patrick Stephens Limited in 1996
Reprinted in February 1997
Reprinted in July 1997
Second edition published by Haynes Publishing in August 1998
Third edition published in February 2000
Reprinted March 2003

British Library Cataloguing in Publication Data
A catalogue record for this book is available from the British Library

ISBN 1 85960 668 7

Library of Congress catalog card no. 99-80194

Published by Haynes Publishing,
Sparkford, Yeovil, Somerset, BA22 7JJ, UK
Tel: 01963 442030 Fax: 01963 440001
Int. tel: +44 1963 442030 Fax: +44 1963 440001
E-mail: sales@haynes-manuals.co.uk
Web site: www.haynes.co.uk

Haynes North America, Inc.
861 Lawrence Drive, Newbury Park,
California 91320 USA

Printed and bound in England by J. H. Haynes & Co. Ltd.

Contents

Foreword by Ing. Fabio Taglioni   6
Introduction and Acknowledgements   7

Chapter 1   Origins   9
Chapter 2   Desmodromics   17
Chapter 3   Production Overhead Camshaft Singles (Narrow-Case)   22
Chapter 4   Oddballs   29
Chapter 5   Desmodromics Reborn and the Wide-Case Singles   36
Chapter 6   The Birth of the V-twin: The 750 Round-Case   44
Chapter 7   Imola and the Desmodromic 750   55
Chapter 8   Production Mainstays   69
Chapter 9   The Isle of Man and the Mike Hailwood Replica   81
Chapter 10   The Pantah: 500SL and 600SL   94
Chapter 11   Racing Pantahs and the 750F1   102
Chapter 12   The Cagiva Take-over   114
Chapter 13   The 851: Four Valves and Water-cooling   129
Chapter 14   American Buy-Out   152
Appendix   Ducati Motorcycles 1952–2000   175

Index   183

Colour Section between pages 96 and 97

Foreword

When Ian Falloon asked me to write the introduction to his new book on the history of Ducati motorcycles, I was delighted to oblige. He and his wife visited me at my home in Bologna where we discussed many details about the history of the company and my designs.

When I started at Ducati in 1952 the only development work that was being done was on the Cucciolo, but as I began my collaboration with the company and started on my first projects, the work on the Cucciolo was suspended. The first Ducati motorcycle design of mine to be built was the 100 cc Marianna, then the 125, 175, 250 and 350, all with a single overhead camshaft. My final designs were the Pantah series 500, 600, 750, 850, 900, until the 955, all unequalled and memorable because they have been the only engines to use the indestructible desmodromic valve system.

My best motor, and the best looking motorcycle, was the 750 twin, made world famous by many Italian riders such as Bruno Spaggiari, and foreigners Paul Smart and Mike Hailwood. Nearly all the riders of the racing Ducatis were excellent, and enthusiastic, because these motor-cycles fulfilled their ambitions. They gave everything, and I tried to contribute by giving them the best equipment possible.

I have designed many motorcycles over my 40-year period at Ducati, and all have gone into production except the 1,000 cc V Four, which was considered too expensive.

I hope Sig. Falloon has a lot of success with this book.

Ing. Fabio Taglioni
Bologna
October 1995

Introduction and Acknowledgements

For the best part of my adult life I have had an association with Ducati motorcycles bordering on the obsessional. There is no rational explanation for it, and I have been badly hurt crashing them, but the seduction of their superb engineering and their excellence as motorcycles persists. However, not all Ducatis are great motorcycles, and in this story, while endeavouring to document most models, I have also made judgements regarding their relative excellence or historical importance. More than most manufacturers, Ducati has had peaks and troughs, and this is largely part of their appeal. The Japanese or Germans rarely build a bad motorcycle, but then their products seldom achieve the level of inspiration that is found in the best Ducatis. The peaks are undoubtedly associated with racing success, either directly with the actual bikes themselves, or the spin-off with street versions of race replicas. The troughs occurred when the bureaucrats, rather than the engineers, decided what the public wanted. This happened more than once, but throughout the history of Ducati it was the conviction and brilliance of Fabio Taglioni that kept the company on the right track. It is no coincidence that Taglioni has been associated with all the peaks, including the most recent successes.

The constraints of this book have been such that inevitably there will be exclusions. There are just too many models for them to be detailed individually, and I have concentrated on the more recent history because the earlier period has been comprehensively covered by other commentators. Only the motorcycles from Bologna are covered, and the racing bikes are either the factory bikes or particularly significant privateer machines. The plethora of Ducati singles, both four- and two-stroke, overhead valve and overhead camshaft, have by necessity been covered only briefly, and not exhaustively. They have an historic importance, but to most enthusiasts they are not as relevant as the later twins, and I have concentrated on those particular models that I feel are of more historical interest. I apologise to any singles fanatics who feel that their bikes are hard done by. While I have endeavoured to be as accurate as possible, often factory power and weight figures are conflicting, a scenario that has existed from the first Ducati motorcycles and continues today. Therefore I have aimed for consistency in quoting figures, generally using workshop manual data in preference to that from brochures.

This book would not have been possible without the help of many Ducati enthusiasts around the world, and I would like to thank everyone who has supported this project: from Italy, my good friend Maurizio Bavaresco, of the Bikers' Restaurant at Valle San Liberale; Ing. Fabio Taglioni, and his wife of 50 years, Narina, who entertained us so lavishly at their home in Bologna; Nadia Pavignani, of Ducati's Public Relations Department; Virginio Ferrari, who gave me valuable time during a World Superbike race meeting; and another enthusiastic friend, Gerolamo Bettoni. In Germany: Rolf im Brahm, who was happy to let me use his magnificent range of photographs from ten years of Ducati Calendars; Hartmut Snoek for his help and encouragement; and Thorsten Schulze. Phil Schilling in the US has been most enthusiastic, and Art Friedman from *Motorcyclist* magazine helpful with photos. In Australia the editors of *Streetbike*, Bob Guntrip, and *Australian Motorcycle News*, Ken Wootton, who both allowed me access to their photographic archives, while Shane McCartin provided me with copies of his collection of early Ducati brochures, and Rick Begg many useful photographs.

For the 2nd edition many people at Ducati were forthcoming with assistance. Federico Minoli, Ing. Massimo Bordi, Pierre Terblanche, and Ing. Andrea Forni were particularly obliging with information about new models and the direction of the company. In the Public Relations Department, Paolo Ciabatti, Silvia Frangipane, Eliana Chieruzzi, Cristina Pitton and Daniela Riberti couldn't have been more helpful. David Gross and Kristin Schelter provided the details of the TPG involvement with the company. Finally, I must thank my wife Miriam, who has put up with the many hours of work, and constant Ducati conversation, not only during the first 18 months, but now also for this updated edition.

March 1998

1.

Origins

Back in 1922, when 19-year-old physics student Adriano Cavalieri Ducati was conducting his first experiments with radio, the production of motorcycles could not have been further from his mind. By 1924, from his house in Bologna, he had established radio contact with the United States, a considerable feat at the time, and on 4 July 1926, with his two brothers Bruno and Marcello, he set up a company called the Società Scientifica Radio Brevetti Ducati, building condensers and other radiographic components. While Adriano was a brilliant technician, Bruno assumed the role of manager and administrator, and Marcello that of designer. At this time Bologna was a centre of radio development, with

Guglielmo Marconi, the inventor of the radio, being one of Bologna's most famous sons. Under the fascist dictator Mussolini's policy of modernization, the Ducati brothers' business expanded considerably, and by 1935 they had acquired a new site at Borgo Panigale, an industrial district on the outskirts of Bologna.

On this site they built a huge modern factory to manufacture radios and electronic components, and the prosperity of the company was undoubtedly aided by Mussolini's interest in the widespread availability of radios to further his propaganda. By 1940 the Ducati company also had a large research department and had diversified to include optical and mechanical divisions alongside the

electronic, starting to produce cameras and lenses as well as cash registers and electric razors. Because Italy was largely untouched by the early years of the Second World War the company continued to grow, until the Italian government sought an Armistice with the Allies on 8 September 1943.

That was when things started to go wrong for the Ducati brothers. On the day after the Armistice, German soldiers commandeered the factory at Borgo Panigale, eventually transferring much of the plant and machinery to Germany. There was a further disaster on 12 October 1944, when Allied bombing almost destroyed the factory completely. After the war the Ducati brothers were briefly involved with Allied Naval Intelligence, but attempts to rebuild the company were stricken with financial problems caused by the expense of reconstruction and the general difficulties of the immediate post-war period. On 1 December 1947 the Società Scientifica Radio Brevetti Ducati went bankrupt. However, it was considered too important by the IRI (Istituto di Ricostruzione Industriale) to be allowed to collapse completely, and a joint Government and Vatican financial consortium came to its rescue in 1948, when control of Ducati passed from the brothers to that of the FIM (Fondo Industrie Meccaniche) and IMI (L'Istituto Mobiliare Italiano). Now under government control, the history of Ducati would be affected by a mixture of good and bad political decisions for the next 40 years. In the meantime the Bologna plant had been rebuilt

The three Ducati brothers in the 1980s: Marcello, Adriano and Bruno.

Aerial view of Ducati Meccanica, Borgo Panigale.

Ducati 18 x 24 mm 'Sogno' camera, c.1950. These came with Vitor interchangeable lenses.

Ducati Radio, c.1948.

and started producing 'Cucciolo' motors, condensers, cameras, and cinema projectors, while Milan became the centre for Ducati radios and electronics. The 18 x 24 mm format rangefinder camera, with its assortment of screw-mount lenses, was of particularly high quality, being hailed as a miniature Leica.

The Cucciolo

The 'Cucciolo' (or puppy) was an engine designed for Siata of Turin during the Second World War by a lawyer called Aldo Farinelli. 1945 was a very opportune time to produce such a motor: it was easily installed in a bicycle frame, thus providing cheap and economical transportation. Somehow, amidst the chaos of post-war Italy, the Borgo Panigale plant came to produce these engines, presenting their first example, the T1,

at the Milan Show in September 1946. Using the FIAT foundry at Cameri near Milan, the Cucciolo was so successful that it became the cornerstone of the Ducati company's revival.

The 48 cc four-stroke Cucciolo engine was intended as a cheap, reliable, and economical unit. With only a 6.5:1 compression ratio, the 39 x 40 mm engine, with its 9 mm Weber carburettor, could run easily on the post-war low octane fuel and provide exceptional fuel economy. Perhaps the most interesting feature of the engine was that the 12 mm valves were operated by pullrods rather than pushrods. Starting was by the usual moped method of pedalling while the engine was in gear, and there were two speeds, selected by the pedals via a handlebar mounted clutch lever.

By 1948, with the injection of capi-

tal from the new controllers, the Borgo Panigale plant had been rebuilt and was operating at increased capacity. Demand for the Cucciolo was so strong that a T2 was offered in two versions, Turismo and Sport. With capacity still at 48 cc, the Turismo was detuned slightly with a 5.5:1 compression ratio to produce a mere 0.8 bhp. The Sport retained the 6.5:1 compression of the T1, and power was up to 1.2 bhp at 4,250 rpm. The valve timing was very moderate, and not particularly accurate, with the inlet opening 5°–15° before top dead centre, closing 25°–30° after bottom dead centre, and the exhaust opening 45°–35° before bottom dead centre, and closing 0°–20° after top dead centre.

The T3, which appeared at the Milan Show of 1948, was almost identical to the T2 but with fully enclosed valve gear and a slight bore increase to 43.8 mm, to yield 60 cc. More importantly, this engine was displayed in an entirely new vehicle called the Girino, an unsuccessful three-wheeled device that gave Ducati the impetus to construct their own complete motorcycle. So, with no experience in motorcycle design and construction, they went into a partnership with Aero Caproni, a company that had built aircraft before and during the war but was looking to diversify. This appeared a strange choice, because Caproni were also totally inexperienced in the field of motorcycle design and only one 60 cc motorcycle arose from this alliance. By May 1950 Caproni decided to market their own machines in an expanding, but increasingly competitive market.

In order to maintain sales of the Cucciolo, Ducati supported an attempt on some 50 cc speed records at Monza in March 1951. Ugo Tamarozzi set 12 new 50 cc world records, returning two months later with co-rider Glauco Zitelli to achieve 20 more, notably the 12-hours' at 67.156 km/h (41.73 mph). Not content with these, a team of five riders took another 27 records in November, with Tamarozzi collecting the final two in January 1952. These 50 cc world records were to last five years, demonstrating to the public the

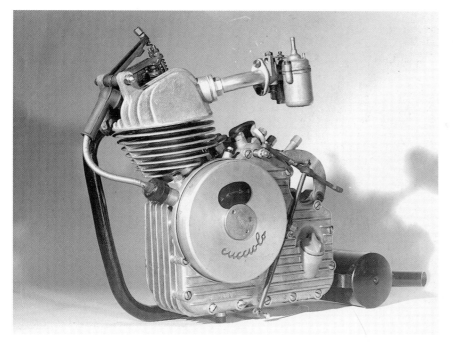

48 cc Cucciolo engine T1.

durability and reliability of the Cucciolo.

They also had the desired effect of keeping the Cucciolo in production for several more years, with small modifications. The final versions, the 55/r and 55/e, were marketed from 1954 as true mopeds, with leading-link forks and swinging-arm rear suspension. The power was now up to 1.35 bhp, but, with its popularity waning, the little Cucciolo was discontinued during 1956. Many thousands had been built over a ten-year period, and while not being of a particularly sporting orientation, they did much to establish the name of Ducati as a motorcycle manufacturer.

The First Singles

Even before the brief relationship with Caproni had soured, Giovanni Fiorio had designed another engine, a 65 cc four-stroke with pushrod-operated valves. Introduced in March 1950 and called the 60 Sport, it was the first real Ducati motorcycle. This engine would form the basis of a complete range of pushrod singles lasting through until the 125 Cadet of 1967. The 44 x 43 mm three-speed engine produced 2.5 bhp at 5,500 rpm, and soon became the 65TS. 1951 was a significant year for Ducati, with all production being concentrated at Borgo Panigale and the company headquarters moving from

The final Cucciolo, the 55E of 1956.

The 65 cc engine of 1952.
(Two Wheels)

Largo Augusto 7, Milan. In addition, in October that year Dottore Giuseppe Montano was made director. Montano, while a government appointment, was a motorcycle enthusiast and a racing supporter, and he could see the promotional benefits of a successful racing programme.

The 65 soon grew to 98 cc and was displayed at the Milan Show in January 1952 in two forms, the 98N and 98T (with twin seat). With a power output of 5.8 bhp at 7,500 rpm, this 48 x 52 mm engine with its 8:1 compression ratio was the most sporting Ducati yet. The 98s had a pressed-steel spine type of frame, telescopic forks, and swinging-arm rear suspension. With 17-inch wheels, their weight was 89 kg (196 lb) and they were good for 87 km/h (54 mph).

The other model displayed at the Milan Show was the complete antithesis, and ultimately a failure. Attempting to compete directly with Vespa and Lambretta scooters, the Cruiser, as it was known, was the world's first four-stroke scooter, with a 7.5 bhp 175 cc ohv engine designed

One of the first Ducati motorcycles, the 1952 65TL.

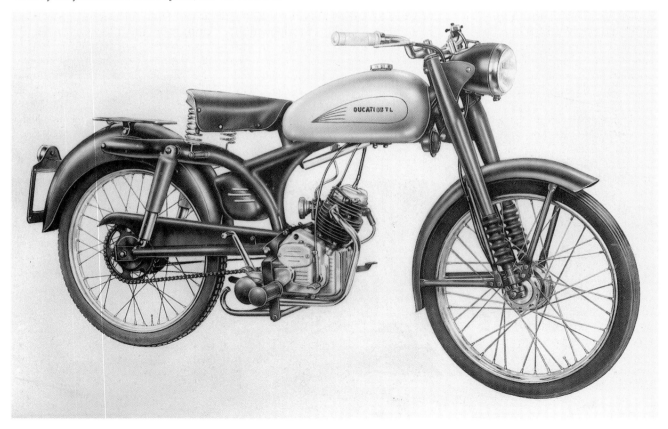

The disastrous Cruiser, the first of Ducati's mistakes.

The first sporting Ducati, the 98N of 1953. It has an oil-cooler in front of the sump.

by Fioro. Among the features of the Cruiser were an electric starter and an automatic gearbox, both contributing to its excessive weight and complexity. Within two years the Cruiser was dead, the first of several poor marketing decisions by Ducati, and one they would amazingly repeat in the next decade.

Both the 65 and 98 continued to be produced during 1953 and 1954, and the first more sporting model, the 98S or Sport, appeared at the Milan Show of 1953. This had a finned oil-cooler attached to the front of the sump and produced 6.8 bhp for a top speed of 90 km/h (56 mph). By this time Ducati Meccanica had been created as a separate organization alongside Ducati Elettrotecnica. They both still operated in Borgo Panigale, but in adjoining factories on a street renamed Via Antonio Cavalieri Ducati. (Antonio was the father of the three Ducati brothers and had been an eminent engineer and designer of water systems.) Ducati Meccanica gave Montano the opportunity to hire a new designer to spearhead a racing programme. He could see that the potential of the ohv 98 was limited as a competition design, so he looked at some of the other successful motorcycle manufacturers in Bologna and in 1952 found, at nearby Mondial, a 32-year-old engineer by the name of Fabio Taglioni. It turned out to be an inspired choice. Taglioni was a brilliant designer, and Montano gave him the freedom to develop his own ideas. It was also a bonus for Ducati. They

would now achieve results totally out of proportion to their size and influence, and eventually become the premier Italian motorcycle manufacturer. None of this would have been possible without Fabio Taglioni.

Fabio Taglioni and the Gran Sport

Born on 10 September 1920 and a graduate of Bologna University, Taglioni had been involved with the FB Mondial racing team. With designs by Alfonso Drusiani, Mondial had just won three successive 125 cc road-racing world championships, and Taglioni came to Ducati with impressive credentials. Montano decided that they needed a motorcycle capable of success in the important Milano–Taranto and Giro d'Italia races, so Taglioni set about designing a completely new, bevel-

gear driven, overhead camshaft engine that would not only be a successful racing engine, but would also provide a basis for future development. The 100 cc Gran Sport, nicknamed the Marianna, was an instant success and would be the foundation for a line of classic singles lasting two decades.

By February 1955 the prototype Gran Sport was being tested at Modena. One month later it was officially released, and a team was entered in the Giro d'Italia only a few weeks later. Gianni Degli Antoni easily won the 100 cc class for the nine-day event at an average speed of 98.90 km/h (61.5 mph). In its debut, the Gran Sport had performed beyond even Taglioni's expectations.

The reasons were not that difficult to see. From the outset the Gran Sport had been designed as a racing

Taglioni's first masterpiece: the 98 cc Gran Sport of 1955.

Gianni Degli Antoni prepares his Gran Sport for the 1955 Giro d'Italia.

engine of the highest quality and was of considerably more advanced specification than the Ducati ohv 98, or the Laverda pushrod ohv singles that had beaten them so convincingly in 1954. This approach would also serve Ducati well 30 years later, when they designed the eight-valve twin also as an uncompromised racing design that could be adapted for street use. By using bevel-gears to drive the overhead camshaft, Taglioni chose the best engineering solution, but it was an expensive one. Bevel-gears required careful manufacture and assembly, so the first Gran Sports were high-priced, limited-production racing bikes, albeit with a horn and headlight to comply with Italian FMI regulations.

Displacing 99.66 cc, the 49.4 x 52 mm Gran Sport, with its 8.5:1 compression ratio and 20 mm Dell'Orto carburettor, produced 9 bhp at 9,000 rpm. It featured many design specifications that would not only carry through to the production overhead camshaft singles, but also the later V-twins. Some, like the vertically split crankcases with unit gearbox and finned sump, along with the predominance of ball and roller bearings, are even present today in the Pantah and current eight-valve engines. The cylinder head had the same 80° included valve angle that would last until the Mille V-twin of

1985, as would the camshaft drive by a vertical shaft and bevel-gears from the right side of the pressed up three-piece crankshaft. Like all the ohc singles, the finned alloy cylinder was inclined forward 10°, but the Gran Sport had exposed hairpin valve springs with the cam box cast separately from the cylinder head. The bevel and primary gears were straight cut and the Gran Sport had a four-speed gearbox.

The frame was also a prototype for the range of Ducati singles that was to follow, in that it was a single down-

The 98 cc Gran Sport soon became a 125.

tube open cradle type using the engine as a stressed member. With 17-inch wheels and weighing a mere 80 kg (176 lb), the 100 Gran Sport had a top speed of 130 km/h (81 mph). Success continued for the Marianna in the Milano–Taranto road race of 1955, with Degli Antoni winning the 100 cc class of the 1,400 km event at 103.172 km/h (64.1 mph). This continued until 1958, when, because the Gran Sport had been so successful, the 100 cc class was scrapped altogether. Fortunately, Taglioni always envisaged a larger engine for his masterpiece, and even for the 1955 Milano–Taranto event had produced a prototype 125 Gran Sport.

The 125 was simply achieved by boring the 100 unit to 55.3 mm, and with a 22 mm carburettor 12 bhp was produced at 9,800 rpm. Apart from the use of 18-inch wheels and larger brakes, the 125 was very similar to the 100, and both continued into 1956 with moderate power increases (12 bhp for the 100 and 14 bhp for the 125). There was success again in the Giro d'Italia, with Giuliano Maoggi winning the event outright in 1956 on a 125. In the final Milano–Taranto race, once again both the 100 and 125 Gran Sports were dominant, Alberto Gandossi winning the 100 cc class at 99.744 km/h (62 mph), and Degli Antoni the 125 class at 103.176 km/h

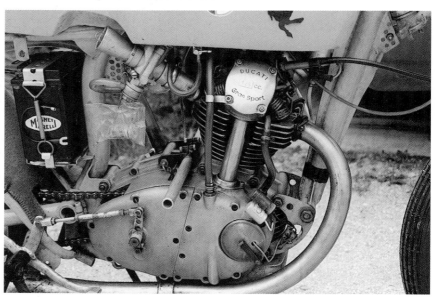

The streamlined Gran Sport of Mario Carini and Sandro Cicero, still maintained in its original condition.

(64 mph). As expected, the Gran Sport engine grew again during 1956 to 175 cc. By both boring and stroking the 100 to 62 x 57.8 mm, the 175 produced 16 bhp at 9,000 rpm, and was the prototype for the 1957 175 cc road bikes, 175 Bialbero, and the later Formula 3 bikes. Taglioni's influence was also becoming evident in the range of pushrod ohv bikes, most notably with the first sporting Ducati, the 98S of 1953. By 1956 this had a small fairing, and was joined by the 125TV with a full cradle frame. The 1956 98S in particular was a very purposeful-looking sporting motorcycle and headed the year's line-up of three 65 cc bikes (65T, TL, and TS) and four 98s (98N, T, TL, and S) alongside the 125TV.

The dominance of the 100 Gran Sport in its class was emphasized in November 1956, when the streamlined private machine of Mario Carini and Sandro Ciceri took 44 world records at Monza. Apart from a 25 mm Dell'Orto carburettor, the engine was standard and the bike was timed at an amazing 171.910 km/h (106.8 mph). The Marianna's reliability was displayed over the 1,000 km at an average speed of 154.556 km/h (96 mph).

1957 brought the first production overhead camshaft road bikes (covered in a later chapter), and not only the end of the 100 cc class, but also the final Giro d'Italia following the tragedy in the Mille Miglia car race only a week later when De Portago's Ferrari 315 ran off the road into the crowd after a tyre burst,

killing nine spectators. In this last Giro d'Italia, Graziano won the event outright, with Mariannas filling the first 12 places. While the single overhead camshaft racers were now superseded by the double overhead versions, there was still one important success left for the 125 Gran Sport, a clean sweep in the 1957 Barcelona 24

Hour endurance race. Here Bruno Spaggiari and Alberto Gandossi completed 586 laps at an average speed of 57.66 mph (92.8 km/h) on a bike intended for the cancelled Milano–Taranto race, with Gran Sports also filling second and third places. The following year Mandolini and Maranghi led home another Gran Sport dominated field: while the number of laps completed was identical, 125 cc Gran Sports this time took the first five places. The stage was set for Ducati's years of dominance in this esteemed event.

However, during 1955 Ducati had decided to contest the 125 cc Grand Prix class, and while the Marianna was ideal for street races and for establishing Ducati's reputation, a more sophisticated engine would be needed. Taglioni would also be given the opportunity to put into practice his idea for desmodromically-actuated valve operation, an idea that he had been working on since 1948.

Taglioni's 73rd birthday. Fabio and Narina Taglioni, with Mario Carini and Sandro Ciceri, at the Bikers' Restaurant in September 1993.

The first desmodromic Ducati, this 125 Grand Prix racer of 1956, demonstrated Taglioni's genius for seeking individual and unique engineering solutions. His commitment to desmodromic valve actuation was such that today every Ducati features it.

2.

Desmodromics

On 25 February 1956, barely one year after the debut of the Gran Sport, a double overhead camshaft version, the Bialbero, was unveiled. It was now Ducati's intention to enter not only the Italian modified sports class with this new racer, but also the World Championship 125cc Grand Prix. This was a massive step for a small company with little racing experience. The mid-1950s was a golden age for Grands Prix in all classes, and competition between MV and Mondial in the 125 class was fierce, with DKW, Montessa, and Gilera also vying for the victor's laurels. Essentially a Gran Sport apart from the cylinder head, the Bialbero was raced in the early Grands Prix of 1956, but with little success.

Fabio Taglioni astride the prototype fully-faired 125 GP, 1955.

While the Bialbero was significantly more powerful than the Gran Sport, initially producing 15.5 bhp at 10,500 rpm and soon increased to 16 bhp at 11,500 rpm, it was still no match for the MVs, let alone the Mondials and Gileras, and with sustained high revs its reliability suffered. The problems of valve float and the minimal valve-to-piston clearance meant there was no room for error if a rider missed a gear, so Fabio Taglioni sought to eliminate valve-springs entirely by a method of positive valve control – desmodromic valve gear. Mercedes-Benz had successfully used desmodromic valve gear on their W196 Grand Prix and 300 SLR Sports racing cars in 1954 and 1955, but apart from Mercedes only Taglioni has managed to make desmodromics work reliably and successfully.

Using the Bialbero engine from the cylinder head downward, Taglioni was able to create his 125 desmodromic racer in an astonishingly short time. Its debut at the non-championship Swedish Grand Prix at Hedemora on 15 July 1956 was one of Ducati's greatest race triumphs. Gianni Degli Antoni, on the fully-faired little desmo, easily won the 125 race, lapping the entire field. This was no hollow victory either, because the competition included a number of privately entered MVs and Mondials. While this first desmo wasn't significantly more powerful than the Bialbero, with 17 bhp at 12,500 rpm, it was the increase to over 14,000 rpm that the desmodromic system safely provided that had made the difference. A shortened big-end life was

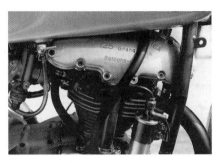

The DOHC Bialbero featured a distinctive cover for the set of camshaft drive gears.

the only price paid for exploiting this capability. Taglioni's desmodromic system differed from others in that it used three camshafts mounted in a magnificent one-piece cambox and cylinder head casting. As with the Bialbero, the opening camshafts were carried on the outer shafts, but the desmo's closing cams were mounted on the single central camshaft, operating the valves by forked rockers. The closing camshaft was driven by a vertical shaft and bevel-gear, this being geared directly to the two opening camshafts. The 31 mm and 27 mm valves were the same size as the Bialbero, but desmodromics allowed more lift, 8.1 mm for the inlet (up from 7.5 mm), and 7.4 mm for the exhaust (compared with 7.0 mm). Carburation was either a 27 mm Dell'Orto like the Bialbero, a 29 mm unit for faster circuits, or as small as 22 to 23 mm for the Italian street circuits.

Setting a precedent that would become a feature of all factory racing singles (and the later Imola twins), twin plug ignition was used. The usual 14 mm spark plug was supplemented by a 10 mm plug mounted near the bevel-gear tube, allowing the ignition advance to be reduced from 42 to 36°. Ignition was by a total loss 6 volt battery and twin 3 volt coils. The compression ratio was 10:1, and much of the lower part of the engine was shared with the Gran Sport. A five- or sometimes six-speed gearbox was fitted, but because there was no room inside the Gran Sport engine-cases for more than four, the fifth or sixth gears were mounted inboard of the clutch in the primary drive compartment. The street origins were also displayed by a blanked-off kick-start and an empty space on the left side of the crankshaft where the Gran Sport carried a generator.

Ducati hoped to create a big impression at the Italian Grand Prix at Monza in September 1956, but tragedy struck when their star rider, 26-year-old Gianni Degli Antoni, was killed while testing at Monza in August. In the race itself none of the Ducatis performed particularly spectacularly, ending the year on a disappointing note after their magnificent display in Sweden. For 1957 it was decided to spend a year developing the desmo for an all-out assault on the Grands Prix in 1958. This also gave Taglioni time to concentrate on the production of the new overhead-camshaft road bikes. Meanwhile, a limited number of double overhead-camshaft 125s, called the 125 Grand Prix, were made available to privateers, and these featured a number of

1957 fully-streamlined factory 125 Desmo.

changes from the previous year, most noticeably in the frame, which now had an additional twin-loop subframe under the engine. The engine also received new crankcases. About 50 of these 125 Grand Prix racers were made between 1957 and 1959, and they were the most competitive 125 racer a privateer could buy at the time. A double overhead-camshaft Bialbero 175 cc version was also available.

While the only 1957 World Championship event that the desmos raced in was the Italian Grand Prix at Monza, this, like the previous year, was a disaster. Alberto Gandossi fell while in the lead on the first lap, bringing down most of the field. Non-desmo Ducatis were also entered for the non-championship Swedish Grand Prix (where this time they

took the first five places), but in the Italian Formula 2 and 3 classes Franco Farnè and Bruno Spaggiari were virtually unbeatable. The 125 desmo now produced 18 bhp at 12,500 rpm, and, with a new double-cradle frame, was ready to take on the might of the other Italian factories.

However, before the start of the 1958 season Moto Guzzi, Gilera, and Mondial announced their retirement from Grand Prix competition. This would leave MV Agusta as Ducati's principal opposition, but with Carlo Ubbiali being joined by reigning World Champion Tarquino Provini they would be a formidable team. Ducati's own team was headed by Luigi Taveri, and consisted of Alberto Gandossi, Bruno Spaggiari, sometimes Romolo Ferri and Franco Villa, Dave Chadwick for the opening Grand Prix at the Isle of Man, and, later, trials ace Sammy Miller. The fully-streamlined 'dustbin' fairings of the previous two years were now banned, and in several pre-season events the desmos performed impressively. Ducati went to the Isle of Man with an air of confidence, and a speed advantage over the MVs.

Ubbiali on the MV won at the shorter Clypse Isle of Man circuit after Taveri retired, but Gandossi retaliated with a win at Spa in Belgium. After the Isle of Man new, higher-lift camshafts had given the desmo single an increase to 19 bhp, and throughout the season the motorcycle was continually developed. No two were identical, with not only

The 175 DOHC Bialbero.

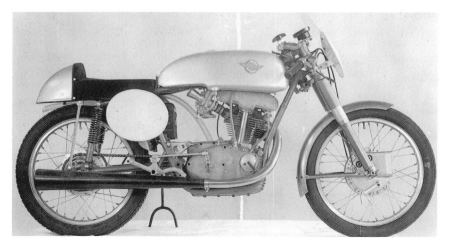

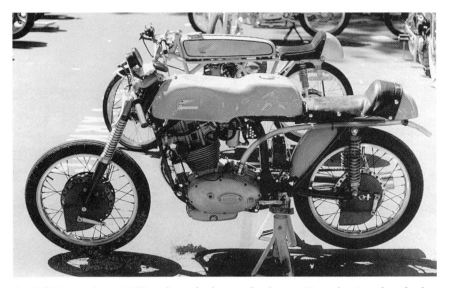

A 125 Desmo from 1957 with single down-tube frame. Note the Amadoro brakes with large air scoops. (Phil Schilling)

contest the 1959 series of Grand Prix and Italian championship races on a reduced scale with both the single cylinder desmo, and the new twin. Joining Gandossi and Spaggiari were Taveri and a promising English newcomer, Mike Hailwood.

After the success of 1958, everyone expected 1959 to be a repeat performance, but, unfortunately for Ducati, this didn't materialise. Hailwood's success in 1958 on a dohc Grand Prix, along with his father Stan Hailwood's setting up of Ducati Concessionaires in Manchester as distributors, prompted the factory to loan Hailwood a 125 cc desmo single for the season. It was only Hailwood's exploits that brought any real results, and he won his first ever Grand Prix victory at Ulster in August, eventually ending up third in the 125 cc World Championship. At the end of the 1959 season Ducati retired from racing, selling off the works desmos but substituting the desmodromic heads for the dohc valve-spring type. These continued to be successfully raced for many years, often with the single down-tube Gran Sport type

different petrol tanks and seats, but also crankcase castings and frames. Further Ducati victories came in Sweden and at Monza, where Spaggiari led a top-five clean sweep. His winning speed was 155.827 km/h (96.8 mph), and this was one of Ducati's greatest triumphs.

Unfortunately, while humiliating MV in front of their home crowd, Gandossi still just failed to beat Ubbiali for the 125 cc title. However, on the domestic front Ducati won all the 125 cc championships in 1958. Having proved that desmodromics worked, the factory decided to

The same 1957 125 Desmo with its strengthened single down-tube frame. (Phil Schilling)

The 1957 GP 125s used downward-facing air scoops on their brakes to avoid overheating beneath their original dustbin fairings. (Phil Schilling)

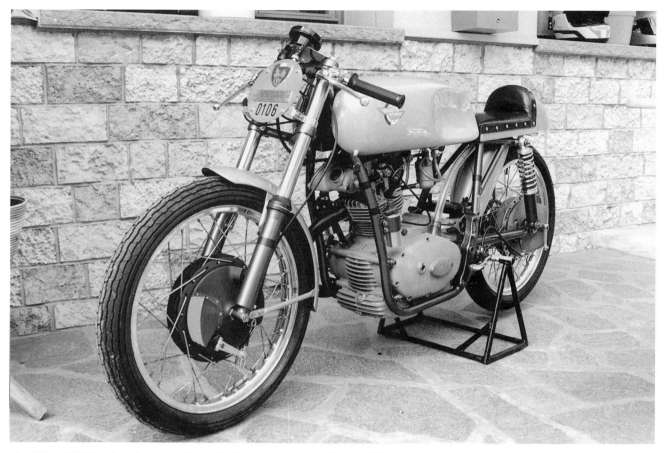

A 1958 125GP, still with the double cradle frame, but now with a DOHC valve-spring cylinder head.

frame of 1956 and 1957 rather than the later full-cradle double down-tube.

There was one more interesting development to the 125 Grand Prix that needs to be documented, and this occurred at the end of the 1959 season. Australian Ken Kavanagh had successfully raced a 125 Grand Prix during 1959 and persuaded the factory to supply him with a 220 – built out of a 69 mm bored 175 dohc Bialbero – to use to help promote Ducati in Australia in a series of races held during the antipodean summer season. Displacing 216.13 cc, and with a 9:1 compression ratio, the 220 produced 28 bhp at 9,600 rpm. Carburation was by a 29 mm Dell'Orto, and because of its success several similar 220 cc machines were later built.

Racing Twins and Fours

The first indication that Ducati were interested in building larger, multi-cylindered motorcycles came at the Milan Show in December 1956, with the unveiling of a 175 cc double overhead camshaft parallel twin with

exposed valve springs. This was raced by Leopoldo Tartarini in the final, 1957, Giro d'Italia, but it retired in the third stage. Originating from drawings first sketched by Taglioni in 1950, it was an interesting, if complicated design, with the pressed up crankshaft

consisting of two flywheel assemblies clamped by Hirth (radially serrated) couplings. A jackshaft was driven off the middle of the crankshaft, and this drove the twin overhead camshafts by a train of spur gears. While the 49 x 46.6 mm 175 produced considerably

The 125 cc twin that Franco Villa rode to third place in the 1958 Italian Grand Prix.

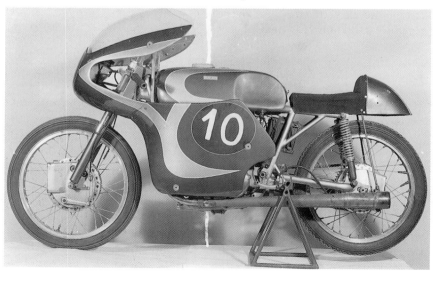

more power than the 175 cc single cylinder Gran Sport – 22 bhp at 11,000 rpm – the narrower power band and increase in weight to 112 kg (247 lb) largely negated this benefit. The 175 became the basis for a 125 cc Grand Prix machine first raced by Franco Villa at the Italian Grand Prix at Monza in 1958, where it finished third in that remarkable Ducati first-five clean sweep.

This 125 was intended to replace the single by producing more horsepower through increased revs, and the 42.5 x 45 mm engine produced 22.5 bhp at 13,800 rpm. A similar three-camshaft desmodromic valve system to the single allowed the engine to rev to an amazing (for the time) 17,000 rpm, but the power band was extremely narrow and the bike difficult to ride despite having a six-speed gearbox. As with the 175 twin, the 125 was also too heavy at a claimed 92 kg (203 lb), and the handling was less than satisfactory. Compared with the single, the twin (of which only three were built) didn't achieve much success. Breakages in the camshaft drive gear-train often occurred, with disastrous results, and the bikes were sold at the end of the 1959 season, two of them ending up being raced by Mike Hailwood.

It was during 1959 that Stan Hailwood commissioned a 250 cc version for Mike to race in 1960. Revealed to the press in February 1960, the 250 shared the same 55.25 x 52 mm dimensions with the 125 cc single, but in other respects was a scaled-up 125 twin. The power was 43 bhp at 11,600 rpm, and it was a very fast motorcycle with a top speed in the region of 218 km/h (135 mph), but it handled poorly and was considerably overweight. At about the same time, Ken Kavanagh, about to undertake his successful series in Australia, persuaded the factory to build a 350 cc desmo twin for the 1960 season. This appeared in time for Kavanagh to race at Imola in April but an accident prevented him from riding it until the Isle of Man, by which time Hailwood also had a similar machine. With a bore and stroke of 64 x 54 mm, the 350 produced 48 bhp, but the engines vibrated badly and the bikes needed a lot of development to be competitive. At the end of the season John Surtees

bought both Hailwood's 250 and 350, followed a few months later by Kavanagh's. They received new frames and leading-link forks by Ken Sprayson, and Phil Read rode a 350 at the Isle of Man in 1962 where it blew up in practice. They were raced unsuccessfully for a couple more domestic British seasons.

There was, however, to be one more multi-cylindered disaster. Seeing the limitations of a single, or even twin, at Grand Prix level, Taglioni designed a 125 cc in-line four-cylinder engine in 1958. This idea was advanced for the time, but with Ducati's withdrawal from competition at the end of 1959 the design languished until the Spanish Mototrans concern persuaded Ducati to produce it five years later, in 1964, by which time it was obsolete in a few design areas. There were four non-desmo valves per cylinder and a very wide 90° included valve angle. The double overhead camshaft 125 used a train of gears on the left side of the engine to drive the camshafts. With a compression ratio of 12:1 and four 12 mm Dell'Orto carburettors, the 34.5 x 34 mm engine produced 23 bhp at 14,000 rpm, hardly outstanding considering that the 125 cc twin had produced 22.5 bhp in 1958. Even with 12 months of development the power

was only increased to 24 bhp at 16,000 rpm, and Ducati realized that it would never be competitive at Grand Prix level. Only two bikes were built, and during 1966 the 125 four quietly disappeared.

The entire parallel twin and four cylinder episode was interesting in that they were the first Ducatis designed exclusively for racing bearing no relationship to any road bikes. Because they were so unsuccessful compared to the Gran Sport derivatives none of their features ended up on the production line, but they certainly had the effect of creating a Taglioni philosophy that would prevail in the future: that of producing a motorcycle with a balance of power and weight. There was no point in an unnecessarily complex and heavy motorcycle if this did not translate into improved lap times. Also, what good was a powerful motorcycle if it did not handle well or the powerband was so narrow that it was unrideable? Not only was it significant that the desmodromic Grand Prix racer was closely derived from a road bike (albeit a catalogued racer with lights), but all future Ducati success would emphasize a broad range, rather than outright power, and a balance between power and weight.

John Surtees commissioned a Reynolds frame for the 250 twin in 1961. (Two Wheels)

3

Production Overhead Camshaft Singles (Narrow-Case)

Following the success of the Gran Sport in the 1955 and 1956 Giro d'Italia and Milano–Taranto races, it was inevitable that the Gran Sport engine would be used as a basis for a range of production motorcycles. Given Taglioni's ability to generate designs amazingly quickly, it wasn't surprising that Ducati's first production bevel-gear motorcycle, the 175 Sport, was on display at the Milan Show in December 1956. This was followed shortly afterwards by a slightly detuned version, the 175T.

100/125/175/200

The 175 engine was to form the basis of the entire range of production singles (and also the subsequent Spanish Mototrans versions) until their demise in 1974. It differed from the Gran Sport in a number of design details, most notably in the use of enclosed, rather than exposed, hairpin valve springs. With a bore and stroke of 62 x 57.8 mm, and a compression ratio of 8:1, the 175 Sport produced 14 bhp at 8,000 rpm. The weight was 104 kg (229 lb), and though only a four-speed gearbox was used, performance was lively with a claimed top speed of 130 km/h (81 mph). The 175T had a 7:1 compression ratio and produced 12 bhp at 6,000 rpm. Top speed was 109 km/h (68 mph). The Sport featured the distinctive scalloped petrol tank that would last through to the 200 Elite.

In September 1957, 100 and 125 cc Touring and Sport versions of the overhead camshaft single were displayed, to go into production during 1958. The 125 Sport, sharing its 55.25 mm bore and 52 mm stroke with the Grand Prix, produced 10 bhp at 8,500 rpm with a compression ratio of 8:1. The 100, with the same 49.4 x 52 mm bore dimensions as the first Marianna, produced 8 bhp at 8,700 rpm. Both these Sports were styled after the F3 and weighed 100.5 kg (221.5 lb), with the 125 having a surprising maximum speed of 112 km/h (69 mph). The 175S of 1958 continued with the scalloped petrol tank, and was the first to feature the strange dual muffler that would also categorize the later 200 Elite. After about a year of production the 100 was discontinued, but the model range actually expanded during this period as the 125TS and 175TS were added, and the 175 grew to 200 cc. The 125 Sport remained a popular model, particularly in Italy, until 1965.

By simply boring the 175 by an additional 5 mm, to 67 mm, the 200 Elite was created for the 1959 season. With 18 bhp at 7,500 rpm, the 111 kg (245 lb) Elite had a claimed top speed of 135 km/h (84 mph). The styling followed that of the 175 Sport, but for 1959 both models received 18-inch wheels. The Elite soon gained a reputation as a first rate sporting motorcycle and did much to establish the Ducati name in export markets. There were other 175 and 200 models for 1959, notably the Americano sharing the dual muffler and valanced mudguards. The 175 Americano was an extraordinary motorcycle with its twin air horns, high 'cowboy' style handlebars, and chrome-studded seat. It was difficult to imagine that

The 175T of 1957. One of the first production bevel-gear Ducatis.

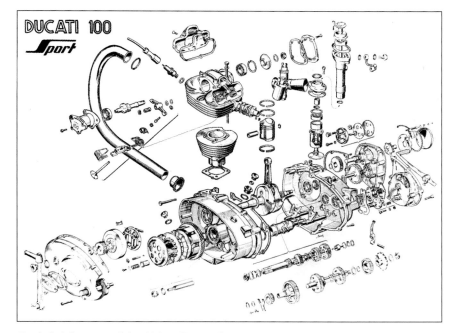

Exploded diagram of the 100 cc Ducati Sport engine.

beneath that exterior lurked much the same engine and running gear as the 200 Elite. Another significant, if not totally successful, model was the 175 and 200 Motocross. Though this lasted only through to 1961, it was a prelude to a much more successful range, the Scrambler or SCR, later to become the backbone of the overhead camshaft line up.

During this period a wide variety of specifications was offered with the range of 175s and 200s, much depending on the requirements of importers in specific countries. In the UK they even had different names, with the 125 Monza and Monza Super, 175 Silverstone and Silverstone Super, and 200 Super Sports and Elite being listed in 1960. For the domestic Italian market there was also the touring 175TS and 175 'Due' Selle with an 11 bhp engine.

The 175 Sport of 1958 with its dual muffler.

The 125 Sport is still to be seen in Italy.

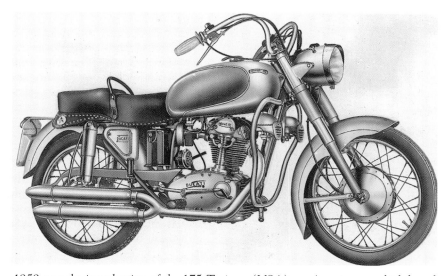

1959 saw the introduction of the 175 Turismo (USA), or Americano, which lasted until 1963.

As the engine grew to 250 cc, the 175s and 200s were phased out. The 125 engine eventually became a 160, and by 1962 the 175 was discontinued. The 200 Elite soldiered on for a few more years, still being offered until 1965, while in 1962 the 200GT was created out of the new 250 Diana. Perceived as an underpowered 250, this was a sales disaster, and was dropped after only a year. The writing was on the wall for the smaller-engined Ducatis, and the success of the new 250 only reinforced this. The public then, as now, wanted larger engines, with more performance.

125/175/250 Formula 3

In 1958 the Formula 3 became Ducati's production racer, superseding the Gran Sport that had been available since 1955. If one were to make an analogy with modern Ducatis, the Supermono would be the closest equivalent to both the Gran Sport and the F3. They were intended for the non-Grand Prix privateers and were made in very limited numbers, being assembled by racing mechanics. Also they were extremely expensive and used unique components. 175 F3 owner Phil Schilling estimates that less than 100 of all types (125/175/250) were built over a five-year period, perhaps some 50 of them being 175s.

Looking like racing versions of the 100 and 125 Sport, the F3 actually owed more to the Gran Sport than the production bikes. Unlike the street bike, the engine-cases were sand-cast rather than die-cast, and internally the engine was completely different. From the Gran Sport came the straight-cut primary and bevel-gears, along with special camshaft, rockers, con-rod, piston, clutch, and gearbox. Virtually nothing was interchangeable with the street 125/175 Sport. The frame was lighter, lower, and longer than the standard model, and used different forks and shock absorbers. The dimensions were such that neither the petrol tank nor seat

were interchangeable between the two. However, by far the most startling differences on the 175 and 250 were the brakes. They had the same double-sided Amadoro front, and vented rear, brakes that were used on the Bialbero and factory racers. These were so unusual that Phil Schilling always referred to his 175 F3 as the Ducati 'with the funny front brake'.

Interestingly, all the F3s came with complete street equipment that included a headlight, muffler, tail light, and number-plate holder, but the intention for the bike was clear. It was meant for the track. The 125 F3 featured the same engine specifications as the 125 Gran Sport (but with enclosed valve gear), and the 175 shared its 62 x 57.8 mm engine dimensions with the 175 Bialbero and 175 road bikes. The 175 F3 produced 16 bhp at 9,000 rpm, with a maximum of 9,800 rpm, and was able to achieve 100 mph (161 kph).

Given the specifications, one could assume that the 175 F3 had a spectacular racing career, but generally only factory-prepared bikes were successful. Franco Villa won the supporting Formula 3 race at the 1958 Italian GP (where Ducati had filled the first five places in the 125 Grand Prix), and Franco Farnè the Class 4 Lightweight race at Daytona in 1959. At the Barcelona 24 Hour race of 1960 eight 175s were entered, with victory going to Franco Villa and Amedco Balboni

Unlike the 125, the 175 F3 featured the Amadoro brakes of the factory racers. (Phil Schilling)

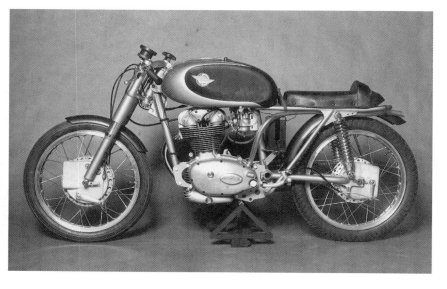

The F3 engine. Virtually no part was interchangeable with the street version.
(Phil Schilling)

at an average speed of 59.25 mph (95.35 km/h). Most F3s were raced by privateers, but they were too expensive for many. The lightweight class eventually grew to 250, so the 175 became obsolete, and a limited number of 250 F3s were made during 1961. Pressure from Ducati's export markets, particularly Berliner in the US, had led Taglioni to develop a 250 cc version of the 175 F3 in 1960. With a special 74 mm cast iron liner, the 250 F3 produced 32 bhp at 9,000 rpm, and Franco Villa was sent to contest a series of road races in the US. So successful was this racing effort that it established Ducati in the US as a manufacturer of reliable and competitive racing machines, and also paved the way for the release of a production 250.

By 1962, production of these beautiful and purposeful racing motorcycles was finished, but they remain as some of the best examples of Ducati's commitment to fine engineering and exquisite construction. There would be no more catalogued production racers, apart from a small number of Mach 1/Ss in 1965 and 1966, until the 600TT2 of 1982.

250 Monza, Diana, and SCR

Following on from the success of the prototype racing 250 F3, a 250 street bike was displayed in April 1961. This new motorcycle would form the basis of the overhead camshaft

production range until the wide-case single of 1968, and was available in two versions, the touring Monza and more sporting Diana. The first Monza had high handlebars and the new engine shared the same bore and stroke (74 x 57.8 mm) as the 250 F3. With a Dell'Orto UBF 24BS carburettor, and an 8:1 compression ratio, the claimed power was a pretty unrealistic 22 bhp at 7,200 rpm. Weight was only 125 kg (276 lb), so the performance was more than respectable for its day, and top speed was claimed to be 80 mph (129 km/h). The Diana (Daytona for the UK), with clip-on handlebars, had a claimed power output of 24 bhp. Its weight, at 120 kg (265 lb), was slightly less than the Monza, and top speed was in the region of 85 mph (137 km/h). There was also the option of a larger, SS1 27A remote float-bowl carburettor for the Diana. The styling for the 250 was completely new, with a different petrol tank, seat, and side panels from the 175s and 200s. The third 250 cc model to emerge during 1962 was the 30 bhp 250 Motocross, the 250 SCR. Primarily intended for the US market, this was based very closely on the earlier 200 Motocross.

With Ducati dubiously preoccupied throughout 1962 and 1963 with the new range of two-strokes, the only new ohc model was the 250

The first sporting 250 was the Diana of 1962. This is the UK version, the Daytona.

Mark 3 Super Sport for the US in mid-1963. This modified Diana was a true production racer and offered the 30 bhp, 10:1 compression ratio engine, with the SS1 27A carburettor and 40 watt flywheel magneto ignition, of the 250 SCR. Full racing equipment, including clip-ons, racing guards and tyres, and a competition plate, were also included. In April 1964 the Mark 3, Monza and Motocross received a five-speed gearbox along with the 250GT (essentially a Diana with a Monza engine). A few months later one of Ducati's all-time classics, the 250 Mach 1, was released.

250 Mach 1

There have been several occasions throughout Ducati's history when one particular production model has stood out like a beacon from the rest of the range, and the Mach 1, first displayed in September 1964, was undoubtedly one of these. Purely from a performance point of view the Mach 1, based on the US 250 Mark 3 Super Sport, was outstanding, with its claim of a top speed of 106 mph (170.6 km/h). In 1964 this placed the Mach 1 firmly at the top of the 250 cc

class, but it wasn't a claim that was always substantiated. In February 1965, for instance, *Motor Cycling* could only manage a best of 83 mph (134 km/h), because the bike was too overgeared.

Of all the production street narrow-case singles, the Mach 1 was the most outstanding. It was the first top-of-the-line limited production street Ducati developed from a successful racer and offered the highest standard of performance for its day. Because of its significance, the Mach 1 justifies more detailed examination.

While Ducati had officially withdrawn from Grand Prix racing at the end of 1959, the factory continued to support various racing events that would help develop the road bike range. The most notable venue was that of Montjuich Park in Barcelona for the annual 24 Hour endurance race, and it has always been one of Ducati's happiest hunting grounds. The first 250 had been entered in 1962, when Ricardo Fargas and Enzo Rippa took a prototype Mototrans 250 to victory, but a more significant win was in 1964 when Spaggiari and Mandolini rode a 284 cc factory

prototype. With a bore of 79 mm, this was the first Ducati displacing more than 250 cc, and its success prompted the factory to release a limited number of Mach 1/S production racers. Like the F3, these had straight-cut primary and bevel gears, and special sand-cast crankcases. Those of the Mach 1/S were stronger than earlier designs, and a forerunner of the subsequent wide crankcase of 1968. A 250 and 350 Mach1/S were offered in January 1965, and they had a twin spark-plug cylinder head producing 34 bhp at 8,500 rpm for the 250, and 39.5 bhp at 8,000 rpm for the 350. Because they had been designed to be strong and reliable in endurance events, they weren't a particularly light or compact bike at 280 lb (127 kg) on a 56-inch (1,422 mm) wheelbase. The most notable feature of the Mach 1/S was its double down-tube full-cradle frame and much wider engine mounts, both front and rear. The 1965 version used a Mach 1 style petrol tank, but was not particularly successful. The Mach 1/S was also offered in 1966, when it had an Oldani front brake and a special fibre-glass racing petrol tank. It may not have been the ideal racer

One of the all-time classic Ducatis, the Mach 1.

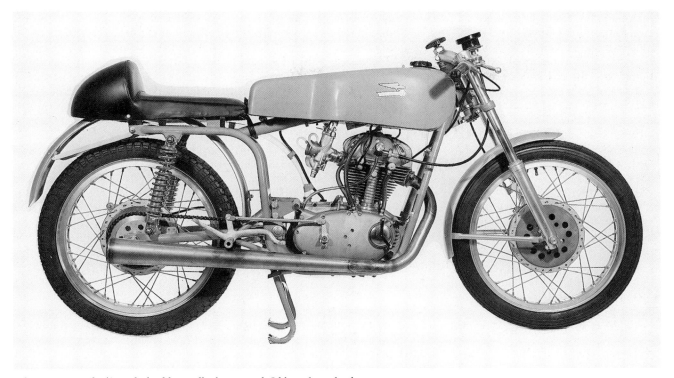

The 1966 Mach1/S with double cradle frame and Oldani front brake.

for the privateer, but its street derivative, the Mach 1, was definitely the bike that Ducati enthusiasts had been waiting for.

The Mach 1 engine had a higher compression piston, giving a 10:1 compression ratio, and had larger (40 and 36 mm) valves along with a grey coded camshaft. As with all the overhead camshaft singles, the valve springs were the hairpin type, and the valve timing figures were inlet opening 62° before top dead centre and closing 76° after bottom dead centre, and exhaust opening 70° before bottom dead centre and closing 48° after top dead centre. With an unfiltered Dell'Orto SS1 29D carburettor, the claimed power was 27.6 bhp at 8,500 rpm. The five-speed gearbox was operated by a rear-set rocking gearchange pedal, and while clip-on handlebars were specified, there was also the bizarre option of a Mach 1 with rear-set foot controls and high, touring-style handlebars.

Despite the output of the alternator being increased to 60 watts (from 40) for the five-speed 250s, the electrics remained a cause for concern, with the six-volt 25W headlight particularly poor. But Marzocchi

suspension front and rear, a light weight of 116 kg (256 lb), and a short wheelbase of 1,350 mm (53.15 inches), ensured that the Mach 1 had the right ingredients for a top 250 cc sporting streetbike in the style of the 500 cc BSA DBD34 Clubmans Gold Star and Velocette Thruxton. Brakes were the 180 x 35 mm front and 160 x 30 mm rear drums fitted to the rest of the range, as were the 18-inch wheels with steel rims, but the red and silver Mach 1 was the only one with a red frame. It was also noted for a wildly optimistic 150 mph (241 km/h) Veglia speedometer.

For the US market the 250 Mark 3 continued to be the top performance model as it had been during 1963 and 1964, but for 1965 it was very much a renamed Mach 1 (with magneto ignition). The factory even claimed a higher top speed of 177 km/h (110 mph) for the Mark 3, which also came equipped with a supplementary 100 mm white-faced Veglia tachometer and a racing plate over the headlight. The weight for the Mark 3 of 1965 was slightly less than the Mach 1 too, at 112 kg (247 lb). *Cycle World*, testing a Mark 3 in August

1965, achieved a top speed of 97 mph (156 km/h).

The Mach 1 continued in production until 1966, as did the Mark 3, now with normal foot-rests rather than rear-sets. The Mach 1 was discontinued in 1967, leaving only the Mark 3, but with battery and coil ignition rather than the flywheel magneto. However, even with the new wide-case replacement

The Mach 1 used a Dell'Orto SS1 29D carburettor.

imminent, the Mach 1 (and narrow-case Mark 3) continued to be the favoured choice amongst privateer racers because they were so much lighter, and the problems of a fragile kickstart mechanism less significant. In 1969, Alistair Rogers on a Mach 1 racer gave Ducati its first TT victory – the 250 at the Isle of Man – at an average speed of 83.79 mph (134.84 km/h).

160/250 Monza, 250GT, 250 SCR, 350 Sebring

The importance of the US market for Ducati really became evident from 1964 with the release of a number of basically non-sporting models. The 160 Monza Junior was created out of the earlier 125 by increasing the bore to 61 mm, while retaining the 52 mm stroke, to achieve 156 cc. With an 8.2:1 compression ratio and a Dell'Orto UB 22BS carburettor, this engine was placed in the same frame as the 250 Monza, where it looked too small and out of place. The 160 also received 16-inch wheels front and rear, and there was still only a four-speed gearbox. The 106 kg (234 lb) machine was only able to reach a top speed of 102 km/h (63 mph). Most commentators couldn't understand the logic of putting a smaller engine in a 250, but Ducati kept making the 160 Monza Junior until 1966; then, in 1967, with US demand at an end, 1,800 were dumped on the UK market as part of a consignment of 3,400 motorcycles purchased by Scottish entrepreneur Bill Hannah. They were still being sold at a discount price in 1972.

The styling was altered for 1965 with a new square petrol tank, side covers and seat, and there was a similar third, and final, edition in 1966, now with a square headlight surround. Otherwise the 160 remained unchanged throughout its production and was definitely not one of Ducati's triumphs.

The 250 Monza mirrored the 160, but for some reason the squarish styling changes happened a year later. So the five-speed 250 Monza appeared in 1964 looking identical to the earlier four-speed model, and continued unchanged through 1965. Engine specifications were the same

as the first version, and for 1966 the 250 Monza shared its styling with the 160 Monza Junior.

Fitting in between the Monza and Mark 3, the 250GT was essentially a Mark 3 with the detuned Monza engine (along with battery and coil ignition), and was only available for 1964 and 1965. The final model in this range of rather mundane touring singles was the 350 Sebring. Like so many Ducati engines, the largest narrow-case single, the 350, had its origins on the race track. Franco Farnè had taken a 350 Mach 1/S racer to victory in the 350 class (and tenth overall) in an international race run in conjunction with the Sebring 12 Hour car race, in central Florida, in April 1965. Hardly a high profile event, it was, however, considered sufficiently prestigious to name the new 350 the Sebring.

Unfortunately, the production version shared little with the racer, and was in reality a Monza with a larger engine. By boring and stroking the 250 to the almost square dimensions of 76 x 75 mm, 340.327 cc was obtained. With an 8.5:1 compression ratio, and the Dell'Orto UBF 24BS carburettor of the 250 Monza, the 123 kg (271 lb) Sebring was a particularly sluggish performer with a top speed of only 125 km/h (78 mph). There were two versions for 1965, the US model almost identical to the 250 Monza, and the European model

mirroring the 250GT. For 1966 the Sebring had the square styling of the 160 and 250 Monzas of that year, and, with no change in engine specification, the claimed top speed had amazingly risen to 142 km/h (88 mph).

Throughout the continuing changes to the range over this period, the 250 Motocross (SCR) remained in production, largely in the same form as it had appeared in 1962 but now with the five-speed gearbox. With a more highly tuned engine than the Monza, the Motocross had a 9.2:1 compression ratio, a Dell'Orto SS1 27A carburettor with air cleaner, and a totally open exhaust system. For 1965 there were 19-inch wheels front and rear, and the weight was 109 kg (240 lb). The 1966 version had a different headlight, an 18-inch rear wheel, a battery to power the lights, and the weight was up to 120 kg (264.5 lb).

By 1968 the entire range of narrow-crankcase models had been superseded by the new wide-crankcase type, even though unsold stocks continued to be available long after production had finished. There had been too much emphasis placed on the mundane touring models, and problems with reliability and finish did little to endear these to the motorcycle-buying public. The only lines to continue as a wide-case were to be the 250 Monza, the Mark 3, and the Scrambler.

The 1966 350 Sebring, the largest narrow-case single.

4.

Oddballs

While today the name of Ducati motorcycles is associated with the production of some of the best-ever sporting and racing motorcycles, throughout its history the company has produced a surprising variety of unmemorable products. Most of these lesser models were produced during the 1960s, being the more mundane overhead camshaft bevel-gear singles outlined in the previous chapter, and an even less noteworthy range of entry level motorcycles. These outnumbered the entire line up of ohc bikes, both in production and model range. Some had two-stroke engines, while others had four-stroke engines with pushrod-operated valves. The two-strokes were born in 1958, finally dying in 1977 with the 125 Six Days, while the pushrod singles finished in 1968. As part of a period of diversification of Ducati products that included outboard motors, lawn-mowers, and even the distribution of British Triumph cars, they were the result of poor management decisions. As would happen in the future, Taglioni refused to be involved with most of these projects, and he was ultimately proved right.

Pushrod Singles

Until the advent of the Gran Sport in 1955, Ducati's road motorcycles were built around a range of pushrod overhead valve singles, which formed the basis of production until 1957, when the first overhead camshaft street bikes were released. Even after this, the overhead valve models continued to be sold in a range of capacities, and in 1957 the 85 Turismo and 85 Sport

joined the 65, 98, and several 125s. At the request of Berliner in the US, the 98 cc Bronco appeared in 1959, and by 1960 the ohv model range was the 85T and S, 98 Bronco, Cavallino and TS, and 125 Aurea. The Aurea was an unusual model in that it used the twin cradle frame of the 1956 125TV, with the more sporting headlight and petrol tank of the 125 cc overhead camshaft bikes. The overhead valve motorcycles were definitely budget Ducatis, as the 125 Aurea, despite looking like a 125 Sport, only developed 6.5 bhp at 6,500 rpm from its 55.2 x 52 mm engine. The compression ratio was 6.8:1, and an 18 mm Dell'Orto carburettor was used. Performance didn't match that of the contemporary overhead camshaft 125TS with its 10 bhp.

The 98 Bronco and 98TS used the 48 x 52 mm 98 cc engine that had first appeared in 1952. With a compression ratio of 7:1, they made

6 bhp at 6,800 rpm. Both these, and the 125 Aurea, had a four-speed gearbox, and the TS boasted a more sporting riding position. The 98s weighed 87 kg (192 lb) and the top speed for the TS was about 53 mph (85 km/h).

The Bronco continued to be produced in 125 cc form and during 1964 it received a slightly restyled 125 cc engine, with square finning, but still with the engine specifications of the 125 Aurea. Then in 1966 a new 125 cc overhead valve engine was designed, with dimensions of 53 x 55 mm. This 121.3 cc engine was installed in a model known as the 125 Cadet/4 Lusso (the 4 denoted four speeds, while lusso means 'luxury'). There was a more powerful engine (with 8.4:1 compression), able to propel the 72 kg (159 lb) Cadet to a top speed of 95 km/h (59 mph). By 1967 the Cadet/4 was joined by the Cadet/4 Scrambler, with a high-rise exhaust system and a 16-inch rear

The 1957 85 Sport was styled along the lines of the ohc 175 Sport.

A 98TS of 1958. In the background is a Cucciolo made under licence by the French company Rocher.

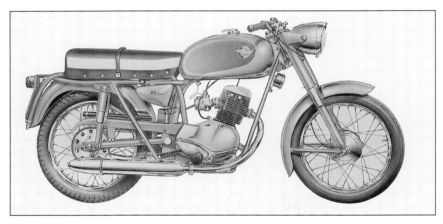

The 125 Aurea of 1961.

versions had slightly more power (1.5 bhp) and went a claimed 50 km/h (31 mph). The frame was of pressed steel, but, unusually for a moped, the Brisk had telescopic forks and a swing-arm with dual shock absorbers.

Using the same 1.5 bhp engine, but with a three-speed gearbox and dual seat, was the Piuma 48 Export. For the British market the Piuma was called the Puma, and released in 1962 with a single seat. The 48 cc Sport models were also based around the same power unit, but with a 9.5:1 compression ratio, and a larger Dell'Orto UA15S carburettor without an air filter, power was increased to 4.2 bhp at 8,600 rpm. Using a double cradle tubular-steel frame, the Sport also looked like a smaller version of the then current 125/175/200 overhead camshaft model, right down to the shape of the petrol tank and the red and gold paintwork. The basic Italian market Sport 48 was styled as the 125 Sport, with clip-on handlebars, a dual seat, and the speedometer in the front headlight. It was a real motorcycle in miniature, but some had pedals, rather than a kickstart, for starting, which looked out of place. The performance of this 54 kg (119 lb) machine was up considerably on the regular Brisk or Piuma, with the top speed a claimed 80 kph (50 mph).

Other markets received slightly different versions. There was the Sport 48 Export, identical but for

The final push-rod single was the 125 Cadet/4 of 1967. (Two Wheels)

wheel. Very few were made, and production didn't continue beyond 1968.

So ended the pushrod single that had started out 15 years earlier and had been entirely eclipsed by Taglioni's Gran Sport and its successors. As with the complete range of two-strokes, these final pushrod 125s weren't missed. They have become categorized with other failures, the later parallel twins, the Giugiaro 860, and the Weber carburetted Pantahs.

Two-Strokes

In an endeavour to expand their customer base for motorcycles, Ducati decided in 1961 to market a range of moped and lightweight two-stroke motorcycles, initially in 50 cc but later joined by an 80 cc sports model. There had been a two-stroke 48 Sport offered briefly during 1958, and the new engine was based on this design. The 50 cc range of five models started with the single speed 48 cc Brisk, and culminated in the three speed 48 cc Sport. The Brisk/1 (single speed) certainly didn't live up to its name, and was a moped of very modest specification and performance. The single cylinder 38 x 42 mm two-stroke displaced 47.633 cc, and with a 7:1 compression ratio produced 1.34 bhp at 4,200 rpm. Weighing only 45 kg (99 lb), the top speed was a mere 40 km/h (25 mph). Subsequent

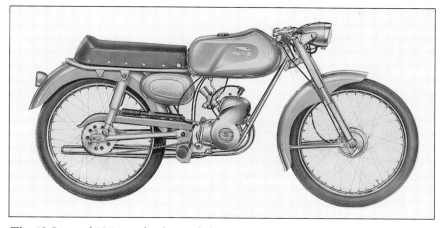

The 48 Sport of 1964 used a fan-cooled engine.

a fuel tank styled along the lines of the 200 Elite, and the Sport 48 USA (called the Falcon 50) that had the Italian market version's petrol tank, but higher handlebars and a single seat. According to the factory brochures, all models had a 'voluminous toolbox'.

The Setter 80 (Super Falcon 80 in the US) appeared at the same time as the 48 and used a similar two-stroke engine displacing 79.807 cc. The bore and stroke were 47 x 46 mm, and with a 7.1:1 compression ratio power was 4.25 bhp at 7,200 rpm. The weight was 62 kg (137 lb), and the top speed 75 km/h (47 mph), even less than that of the 48 Sport. Needless to say, the Setter 80 wasn't a spectacular success and was discontinued during 1964. In its place was a new range built around a 94 cc engine.

Several new models joined the Brisk 48/1, Piuma 48 (three-speed), and 48 Sport (now with a fan-cooled engine). Because of Italian laws prohibiting 50 cc motorcycles to exceed 1.5 bhp and 40 km/h (25 mph), the 48SL was created using a fan-cooled version of the Brisk engine (with only 1.3 bhp at 4,300 rpm), mounted in the full cradle frame of the 48 Sport. The same motorcycle, with the new 94 cc engine in place of the 48 cc unit, became the 100 Cadet and would last, with minor changes, until 1968. The fan-cooled 94 cc engine had a bore and stroke of 51 x 46 mm, and produced 6 bhp at 7,000 rpm.

In addition to the Cadet there was also the 100 Mountaineer and two scooters, the 48 and 100 Brio. The 100 Mountaineer was similar to the Cadet, but for a high-level exhaust, rear rack, and 16-inch wheels, while the Brio was a genuine scooter in the Vespa and Lambretta mould. Harking back to the disaster of the Cruiser, the equally uninspired Brio used the three-speed engine of the Piuma and Cadet.

Small changes occurred for the

1966 saw the introduction of the Brio scooter. Here it is from a publicity photo, with the Piuma 48.

1966 season, most noticeably with the creation of the Piuma Sport 50, which had a pressed-steel frame and used the three-speed 4.2 bhp engine of the 48 Sport. The styling was similar to that of the larger sporting Ducatis, but without the performance to match. The 49 kg (108 lb) machine had a top speed of 80 kph (50 mph). The 48SL was uprated to the 50SL. No longer with fan-cooling, and with a larger 38.8 mm bore, capacity was now 49.66 cc, and it had a four-speed gearbox. The compression ratio was 9.5:1, and the styling was similar except for the exhaust now being on the right side. Both the 100 Cadet and Mountaineer retained the fan-cooled engine, but with a foot-operated four-speed gearbox rather than the previous hand change.

While the 94 cc Brio continued into 1967 largely unaltered except for a name-change to 100/25, it still had the fan-cooled engine. The rest of the range came in for some revision. The 50SL/1 received a higher compression ratio of 11:1, lost its air filter, and gained a new style of petrol tank with twin filler caps, a styling feature that would be used on the first Mark 3 Desmo singles a year later. The 100 Cadet and Mountaineer were no longer fan-cooled, and received a new air-cooled cylinder head with a chrome bore. The capacity was increased to 98 cc with a 1 mm bore increase.

The Brio continued through to 1968, when it was joined by the 50 cc Rolly moped, and some new 50 cc

The 1968 100 Mountaineer used an air-cooled cylinder head. (Two Wheels)

sporting bikes. Following on from the 50SL/1 came the 50SL/1A, identical but for a different petrol tank, and the 50SL/2 and 50SL/2A. These were styled more like the Cadet, with a square type of headlight, the 2A

getting higher handlebars. The 100 Cadet and Mountaineer were available into 1969, and the last versions, 50 and 100 cc Scramblers, finished production in 1970. While there had been significant numbers of these two-stroke machines made, most weren't exported, and they have done little to enhance the reputation of Ducati as a premier motorcycle manufacturer. It must be borne in mind, though, that a good proportion of Ducati motorcycle production through the 1960s was that of two-strokes, but if the management hadn't finally listened to Taglioni and re-entered the world of competition in 1970 with new designs the company might have faded from the scene altogether.

Amazingly, considering its lack of success, the two-stroke was resurrected in 1975. As in the 1960s, some poor managerial decisions were made at this time. Not only was production

The sporting 50SL/1 of 1967 featured twin petrol filler caps.

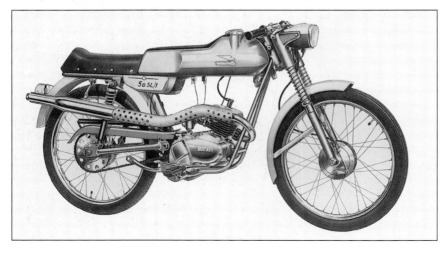

The 1968 100 Cadet.

of the 750 and 250/350/450 singles being ended, but their replacement by the Giugiaro-styled 860 and the parallel twins was a dubious move. Two 125 cc two-strokes were proposed, the 125 Sperimentale street bike and the 125 Regolarità. Only the Regolarità Six Days made it into production, but because it wasn't a real enduro bike, it didn't sell well. This wasn't really surprising considering Ducati had no real experience in off-road competition. It had a completely new 54 x 54 mm 123.7 cc engine with a 10.5:1 compression ratio, a Dell'Orto PHB 30 carburettor, and a six-speed gearbox. The weight was 108 kg (238 lb). In 1977 an improved 125 Six Days was offered, with a larger 32 mm Bing carburettor and a 14.5:1 compression ratio. The revised 125 Six Days had a new petrol tank, and laid-forward twin Marzocchi shock absorbers. The weight was much less than the Regolarità, at 97 kg (214 lb), but this also wasn't a success. Both Six Days'

had obsolete suspension, and were unremarkable bikes competing against some highly specialized off-road motorcycles. They were defi-

nitely not among Ducati's more memorable models, and served only to prove that the company should concentrate on what it had always

The last Ducati two-stroke, the 125 Six Days of 1977.

done as well as, if not better, than other manufacturers.

The Apollo

During the 1960s the US market became increasingly important to Ducati, which had appointed Berliner as its US distributor in 1957. Berliner's aggressive approach gave them considerable influence with the Ducati management. One of the results of this influence was the Apollo, and even though it was a joint project, ultimately it created more financial problems for the company.

At the instigation of Joe Berliner, Ducati was commissioned to build a police bike that could compete with Harley-Davidson. This was no problem for Fabio Taglioni, who had always been a very prolific designer, and a 1,260 cc V-4 five-speed engine was soon on the drawing board. By the end of 1963 a motorcycle had been constructed, and from a firm that was known primarily for single cylinder motorcycles of up to 250 cc, this was a dramatic departure. It was

also the largest capacity motorcycle to emanate from a European manufacturer since the Second World War.

In retrospect the Apollo was many years in advance of its time. Even if it had been built ten years later it may have been more successful, but it was far too heavy and powerful for the available tyres of 1964. Typically of Taglioni, it was a brilliant concept. Two siamesed 90° V twins created a 1,257 cc V-4. To keep the engine as compact as possible, the stroke was very short, and with cylinder dimensions of 84.5 x 56 mm it was also extremely oversquare for the day. The bore/stroke ratio of 1.5:1 was greater than that of any other Ducati before or since, except for the racing 926 of 1993. The Apollo also featured the different cylinder finning on the front and rear cylinders that would later appear on the 750 twin and Pantah. Every advantage was taken of the benefits of the V-4 layout, and the crankcases were only 19 inches (483 mm) wide. The valve gear was not driven by bevel-gears and an overhead camshaft, but

followed the practice of the contemporary range of utilitarian singles by using the simpler pushrods and rockers. The specifications of the Apollo were such that it was a very advanced motorcycle. It had a five-speed gearbox, a Marelli electric starter, duplex chain final drive, and Ceriani suspension front and rear. With a modest 1,537 mm (60.5-inch) wheelbase, the dry weight was 270 kg (595 lb).

There were to be two versions of the Apollo, one with twin Dell'Orto carburettors and an 8:1 compression ratio producing 80 bhp at 6,000 rpm, and the other, a sports version, with four Dell'Orto carburettors, producing 100 bhp at 7,000 rpm. Unfortunately the Apollo made too much power for the 5.00 x 16 Pirelli white-wall tyres, so it had to be reduced to 65 bhp. Because it was still a heavy bike, reducing the power affected its performance in comparison to the Harley-Davidsons and BMWs that were its competition as a police bike, and Berliner had a lot of difficulty in selling the concept. Only one example,

The Apollo. Only one complete example survives.

One of Taglioni's more unusual designs, the DOHC 700 twin of 1967.

and another engine, survived, the bike staying with Berliner at their New Jersey headquarters. Later it was sold to Domiracer in the US, and it is now in Japan.

500 Parallel Twin

The influence that Berliner wielded over Ducati was such that they were responsible not only for the Apollo, but also for a 500 cc twin. Intended for the US market, and displayed at the Daytona Show immediately after the US Grand Prix in March 1965, the latter was poorly received. Overweight at 190 kg (419 lb), its performance was sluggish. The 497 cc 360° twin had pushrod overhead valves and dimensions of 74 x 57.8 mm. These were very oversquare for the day and very similar to the 500 Pantah of 15 years later. In other respects too, it was very advanced, having an electric starter and five-speed gearbox. With two 27 mm Dell'Orto SS1 carburettors, claimed maximum power was 40 bhp at 6,000 rpm. There was a large twin leading shoe front brake, along with 19-inch wheels, but it wasn't a project that Taglioni was too interested in so it didn't get into production. Another version appeared three years later, in 1968. A lighter bike at 177 kg (390 lb), it was an improvement over the earlier model, but there wasn't enough dealer interest to justify putting this into production either. Amazingly, the 500 cc parallel twin was resurrected seven years later, and was again a disaster.

Taglioni did design a more interesting 700 cc parallel twin, of which a prototype was constructed. This bike was intended for the Italian Carabinieri, as a replacement for their Moto Guzzi Falcone singles, and was built in two versions in 1967. One, a sports version with chain-driven double overhead camshafts, was claimed to produce 80 bhp at 7,500 rpm, while the pushrod police version produced 70 bhp at 6,500 rpm. Still, the question of vibration wasn't addressed, and it came at a time when the overhead camshaft singles were being updated, so the resources weren't there for it to go into production.

5.

Desmodromics Reborn and the Wide-Case Singles

The prototype wide-case Ducati single was displayed at the Cologne Show in September 1967. This revised engine would not only improve on some of the weaknesses of the earlier design, but also allow Ing. Fabio Taglioni to make his dream a reality: the first production engine with desmodromic valve gear. Additionally, the new engine allowed for the capacity to be eventually increased beyond that of the 350 cc of the previous narrow-case, to 436 cc.

While Franco Farnè had debuted a desmodromic 250 at the Italian season opener at Modena on 20 March 1966, this bike was based on the Mach 1/S. It had used crankcases of a new design, with wider front and rear frame mounts, and would form the basis for future designs. There was then a full year of development, during which time Cere and Giovanardi won the 250 cc class at the FIM *Coupe d'Endurance* Imola 6 Hour race on a factory bike, but it wasn't until 1967 that the desmo single was raced again, now with an even stronger, wide-crankcase engine. Initially 350 cc, the new desmo was raced by Gilberto Parlotti and Roberto Gallina at Modena in March 1967. Soon a 250 version joined the 350, and Farnè took it to Daytona to ride in the Expert Lightweight event, but was not allowed to start as the desmodromic single was deemed to be not derived from a road-going model. These 250 and 350 desmodromic bikes were raced in several Italian early season events on street circuits with a reasonable amount of success. The 74 x 57.8 mm 250, with its 36 mm Dell'Orto carburettor, produced 35 bhp at 11,500 rpm, and the 76 x 75 mm 350, with a 40 mm Dell'Orto carburettor, 45 bhp at 10,500 rpm. In 1968, now with Bruno Spaggiari riding, the 250 and 350 desmos achieved more encouraging results, notably fifth in the Italian 350 Grand Prix, but still no outright victories. Making its debut at Rimini in March 1968 was the first 450, actually 436 cc, sharing the dry clutch, twin-plug ignition and straight cut primary and bevel gears with the smaller versions. With a 42 mm Dell'Orto carburettor, power was up to 50 bhp at 9,000 rpm.

In 1969 Gallina, Parlotti, and Spaggiari again rode the 250 and 350, with the best results being Spaggiari's two second-place finishes behind Pasolini's Benelli four at Modena and Cesenatico. While the racing results may not have been spectacular, they were a very useful proving ground for developing the range of street desmos. A similar scenario existed through 1970, but instead of being special factory-prepared engines, Spaggiari's 450 and Parlotti's 250 and 350 derived from the new range of road machines, and had the regular wet-clutch of these bikes. The 450 still featured twin-plug ignition, larger valves, 42 mm Dell'Orto carburettor, and a 10:1 compression ratio, but used die-cast rather than sand-cast engine-cases. It also had a reinforced swing-arm and a 210 mm Fontana front brake and weighed 264 lb (120 kg). They were entered under Franco Farnè's semi-official team quaintly called Scuderia Speedy Gonzales. Once again, while results

The 350SCR of 1968 was the first production wide-case.

were encouraging, particularly at Rimini, Modena, and Riccione, the new singles were no match for the multi-cylindered MVs, Benellis, Lintos, and Patons. For this reason the factory stopped development of the desmo single to concentrate on the 500 V-twin. Ironically, it was the privateers who benefited from all the factory development on the desmo racer, and Ducati singles were, and still continue to be, highly successful in the various classes for which they are eligible. The culmination of this was Charles Mortimer's win in the 1970 250 Production TT at the Isle of Man aboard the Vic Camp Mark 3 Desmo. Here he won at an average speed of 84.87 mph (136.6 km/h).

By 1968, production of the new series of singles was underway. The wide crankcase increased the capacity of the sump to 2.5 litres (0.55 imperial gallons), and there were improved kickstart gears, a problem with five-speed narrow-case engines. There was also a larger crankpin, at 27 mm, and the drive-side main bearing enlarged to 30 x 72 x 19 mm. Because of the wider rear engine mounts and a twin down-tube rear frame section, the frame was stronger at the rear, but this was at the cost of an increase in weight.

125/250/350/450 Scrambler

The first production versions of the wide-case engine appeared in early 1968 as the 350 cc Scrambler, and in the US as the 350 Sport Scrambler. This was followed shortly afterwards by the 250 Scrambler. The Scrambler was to become the most popular of all the wide-case singles, particularly in Italy. It offered full street equipment, with no pretensions for off-road competition as had been evident in the prototype 350 Scrambler of 1967, and the 250, 350, and even the later 450 versions, were essentially similar.

This 350 cc wide-case engine shared the same dimensions of 76 x 75 mm with the 350 Sebring and Mach 1/S racer, and had a 10:1 compression ratio and a high performance camshaft (coded white/green). This had valve timing figures of inlet opening 70° before top dead centre and closing 84° after bottom dead centre, and the exhaust valve opening 80° before bottom dead centre and closing 64° after top dead centre. They certainly required the decompression lever operated from the left handlebar. The 250 had a 9.2:1 compression ratio and no compression release. Using 35 mm Marzocchi forks, the 1968 versions of the 250 and 350SCR had their Veglia speedometer mounted in the Aprilia headlight. They came with 315 mm Marzocchi shock absorbers, later replaced by 310 mm items, with the option of stiffer suspension available. Very soon after they were released they were restyled, with a new petrol tank and seat design that would carry through until 1974. The 350 then became the 350SSS (or Street Scrambler Sport) for the US market.

In 1969 the 450 (actually 435.7 cc) became available, and featured a new crankcase, cylinder, and cylinder head castings to accommodate the 86 x 75 mm dimensions. The reason why a full 500 wasn't created was that the 75 mm stroke was the largest that could be used for the throw of the crankshaft to miss the gearbox pinions. To make the engine larger would have required a redesign and retool. Interestingly enough, even though the 450 shared the 75 mm stroke with the 350, the 450 used a con-rod with an eye-to-eye length of 140 mm, rather than the 136 mm con-rod that was used by both the 250 and 350. Certainly with a rod length to stroke ratio of 1.81:1, the shorter rod was not ideal for the longer stroke 350, accentuating piston acceleration.

For the 450 there was also extra gusseting along the top frame tube, exactly like Spaggiari's 1968 450 racer, and a wider chain and sprockets, allowing the use of a 5/8 x 3/8 inch final drive chain. With a 9.3:1 compression ratio, and white coded camshafts of the 250SCR, the 450SCR (and identical Mark 3) produced a moderate 27 bhp at 6,500 rpm. The valve timing was inlet opening 27° before top dead centre, closing 75° after bottom dead centre, and exhaust opening 60° before bottom dead centre, and closing 32° after top dead centre. In 1969 the US model of the 450 Scrambler was marketed by Berliner as the Jupiter. With the 450 came slightly longer (515 mm) Marzocchi forks, and these were also fitted to subsequent 250 and 350SCRs.

All the carburettors were changed during 1969, with the Dell'Orto SS1 29D being replaced by a new square-slide VHB. The 250 received a smaller VHB 26AD (from 27 mm), and the 350 and 450, a VHB 29AD. This required a new air filter and the traditional rounded muffler became the cut-off Silentium type, either long or short. At the start of 1970 the crankpin diameter was increased to 30 mm, and the Scramblers then

The famous glass-sided Ducati transporter with a selection of Scramblers and outboard motors, 1971.

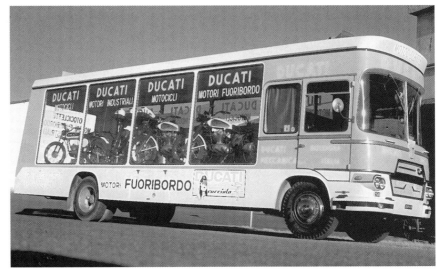

The Scrambler was designed to appeal to a broad range of motorcyclists. (Two Wheels)

remained unchanged until 1973, when they became very similar to the range of Mark 3 roadsters. They now had Borrani 19-inch and 18-inch alloy wheel-rims, and the 350 and 450SCR the same double-sided front brake, headlight, and instruments as the Mark 3. They also featured Marzocchi forks with exposed staunchions and new side-covers. The 250 still had the single brake and fork gaiters (though US versions differed), and all now went back to using the older rounded muffler. In 1973 they received the Ducati Elettrotecnica electronic ignition, and finally a larger, 32 mm diameter crankpin in 1974.

For a short while during 1971 a 125SCR was actually built in Bologna with a narrow-case Spanish Mototrans five-speed engine, complete with Spanish Amal carburettor. This wasn't a success and was soon discontinued, but the final 250 Scramblers of 1974 also used Spanish-built engines.

250/350/450 Mark 3 and Mark 3 Desmo

Soon after the 350 and 250 Scramblers appeared with the new wide-crankcase engine in 1968, so did the Mark 3 and 250 Monza. The Monza was of similar specification and styling to the unremarkable narrow-case version, but the Mark 3 was now quite distinctively styled with a twin filler petrol tank (like the two-stroke 50 SL/1). The 250 engine remained in the same state of tune as it had in the Mach 1, with the same grey-coded camshaft, 10:1 compression ratio, and Dell'Orto SS1 29D carburettor, while the 350 Mark 3 had the even more highly tuned (white/green camshaft) 350 engine from the 350SCR.

For the wide-case Mark 3s the weight was up from the earlier models, at 128 kg (282 lb), so the 250 didn't perform as strongly. Only 143 km/h (89 mph) was claimed for the 250, a far cry from the Mach 1 and Mark 3 of 1965–67. While the 350 Mark 3 was considered the performance model with its top speed of 170 km/h (106 mph), waiting in the wings to enhance Ducati's reputation was Taglioni's engineering *tour de force*, desmodromic valve gear.

During 1968, Fabio Taglioni's dream was fulfilled: Ducati produced the first production motorcycle engine with desmodromically-oper-

ated valve gear. Unlike the 125 Grand Prix desmos with their three camshafts, only one was used, incorporating both opening and closing lobes, and hairpin valve springs were retained to assist in starting. These were from the 160 Monza Junior, and lighter than standard, but were still considerably stronger than the small closing springs fitted to the later desmo twins. Apart from the cylinder head the engines were identical, and there really wasn't much of a performance differential between the two models in standard trim. The desmo engine was fitted to the 250 and 350 Mark 3, creating two new models, the 250 Mark 3 Desmo, and the 350 Mark 3 Desmo. These were virtually indistinguishable from the regular Mark 3 apart from a 'D' on the side-panels and different colours.

All the Desmos used the same white and blue coded camshaft with the inlet valve opening 70° before top dead centre, closing 82° after bottom dead centre, and the exhaust valve opening 80° before bottom dead centre and closing 65° after top dead centre. The performance was up on the Mark 3, with 150 km/h (93 mph) claimed for the 250D, or 160 km/h (99 mph) with megaphone exhaust. The 350D became the fastest production Ducati single offered with its top speed of 180 km/h (112 mph) with megaphone exhaust, but with the standard silencer the maximum speed was 165 km/h (103 mph). Several options were available for the Desmo, these being a high, touring-style handlebar, or a racing uprating kit containing a racing camshaft, a range of main jets, a megaphone, and a full racing fairing. The 1968 models, with their twin filler petrol tanks, Dell'Orto SS1 carburettors, and auxiliary white-faced Veglia tachometer, were amongst the finest Ducati singles, and each bike was provided with a test certificate. All they needed were rear-set footpegs to go with the clip-on handlebars.

With the release of the new 450 engine in the Scrambler in 1969, it wasn't long before there was also a 450 Mark 3 and 450 Mark 3 Desmo. The 450 Desmo used the same camshaft as the other Desmos, and the lower, 9.3:1 compression ratio of the 450 SCR. All the 450s had the new type of Dell'Orto VHB 29 square-slide carburettor, a single filler petrol tank, and the cut-off Silentium muffler, and soon these were shared with the 250 and 350 Mark 3 Desmo. The 450 also had an individual speedometer and tachometer, rather than the headlight-mounted speedo and white-faced Veglia, and these too would become standardized throughout the range of Mark 3s and SCRs during 1970. For the US, Mark 3s and Desmos were fitted with a Scrambler petrol tank and the higher handlebars. *Cycle* tested all three Desmos in February 1970, and found the power characteristics distinctly different, with the 250 and 450 having wide powerbands, and the 350 tuned as 'a street dragster' with power coming in at 6,500 rpm. As they all used the same camshaft and carburettor, this was probably a function of the short con-rod. The 450 was the strongest performer, with a standing quarter-mile time of 16.60 seconds, followed by the 350 at 17.63 seconds, and the 250 at 18.94 seconds. Because they shared cycle parts, the kerb weight ranged from 299 lb (136 kg) for the 450, to 292 lb (132 kg) for the 250, with the 350 in between at 292 lb (132 kg). They found all bikes overgeared, and strangled by the Silentium exhaust system, and with a megaphone the 350 went through the quarter mile in 15.15 seconds.

Also during 1970, a street replica of Spaggiari's racing desmo was offered but unfortunately not put into production. Called the 450 Desmo Superbike, it was to have been available on special order only. While based on a production 450 Desmo, this magnificent machine had genuine rear-set controls and Ceriani racing forks with twin hydraulically-operated Campagnolo disc brakes, surely a first for a street bike. The engine was virtually identical to Spaggiari's, but for a slightly smaller 40 mm remote float bowl Dell'Orto carburettor (which necessitated a cut-out in the petrol tank). It had larger valves, stronger crankshaft and bearings, 10:1 compression, and the option of twin ignition. With a short Silentium exhaust, power was claimed to be 40 bhp at 9,000 rpm. Its

The 1968 350 Desmo had twin filler caps and a Dell'Orto SS carburettor. (Two Wheels)

18-inch Borrani alloy rims were fitted with Dunlop KR83 racing tyres, and the claimed weight was only 297 lb (135 kg), with a top speed of 120 mph (193 km/h).

450 R/T

Certainly one of the more interesting bikes emanating from Bologna during this period was the 450 R/T. While using a production 450 Desmo engine, it had a frame and cycle parts totally unlike any other Ducati. The frame owed more to the 750GT, and was almost half that of the larger bike, also using tapered roller steering-head bearings in place of the ball-bearings of all the other singles. First displayed at the 1970 Bologna Show, the R/T was, like so many Ducatis, created primarily for the US market.

R/T was meant to stand for 'Road and Track', but as *Two Wheels* magazine stated in January 1972, it could also have been interpreted as 'Race and Trail', 'Rorty Thumper', or even 'Revenge on Two-strokes'. The R/T was a much more serious dirt bike

than the Scrambler, and this was demonstrated in August 1971 when, with Morini unable to prepare a team of bikes for the International Six Day Trial, Ducati provided a complete line-up of seven 250, 350, and 450 R/Ts for the Italian Trophy team. Looking very much like standard 450 R/Ts, these factory bikes had an unusual twin muffler reminiscent of that of the 200 Elite, but were no match for the CZ and Jawa two-strokes.

The engine of the R/T was identical to that of the 450 Desmo previously described, except for a compression release valve fitted behind the bevel-gear tube. It was available in two versions, the first being without lights and having an open high-level exhaust. The other version had lights, instruments, and the normal Scrambler exhaust system. With its 21-inch front and 18-inch wheels mounted with Pirelli Cross tyres, the R/T was aimed more at the off-road market than the street, and the specification of a sump guard,

The 450 R/T was the only desmo with a compression release valve.

The 450 Mark 3 of 1974 still used a rocking gearshift pedal.

chain guide, and chain oiler confirmed this, as did the tiny 160 mm front brake from the 160 Monza Junior.

When it came down to it, at 128 kg (282 lb) the R/T was still too heavy to be considered a serious dirt bike, and it didn't remain in production as long as the non-desmo Scrambler. Production had ended by 1973.

239/250/350/450 Mark 3 1971–74

Whereas the Mark 3 and Mark 3 Desmo were virtually indistinguishable from 1968 until 1970, they both came in for a significant redesign in 1971, and in the process two distinct models were created. But for a new petrol tank the Mark 3s of 1971 were still quite similar to those of 1970, and these continued through 1972. For 1973 they were restyled with a new seat, side-covers, instruments, and headlight. More importantly they now received the 35 mm Marzocchi forks of the Desmos along with the Grimeca double-sided front brake and Borrani alloy wheel-rims. The final Mark 3s of 1974 had tank badges rather than decals, along with steel wheel-rims, just like the

750GTs of the same era.

The US market singles of 1973 differed to those elsewhere, with two models complementing the 450 R/T. After a year in which no street singles had been imported, in October 1972 Berliner advertised the new 250 Road, with the exclamation, 'It's back!' The 250 and 350 Roads used a combination of parts from the Scrambler, Mark 3, and R/T. Styled very much like a Scrambler, they had a dual seat like a Mark 3, Mark 3 instruments and headlight (with chrome wire 750GT headlight holder), and 18-inch Borrani alloy wheels with a single leading shoe front brake. While the frame was that of the Scrambler, the swing-arm incorporated the snail cam chain adjusters of the 450 R/T. Engine-wise, these US models were similar to their European counterparts, using electronic ignition, but an Amal 30 mm carburettor and a new silencer. Like the R/T they also had a steel sump guard, but they weren't a success and ceased to be available for 1974.

There were also two touring models in 1971 and 1972, based on the Mark 3 and designed primarily for police forces. The T and TS (differ-

entiated only by their camshaft) had a shorter and rounder petrol tank, valanced mudguard, and panniers. Rather heavy at 160 kg (353 lb), the performance wasn't too exciting either, with 140 km/h (87 mph) claimed for the TS and only 128 km/h (80 mph) for the T. The only redeeming feature of the T and TS was in the use of a 12-volt electrical system, and they were discontinued during 1973.

One rather unusual model of 1974 was a 239 cc Mark 3 built specifically for the French market to circumvent taxes on motorcycles over 240 cc. With a 72.5 mm piston, these 239s also used a Dell'Orto PHF 30 mm carburettor, and had regular coil valve springs replacing the hairpin type, along with 12-volt electrics. The 239 also received the reinforced 450 frame, and in many ways was the most developed of the overhead camshaft singles.

250/350/450 Desmo 1971–74

The Mark 3 Desmo became an even more sporting motorcycle with the creation of a new Desmo single for

The 450T became available during 1971.

The 'Silver Shotgun', a 250 Desmo of 1972. (Two Wheels)

1971 and 1972. This was the model nicknamed 'The Silver Shotgun' by the Australian magazine *Two Wheels* in their long-term test of a 450 in January 1974. While the 250, 350, and 450 cc desmodromic engines were unchanged (apart from larger timing side main bearings), the rest of the motorcycle was considerably updated. Most obvious was the metalflake silver paint scheme for the fibreglass petrol tank, side covers and solo seat, but the Desmo was now a genuine cafe racer with rear-set footpegs to complement the clip-on handlebars.

Most of the improvements came with the running gear. Borrani 18-inch alloy wheel-rims replaced the previous steel type, and the front brake became a Grimeca double-sided single leading shoe instead of the rather weak single leading shoe that had been fitted from 1957. The forks were considerably uprated from the

Cockpit of the 1972 450 Desmo. (Two Wheels)

previous spindly 31.5 mm units, with a new type of 35 mm Marzocchi fork with exposed staunchions. As expected, the performance was similar to that of the earlier Mark 3 Desmos. *Motociclismo* managed a maximum speed of 158.632 km/h (98.57 mph) from their totally standard 450 Desmo test bike in 1972.

For some reason the silver Desmos have become an endangered species and not too many are to be seen these days. This is probably because they were mainly sold on the local market, and is a pity because I prefer these to the later yellow type. They had a more

pleasing Aprilia headlight (with the speedometer mounted in the shell), the white-faced racing Veglia tachometer on its individual bracket, and more attractive levers and controls. They still used contact breaker and coil ignition, the smaller tail-light of the 750GT and 750 Sport, and I find the styling of the seat more in keeping with the overall design.

The Desmo single was given to ex-racer Leopoldo Tartarini (of Italjet) for a slight restyle for 1973. Thus appeared the distinctive yellow colour scheme, to match the 750 Sport, along with a new seat incorporating the tail-light. This final version featured electronic ignition, by either Ducati Elettrotecnica or Spanish Motoplat, and the larger 32 mm crankpin. They also received a revised instrument panel with Smiths instruments, and a new style of CEV headlight. With the new colour scheme came replacement of the fibreglass petrol tank by one in steel.

In all other respects the specification was identical to that of 1971–72, but in 1974 Ceriani 35 mm forks, with a 280 mm Brembo disc and 08 caliper, replaced the Marzocchis and their Grimeca double-sided single leading shoe drum brake. These forks were not fitted to any other models in the Ducati range and were unique to the Desmo single. Because of the use of the front disc brake and 750 style

The 1972 Desmos now had rear-set controls. (Two Wheels)

hub, the 18-inch WM2 Borrani had 40 spokes rather than the 36 of the drum-braked versions, and the fibreglass front mudguard was bolted, rather than clamped, to the fork legs. New con-rods and pistons were also used in some of the final 450s when the 86 mm piston of the 860GT, with its 20 rather than 22 mm gudgeon pin, was fitted.

These very last Desmo singles were an intriguing contradiction between ancient and modern. With a race-bred chassis, lightweight Borrani alloy rims and a disc brake, along with a hand-built engine featuring items like polished rockers, it still had 6-volt electrics and an 80 watt alternator. In 1974 there weren't many bikes available with a modern electronic ignition and a 1950s lighting system. The basic design was beginning to show its age and even the fuel crisis of 1974 couldn't save the exceedingly fuel-efficient single without a major redesign. It was unfortunate that Ducati decided to replace these singles with the unremarkable parallel twin, because the changes made to the French market 239 showed that there was development life left in the design.

The yellow Desmos were more widely exported than the silver versions, and tested by several magazines. *Bike* tested a 350 Desmo with a non-standard exhaust and achieved a top speed of 98.47 mph (158.5 km/h) in August 1974, and in April 1975, they managed 99.97 mph (160.9 km/h) out of a 450 Desmo, again with a non-standard exhaust. These were still light bikes, with all Desmos weighing a claimed 127 kg (280 lb) dry. *Bike* weighed their 350 test bike at 294 lb (133 kg) with a gallon of fuel, and their 450 at 308 lb (140 kg) with a full fuel tank.

In standard trim none of the singles, not even the Desmo versions, were particularly fast motorcycles. A lot of earnest modification was required to obtain serious perform-ance from a Ducati single and at higher speeds they were a decidedly lively device due to the light weight, short wheelbase, stiff suspension, and quick steering – quite unlike the later larger twins renowned for their slow steering and more stable handling. Having owned one of the last 450 Desmos myself, I am not overly enthusiastic about such spirited motorcycles on the road, preferring the stability of the larger Ducatis. The intoxication of a Ducati single is on tighter roads (preferably smooth) where the directness of the steering combines with the torquey engine and excellent handling. There was something inherently correct about the balance of these motorcycles, which have achieved cult status in consequence of many commentators waxing lyrical about them. Unfortunately, while the final Desmos were beautifully crafted they were, by 1974, obsolete, and no longer a serious commercial proposition.

The final 450 Desmo of 1974, now with Ceriani forks and a single front disc brake.

6

The Birth of the V-twin: The 750 Round-Case

On 20 March 1970, Ing. Fabio Taglioni made his initial sketches of an idea for a V-twin. This would be the classic round-case 750 engine and was, in his view, his best design. The basis of the 750 was essentially that of taking two singles and placing them on a common crankcase with the cylinders 90° apart. For Ducati to create a larger capacity twin the easiest and cheapest way was to utilize technology from the current range of singles, and, as always, Fabio Taglioni sought an uncompromised and unique engineering solution.

Taglioni could well remember the racing success, not only of the singles and fours from Moto Guzzi, Gilera, and MV, but also the 120° 500 cc Moto Guzzi twin. This bike retained the horizontal front cylinder of a single to maintain a lower centre of gravity with the rear cylinder facing

The prototype 750 emerged in August 1970, only months after the initial designs were formulated. It had Dell'Orto SS1 carburettors and a snail cam chain adjustment similar to the 450 R/T.

slightly rearward. There were other advantages too, not the least of these being a good flow of air to cool the rear cylinder. When Ducati decided it was time to move into the large capacity market, as Moto Guzzi, Honda, and all the British manufacturers were doing, these ideas influenced him.

Taglioni only had limited resources at his disposal, and there was a certain marketing risk involved in developing and trying to sell a larger capacity bike when the company was known only for smaller singles. There was also the stigma of the failure of the 1,260 cc V-four Apollo, a concept that in retrospect had been 25 years ahead of its time. Because of this failure Taglioni first developed his 'L' twin not only as a street bike but as a racer, both for 500 cc World Championship events and 750 cc events. He was always a true believer in the premise that 'racing improves the breed'.

Being an engineering purist, Taglioni chose the 90° layout for several reasons. He liked the wide cylinder angle for the same reasons that Moto Guzzi had used it in their racers, but preferred 90° because it offered perfect primary engine balance. With this layout the engine could be very smooth, with only some high frequency secondary imbalance, and with a narrow crankshaft there was virtually no rocking couple. In addition, theoretically the twin could be no wider than a single so the engine could be kept low in the frame while maintaining good ground clearance. Cooling to the rear cylinder was less of a problem, and the main concerns were carburation and keeping the inlet tracks of equal length with a good shape.

Taglioni's second drawing was completed exactly one month later, on 20 April 1970, and here he indicated a projected power output of 80 bhp (SAE) at 9,200 rpm from 750 cc. The inclination of the cylinders was to be 15° from the horizontal, exactly as the Apollo. Development of a prototype took place almost immediately. The engine was running within two months and a complete bike was on the road by August. This had a 250 mm double-sided twin

leading shoe Fontana front brake, and an unusual forward, rather than rear-set, footpeg arrangement. On a later version the front brake was from a Scrambler, while another had double front discs with the calipers cast into the fork legs, similar to that of the Dunstall Nortons of the time. This bike was displayed at the Olympia Show in London in January 1971. The first version featured remote float bowl Dell'Orto 29 mm SS1 carburettors, but these became 30 mm Amal 930 concentrics on subsequent models. Many of the ancillary components, such as the Silentium silencers, were sourced from the contemporary range of singles.

The 500 GP Bikes

At a Ducati board meeting in October 1970, the decision was made to re-enter the world of motorcycle competition. The management at this time – director Arnaldo Milvio and general manager Fredmano Spairani – were particularly enthusiastic about racing, and they had been instrumental in encouraging Taglioni to develop the 750 twin. The plan was to initially build ten 500 cc V-twin bikes, and race in Italian Championship events and some of the 1971 Grands Prix, but only five

bikes actually ended up being made. The intention was not so much to win races as to prove that the V-twin idea was sound, and to promote sales of the 750. Spairani wanted a frame developed by Colin Seeley in England, and a set of 500 cc prototype engine-cases was despatched to him, his brief being to develop a racing frame along the lines of his successful G50 Matchless version. The frame he developed was displayed in February 1971, then raced with limited success as a 500 Grand Prix bike by Bruno Spaggiari, Ermanno Giuliano, and Phil Read during the 1971 and 1972 seasons. In the meantime Fabio Taglioni and his team managed to design and build a complete racing bike, from scratch to race debut, in under six months.

While many of the technical specifications of the 500 were identical to the 750, it had a much shorter stroke, at 58 mm. With 74 mm pistons and 10.5:1 compression, it initially produced 61.2 bhp at 11,000 rpm. All the 500 GP bikes built used two-valve engines with desmodromic valve gear and an 80° included valve angle. Carburation was by remote float bowl Dell'Orto 40 mm SS carburettors, and they used a six-speed gearbox with a dry multi-plate clutch. Ignition was

Bruno Spaggiari on the first 500 racer in early 1971. This is before the Seeley frame and Lockheed front disc brake.

electronic, provided by nearby Ducati Elettrotecnica, but this was generally unreliable in early races. When first raced, they used a Ducati-designed chassis with a single Lockheed disc brake on the front and a twin leading shoe Fontana at the rear. Dry weight was 297 lb (135 kg) and 18-inch wheels were fitted front and rear with 3.00 and 3.25 tyre sizes. Wheelbase was a moderate 56.3 inches (1,430 mm). In June 1971, Phil Read tested the bike with the better-handling Seeley frame, and this' was then adopted on Spaggiari's bike.

Besides the two-valve head, Taglioni also produced a four-valve version, still with the single overhead camshaft driven by vertical shaft and bevel-gears. These heads were taller and had twin splayed exhaust ports, but ultimately they didn't produce as much power as the two-valve versions. Thus they contributed to Taglioni's suspicion of four-valve cylinder heads, even though he persevered with their development through to 1973. Initial power from the four-valve heads gave 65 bhp at 12,000 rpm, but by the end of 1972 this had only risen to 69 bhp at 12,500 rpm. Over the same period the power from the two-valve engine increased to 71 bhp, so the four-valve version was never raced.

Race results during 1971 were disappointing due to a spate of gear-box and ignition problems. The best results had been Phil Read's second to Agostini in the San Remo Grand Prix, and a fourth, also by Read, at Monza in the Grand Prix delle Nazione, where Spaggiari had looked like taking second before breaking a valve. In May 1972, Bruno Spaggiari finished third at Imola, this time beating Paul Smart into fourth. They had finished the other way round one month earlier in the Formula 750 race (see Chapter 7). Unfortunately, no matter how tractable and light it was, nor how well it handled, a twin was never going to match Agostini on the MV triple. Ducati realized this and already had plans to produce a water-cooled 350 triple, and 500 four.

Taglioni had always been a fan of fuel injection, and direct injection was tried on the 500 Grand Prix bike in March 1972. It was then outlawed by the FIM, which ruled it was a form of supercharging. Twin discs now graced the front end. The final 500 appeared in 1973, with belt-driven double overhead desmodromic camshafts, but it was still no MV-beater. This bike is described in Chapter 10.

The MV-beater proposed by Spairani was the previously-mentioned 350 triple, and 500 four. The government controllers of Ducati wouldn't sanction the 500, but a water-cooled 350 cc double over-head camshaft, 12-valve three-cylinder engine, with a seven-speed gearbox, was built and developed throughout 1972. It ran to 16,000 rpm in bench tests, but barely achieved 50 bhp at 14,500 rpm. Already obsolete, and brought in from the British Ricardo company, Taglioni wasn't too keen on the project. By now Spairani was no longer in control, and all racing projects (500 four and 350 triple), along with the 500 GP, were scrapped early in 1973.

A 750 cc version of the 500 with the Seeley frame was tested by Mike Hailwood at Silverstone in August 1971, but Hailwood elected not to ride the bike because the handling needed more development. Taglioni had already developed another frame, based on the Seeley, that found its way to the production 750GT, and evolved into the largely unchanged 750 Sport, 750SS, and lasted through to the final 900SS and Mike Hailwood Replicas of 1982. It formed the basis of the 1972 Imola race-winning 750s and the 1978 Mike Hailwood Isle of Man F1 bike. All these frames have typical Seeley features such as the solidly-mounted chain adjusters.

750 GT

When the production prototype 750 appeared, it had a single Lockheed disc with the distinctive polished aluminium leading axle Marzocchi forks with 'Ducati' cast into the sliders. The first production models appeared in June 1971 and were the epitome of 1970s styling, with silver-painted frames and garish metalflake paintwork in either orange, green, or blue on the fibreglass tank and side-covers. The instrument layout was more like a dashboard, the Smiths instruments being surrounded by plastic and warning lights. What was undeniable now, though, was the way the designers had managed to tidy up the styling of the engine-cases, with beautiful castings for the side-covers and ignition housing. It was obvious that the aesthetics of the engine were as important as the look of ancillary components. In this respect the 750 twin carried on the tradition of Italian engines of the past, that even

The 1972 version of the 500GP, with a Seeley frame and Lockheed disc brakes.

The first production 750GT of 1971 with metalflake paintwork.

if the internals were rather ordinary (as they were on many popular small Italian motorcycles) the motors still looked purposeful and functional. In the case of the 750, however, there was nothing mundane about the internals and, with the MV Agusta 750, it was the most exotic engine in production at that time.

Though obviously utilizing much from the contemporary line of wide-case singles, the 750 'L' twin, as it was called, was considerably uprated. The hairpin valve springs were replaced by single coil springs, to keep the rocker box narrow and allow sufficient air-flow over the individually-cast cylinder heads. The finning on the horizontal head was longitudinal, while on the rear cylinder it was radial. The two 80 mm pistons moved through a 74.4 mm stroke via one-piece connecting rods, not unlike the singles. Compression ratio was a very mild 8.5:1, the pistons being quite heavy full skirt designs with three rings, one of which was a slotted oil scraper. The small end bronze bush size was 22 mm, and eye-to-eye length on the con-rod 150 mm, giving a theoretically perfect stroke:rod ratio of 2:1. The crankshaft itself was a three-piece pressed-up item with the

two connecting rods on one 36 mm pin, rotating on two rows of 18 caged 5 mm rollers. Thus the two cylinders were slightly staggered, the rear to the right and the front to the left, to allow a slimmer overall width and bring the exhaust pipes closer in for better ground clearance. The main bearings were considerably uprated from the 250/350/450 single, being an expensive fibre-caged axial thrust type, 80 x 35 x 21 mm. The crankshaft was additionally supported by two smaller outrigger ball-bearings in the alloy outer cases. Drive to the gearbox was by helical primary gears, the first series having 29 teeth on the crankshaft driving a 71-tooth clutch basket. Unfortunately, Ducati got it wrong with this ratio of 2.448:1, and early engines were prone to clutch slip. From 1974 all round-case engines had the revised primary drive ratio of the 750 Super Sport. Inside the primary drive gear a large, 5 lb flywheel resided, filling up the space between the gear and the main bearing. Removing this seemed to have no detrimental effect to performance, or idling, and was generally the first modification any prospective racer made. The gearbox and all bearings were stronger. In order to keep the

engine as short as possible, Taglioni had chosen to use a direct type gearbox with the layshaft above the mainshaft necessitating that the engine rotated in a reverse direction. The gear selector mechanism on the right side of the engine was identical to that of the singles, fine while new but rather prone to wear, especially if the bike had been ridden in the rain for long periods. Water would then enter the selector box, washing out the grease.

The cylinder-head design owed more to the singles than any other aspect of the engine, and was arguably obsolete before it was even put into production, the wide included angle of 80° having been inherited from the 1955 Gran Sport. Thus while valve sizes were a reasonable 40 mm for the inlet and 36 mm for the exhaust, there would be problems getting sufficiently high compression from racing engines using these heads in the future. Valve adjustment was by replaceable shims on top of the valve stem. Large squish bands were provided, and the offset of the ports (15° inlet and 30° exhaust) contributed to excellent swirl characteristics. Due to the space limitations imposed by the frame the swirl in the front cylinder was clockwise, as the ports were offset to the right, while in the rear it was anti-clockwise with left offset ports. This swirl contributed to excellent cylinder filling and allowed the use of a moderate 38° of ignition advance, even though ultimate horsepower was limited by the cylinder head design.

Surprisingly, the camshafts were particularly racing oriented for such a low compression touring engine. Timing figures were inlet opening 65° before top dead centre and closing 84° after bottom dead centre, and exhaust opening 74° before bottom dead centre and closing 58° after top dead centre. This gave an inlet valve duration of 329°, exhaust valve duration of 312°, and valve overlap of 123° – figures more appropriate for a high performance engine. It was a tribute to the design characteristics that the engine was still eminently tractable with excellent mid-range torque, despite these camshafts.

The camshafts were supported by three identical ball-bearings, and the larger, 17 mm bevel-gear shafts by a double row, self-aligning ball-bearing at the top and two ball-bearings and sleeve at the bottom. The distributor shaft was placed in between the two

The 750 engine camshaft gear train. Between the camshaft drives are the ignition points. (Two Wheels)

camshaft drives, driving an ignition cam inside an exquisitely cast and machined housing. The points may have been difficult to set up because they were both mounted on one backing plate and access was difficult, but the casting was undeniably artistic. The condensers too were located in this housing, not the most practical place if one was trying to ensure that they didn't get too hot. However, the use of points was obviously considered a temporary measure, because the cases were drilled and tapped for electronic ignition installation beside the drive side main bearing, and the 35 mm outlet hole for the wires plugged up. Electrical power was provided by a marginal 150 watt alternator mounted on the right side of the crankshaft. 150 watts was obviously its peak output because those who rode around at night using low revs would be plagued by a flat battery the next day.

The bevel-gear layout on these first V-twins was magnificent, but time-consuming to assemble correctly. A set of nine helical toothed bevels was used for both camshaft and distributor drive, with the hunting-tooth principle used to distribute the shock load of valve opening over several

The bevel-gears in the cylinder head were similar to those of the singles. (Two Wheels)

teeth. The difficulty in assembly occurred because all the lower bevel-gears were dependent on one another for correct meshing. If too tight, the gears whined excessively, overloading the bearings. If they were set up too loosely, they rattled and affected the valve timing, causing power loss. In addition, the heat expansion of the alloy engine-cases needed to be factored in. The lower bevels came as a matched set, with dots machined to assist correct valve timing during assembly. The earliest bevel sets were also heavily dished underneath, and the very first sets came without timing marks.

The oil filtration and lubrication system was carried over from the singles. The only provision for filtration was a gauze filter in the sump, and the centrifugal sludge traps in the webs of the crankshaft. The transmission too was lubricated by engine oil flung off the big-ends. The oil pump was driven off the crankshaft on the right-hand side and was, in deference to the widespread use of ball and roller bearings, a low pressure device. It has to be said that here was an area in which the design was not thoroughly up to date. An owner needed to be scrupulous with the maintenance schedule and heavyweight oil was specified because of the churning by the bevel-gears. Leaving oil in longer than 1,000 miles (1,600 km) risked problems with the big-end bearings due to loss of viscosity and contamination.

The wet clutch comprised 16 plates, and was a slight problem. The clutches on the early bikes in particular, with the lower primary drive ratio, were prone to slipping. It wasn't long before the factory racing bikes were using a dry multi-plate clutch, but it would be over ten years before these made it to the production line.

With two tower shafts of bevel gears driving the single overhead camshaft in each cylinder head from a set of bevel-gears originating at the crankshaft, and primary drive by helical gear, there wasn't a chain in the engine (at least until the advent of an electric start version first displayed early in 1972). All bearings were ball or roller and every shaft, be it crank, gearbox or bevel, was shimmed individually for the correct end float or backlash. This was truly an engine from a different era, designed without any concession to production economics. It was so labour-intensive to assemble (particularly the bevel-gears, which had to be set up individually from the crankshaft) that it took up to eight hours to assemble one engine at the factory and two days for a racing one. Consequently it wasn't possible to produce many, and over the four-year production period (1971– 75) only about 8,000, or less than 2,000 a year, were made, including 750 Sports and 750SSs. Even contemporary Italian manufacturers were moving towards less expensive engines in the early 1970s. Moto Guzzi was building a pushrod twin and the Laverdas had chain primary drives and cam chains like British bikes and Hondas. The Ducati singles and twins, and the MV fours, were really the only bikes left with their roots in the great racing designs of the 1950s.

However, a beautiful engine is worthless if placed in a mediocre chassis, and this is where Ducati came up trumps. The Seeley-inspired frame using the solid sand-cast engine as a stressed member, though not light, was strong, and utilized mainly straight tubes. Steering was slow due to the 29° fork rake and the 60.2-inch (1,530 mm) wheelbase, but stability was unquestioned. The wheelbase length, which resulted from the long engine, was considerably greater than that of the contemporary 500GP Twin racer. In a time when most large bikes used forks with tiny diameter staunchions and small diameter plastic swing-arm bushes, the 750GT was very advanced with its 38 mm staunchions and large bronze bushes. Not only that, but Taglioni had designed the bike with his typical commitment to balance and symmetry. The crankshaft was placed exactly mid-way between the axles and on the same line, and high quality components such as Borrani alloy rims were fitted to reduce unsprung weight. All these factors contributed to many commentators at the time claiming that no bike in the world handled better than the 750GT. The testers at *Cycle* magazine in the USA were particu-

The 750 round-case was one of the best-looking Ducati engines. This is the clutch side of a 750 Sport.

larly enthusiastic about the Ducati 750. To quote from their road test in October 1972: 'When the right-side peg nicks down in an 80 mph sweeper and the bike never bobbles . . . you know that a motorcyclist designed this machine, and he got it right'. Admittedly, the quality of certain components, such as the Aprilia switchgear and the general standard of chroming, was questionable. However, features like the straight pull spokes laced to strong cast hubs, Tomaselli throttle, and stainless steel guards, showed that Ducati had different priorities when it came to building bikes.

It may have handled better than any other bike, but to those brought up on British motorcycles it looked long and weird. By the standards of the day the single opposed piston Lockheed front brake was excellent (most calipers at that time were floating piston types), but even though weight was moderate at 185 kg (408 lb), it was down on power compared to a Norton Commando or Triumph Trident. With heavy 8.5:1 pistons, and tiny 30 mm Amal carburettors (made in Spain) with extremely restrictive air cleaners, the bike was slow. A rider was hard-pressed to coax more than 180 km/h (112 mph) out of it, even though the factory claimed 200 km/h (124 mph). Maximum power was quoted as 55 bhp, and

maximum revs as 7,800 rpm. With a dealer network that was very poor outside Italy, the bike proved a slow seller until its victory at Imola in April 1972. As Ing. Fabio Taglioni observed in 1974: 'When we won at Imola we won the market too'.

The GT, rather than the singles, became the mainstay of the production line-up, but it underwent numerous changes during its manufacture. The very first few examples built in

Until 1974 750GTs used these distinctive leading axle Marzocchi forks, Borrani alloy rims, and stainless steel guards. (Two Wheels)

1971 featured a twin leading shoe rear brake. Those up to engine number 404 had engine-cases with a bolt through the sump (this was also to mount the forward-set foot-rests of the first prototype). The very earliest bikes also had a clutch cover without an inspection plate, and the engine-cases were sand-cast. The first 500 bikes were considered pre-production. In 1972 (after engine number 501), new paint schemes appeared, the silver frame and metalflake paint giving way to a black frame and red or black fibreglass petrol tanks. Veglia instruments replaced the Smiths. There were new seats, and the rear tail-light from the singles.

Problems with the kickstart lever cracking the engine cover led to the installation of a longer kickstart shaft, and new lever after engine number 1500. By now, with Berliner serious about distributing the bikes, US versions had appeared, slightly different to their European cousins. Larger tail-lights and higher, wider handlebars were the most notable alterations.

Some commentators have made the observation that the 750GT appeared with a random selection of equipment from 1974, but this is incorrect. All bikes can be dated from the range of brakes or suspension fitted, bearing in mind that at Ducati batches of engines are always made separately to the bikes, and engine and frame numbers do not coincide. There was nothing random about the way the bikes were assembled, though the shipment of bikes from Italy may have been less methodical. By mid-1973 the fibreglass fuel tank had been replaced by a steel one, with a new colour scheme, and the Lockheed front disc and master cylinder had given way to an Italian Scarab that was essentially a Lockheed copy.

Earlier, the Smiths instruments had been replaced by Veglia, the tachometer in particular becoming a rather unreliable electronic type. I can remember that the 750GT I bought in 1973 had three of these replaced under warranty. The tacho drive on the first series had been similar to the singles, with a floating drive mounted on the front camshaft end cover, and was rather prone to leaking oil. In addition new camshafts were fitted at this time, with the same opening and closing specifications but a new profile, and the new type of Dell'Orto PHF 30 AD and AS carburettor of the type fitted to the 750 Sport. Though these didn't help the bike develop any more horsepower, they certainly aided starting, and they didn't leak fuel as much as the Amals. The stainless guards now made way for a painted steel variety.

At this point – late 1973 – about 3,500 bikes had been built (GTs and Sports), and they all featured the leading axle Marzocchis, which were painted black for the European market but rendered as polished alloy for the USA. Some of these had an electric start mounted over the clutch cover, but they were unusual and it is rare to see one today. The next stage in production demonstrated the greatest variety, which was caused by variability in supply from Ducati's sources of proprietary components.

In the search for a shorter wheel-base, the racing bikes had moved away from the leading axle forks during 1973, and this filtered through to the production line. By early 1974 some GTs appeared with 38 mm centre-axle Cerianis and a single Brembo 280 mm cast iron front disc and forward-mounted 08 caliper. They still had the Borrani wheel-rims, and had reverted to a cable-driven Veglia tachometer with the drive housed in a one-piece cover from the front camshaft. As supply from Ceriani became difficult, Marzocchi also produced a centre-axle fork, but with a Scarab brake caliper mounting for the 278 mm iron disc. These Marzocchis had modified top triple clamps to provide the same trail as the centre-axle models, and steel rims rather than the Borranis. Marzocchi also produced a centre-axle fork with a forward-mounted Brembo 08 caliper, but fewer GTs had this arrangement.

By now not only had the Borrani rims disappeared, but quieter Lafranconi mufflers had replaced the loud, but lovely, Contis. The valve adjustment followed the practice established by 860 of being by screw and locknut, rather than shim. All engines from mid-1974 had the higher crowned rocker covers, whether they were GT, Sport, or SS, irrespective of their method of valve adjustment. Also, the revised primary ratio of the 1974 750 Super Sport was standardized throughout the range. With 32 teeth on the crankshaft and 70 on the clutch drum, the ratio was now 2.187:1, and helped alleviate problems of clutch slip. This ratio was retained until the advent of the Mille in 1985.

The very final examples shared much in the way of ancillary components with the 860 that was in production simultaneously. They had the revised CEV switch-gear and throttle, with the ignition switch now placed under the tank, not between the tank and seat. They also shared the 860 wiring loom and 860 instrument panel with the intriguing 'city/country' horn button switch. The last models had lost a lot of the individual features of the original and it set a precedent that Ducati was to follow in the future. Often it is the earliest examples of particular models that are the most appealing. Throughout the subsequent history of the marque this has happened time and again.

By late 1974, US legislation was making left-side gear shifts mandatory, so the round-case engine was phased out to make way for the square-case 860 that had a left-side gearshift by a crossover shaft behind the engine. The round-case was also too expensive and time-consuming to manufacture, and by 1975 its production had ended, though, like the last singles, it continued to be sold until stocks had run out. Interestingly, demand occurred again three years later, in 1978, when the Australian importers, Frasers in Sydney, requested a batch of both 750GTs and Sports. The factory responded by building 41 GTs and 22 Sports out of spare parts. These, along with some police bikes, were the last of the round-case models.

For some reason the GT has become one of the forgotten members of the Ducati family. Considering the exotic nature of the engine, and its beautiful castings, it is surprising how little status it has in the Ducati classic hierarchy. Once again it comes down to the sporting heritage. Ducatis are perceived as sporting motorcycles, not touring bikes. However, it is important to remember that even the most revered sporting Ducatis had more humble origins. Historically the 750GT is perhaps one of the most important Ducatis ever, the first of the long line of highly successful 90° V-twins. They were also powered by an engine rated by Taglioni as his best design.

Ducati 750 Sport

When Ing. Fabio Taglioni conceived the 750 Ducati in 1970, he always had it in his mind to develop this design as a sporting motorcycle. An early prototype 750 cc engine carried 35 mm carburettors and spun to 9,500 rpm, far removed from the eventual 750GT, and indicating that sometime in the future a higher performance version would appear. Even before the historic Imola victory in 1972, prototype 750 Sports had been displayed, largely based on the GT but with clip-on handlebars and rear-set footpegs, and a more highly-tuned engine. The first prototype was shown to Italian concessionaires in 1971 by the then Ducati directors, Arnaldo Milvio and Fredmano Spairani. It was little more than a sporty GT with a deeply-scalloped tank, and a second prototype appeared in early 1972. This was black with a white frame, had Nippon Denso instruments as on the Honda 750, 32 mm Amal carburettors with no air cleaners, and unique curved Conti mufflers. Braking was by a single Lockheed disc up front, and a single Lockheed rear disc. Alternative versions were also shown, some with a half-fairing, twin Lockheed front discs, and Veglia instruments. The colour scheme was the one eventually chosen for the production bikes, yellow with black frame and 'Z' stripes. By the end of 1972 the 750 Sport was in production, and today it is one of the most sought-after of the older Ducatis. There is no denying that Ducati got it right with the Sport.

The first production Sports used 750GT frames with the wide rear subframe, Veglia instruments, single Lockheed 278 mm iron disc, and the single rear drum brake as on the GT.

One of the prototype 750 Sports of 1972. This one had Nippon Denso instruments, twin Lockheed front discs, and Amal carburettors.

The strange curved Contis never made it to production, and by 1973 the frame was replaced by a neater-looking one with a narrower rear subframe. All 750 Ducatis at this time came with leading axle Marzocchi forks, but there were a number of details that differentiated the Sport from the GT. It must also be remembered that the 750 Super Sport had not yet appeared, and the 750 Sport was the company's top-performance, and top-of-the-line, model.

The appearance of the Sport created quite a stir in the motorcycle press. Everyone was still amazed by the MV-beating performance of the 750 Desmos at Imola, so naturally the bike was expected to perform considerably better than the GT, and they were not disappointed. With only

minimal changes to the engine the 750 Sport now vied for the title of the best-performing 750 on the market. Not only was this a respectably fast bike for its day but it probably handled best too.

The 1973 version looked stunning with its yellow fibreglass tank, seat, and matching guards contrasting with the black-painted engine side-covers. I can clearly remember seeing one in 1973 and thinking how narrow the bike was compared to Honda 750 fours and Kawasaki triples. As a factory option a small half-fairing was available, but as this was only frame, and not steering head, mounted, its effectiveness looked better than it was. At high speed it moved around unnervingly, and with all the instruments and the headlight still

The first production 750 Sport used a 750GT frame.

mounted on the fork legs and triple clamp, no advantage could be made of any reduced steering inertia. Another problem was caused by the clip-on handlebars being splayed out at an uncomfortable angle because the petrol tank lacked sufficient clearance on full lock. Starting was by kickstart only, using a revised, swinging out lever, and fold-up foot-rest. This was a far more satisfactory arrangement than the kickstart on the GT, which more often than not resulted in bruised shins.

However, it was in the engine department that the Sport really showed most improvement over the GT. While engine changes consisted purely of lighter (by around 70 gm) slipper, pistons matched to a correspondingly lighter crankshaft, and larger carburettors without air cleaners, the change was dramatic. The very earliest models also had milled and polished con-rods, but without the dual strengthening rib around the big-end that characterized the later 750 Super Sport rods. The increase of compression to 9.3:1 was much better suited to the quite radical camshaft profiles of the GT, and the use of the

new type of Dell'Orto PHF 32 mm carburettor with unfiltered velocity stacks allowed the engine to breathe more freely. While power was only up to a claimed 60 bhp, the difference in performance between a GT and Sport was considerable. In all other respects the Sport engine was identical to the

GT, despite various claims of hotter camshafts and larger valves.

The cycle parts were identical to the GT, except that the rear 305 mm long Marzocchi shocks were without the top spring covers. All the guards were fibreglass, like the seat and petrol tank, and were of dubious qual-

The first 750 Sports had black engine covers.

ity. In the search for lightness even the rear number-plate holder was made of plastic. Wheels with 19-inch Borrani WM2 front and 18-inch WM3 alloy rims were the same as for the GT, as were the single 278 mm iron disc and single drum rear brake. With these early Sports no provision was made for any pillion passenger, and like the GT, Scarab brake components appeared during 1973, as did the electronic tachometer. They were still an uncompromised sporting motorcycle, with no provision for turn indicators.

By 1974 the 750 Super Sport had entered production, and the Sport was no longer the range leader. Changes in specification began to mirror those of the GT. First there were Ceriani centre-axle forks with a single Brembo front disc. Then, in deference to the UK market, where fibreglass petrol tanks were illegal, came a steel tank in the same shape. Some of these had appeared in 1973 on US market Sports. During 1974

the black-painted cases were replaced by polished cases like the GT and SS. Also like the GT, Marzocchi centre-axle forks with a Scarab front disc were fitted throughout 1974, still with the flat triple clamps, but unlike the GT Brembo-equipped centre-axle Marzocchis were not specified. While engine specifications remained unchanged except for a longer-stemmed inlet valve and the use of the revised primary drive, the very last 750 Sports featured a range of differences. To pull the widely splayed clip-on handlebars back to a better angle, they became offset forward of the forks. This was a considerable improvement over the strange riding position of the earlier models, and made the bike more similar in feel to the 750 Super Sport. The switch-gear and wiring mirrored the final 750GTs and first 860s, with the boxy CEV items and two-into-one throttle. The last item was definitely a retrograde step as throttle action was poorer and the cables were under more stress.

The last Sports also featured a dual seat as an option. US models now had indicators and large tail-lights, but fortunately the Borrani alloy rims stayed. The earlier Sports, while essentially the same, were a purer display of the sporting concept.

As a sporting motorcycle, the 750 Sport was superb. Lighter than the GT, at 182 kg (401 lb) due to the widespread use of fibreglass, and with more power, it was a stronger performer. Handling was the same, but the riding position lent itself to more spirited riding. To quote *Cycle* magazine in its June 1974 issue: 'The 750 Sport has a great engine packaged with a brilliant chassis'. *Cycle* went on to say: 'The Ducati 750, in any of its three incarnations, is still the best handling street machine available.' Elsewhere, too, praise was heaped on this motorcycle. The Australian magazine *Two Wheels* stated in October 1974: 'The Ducati 750 Sport is not just a good bike – it is a truly excep-

The 750 Sport had a neater instrument layout than the GT. This 1974 model has the later off-set clip-on handlebars.

A 1974 750 Sport with polished engine cases, centre-axle Marzocchi forks, and the optional fairing.

tional motorcycle'. In England, *Motorcyclist Illustrated* said, in July 1974: 'The Ducati Sport stands level with the very best that history can offer to match it, and as a sporting machine probably better than almost any other big roadster in production'.

Fifteen years later Ducati acknowl-edged the importance of the Sport when they released the Nuovo 750 Sport, a bike that was unfortunately only a shadow of the original. The round-case 750 Sport epitomizes the very best of Ducati, uncompromised engine and chassis performance, equal to the best in its day. If it hadn't been for the 750 Super Sport, or if it had possessed desmodromic rather than valve spring heads, the 750 Sport would have a higher status among *Ducatisti*. As it is, not many Sports were made and they are amongst the most desirable street Ducatis.

7.

Imola and the Desmodromic 750

23 April 1972 was the day when a brace of specially-prepared desmodromic 750 racers took on the best the world's manufacturers had to offer, and trounced them convincingly. It was the inaugural Imola 200, the 'Daytona of Europe', for Formula 750 machines, racing 750 cc machines with production-based motors. The win at Imola marked the transition for Ducati, from a relatively small and unknown Italian manufacturer, primarily of small-capacity single cylinder bikes, to that of a marque equal to any other. Within Italy, and to certain *cognoscenti* in other countries, Taglioni and Ducati were respected for technical excellence and innovation. Yet, in production terms, Ducati was a minor manufacturer of motorcycles. Imola changed that.

The impetus for developing a racing 750 had occurred back in July 1971. In a one-off ride, Mike Hailwood was to race a prototype Formula 750 machine at Silverstone in August 1971. However, although Hailwood tested the bike, and recorded a sixth-fastest practice lap for the F750 race, he elected not to race it in the event, telling *Motor Cycle* that 'it did not handle well enough. This isn't surprising because it is only three weeks old and has never been raced before; it just needs a bit of sorting out. It should be good then'.

This 750 was more closely related to the 500 racer than the 750 street bike that had only just gone into limited production. The sand-cast crankcase was identical to that of the 500 Grand Prix bike, but it had the bore and stroke, 80 x 74.4 mm, of the production bike. It also had the dry clutch and six-speed gearbox of the 500, and a single overhead camshaft driven by bevel-gears. This was also the first 750 twin with desmodromic valve gear, and it reputedly allowed 75 bhp to be developed, with the engine revving to 11,500 rpm, using 40 mm SS Dell'Orto carburettors. The frame, likewise, was from the 500, being one of the batch made by Colin Seeley earlier that year. Up front, only a single Lockheed disc graced the Marzocchi leading axle front end, and this was insufficient for the more powerful 360 lb (163 kg) machine. The handling problems mentioned by Mike Hailwood were obviously the result of slotting a 750 engine into a 500. The bike would need to be redesigned for the inaugural Imola 200 the following year.

With the support of Fredmano Spairani, Fabio Taglioni was given the brief to make an all out assault on this important race. It was being heavily promoted, and nine different factories had entered works-supported teams. In order to assess the level of competition, Taglioni made the trip to Daytona in March 1972, and came away impressed by the well developed Japanese racers. He realized that he couldn't tackle them head-on, he didn't have the resources. Utilizing proven technology from the 350 Desmo and 500 racers, he aimed to build a balanced machine, with handling and braking matched to useable horsepower.

Upon his return from Daytona, serious work began on developing the Imola bikes. Surprisingly, Taglioni started with standard 750GT street bikes. They had 750 engine numbers, indicating that bikes were just taken off the production line and into the racing department. The frames still had centre-stand mounts and stock frames. They also had machined production leading axle Marzocchi forks, but there was more to these bikes than met the eye. The engines, while using standard 40 mm inlet and 36 mm exhaust valves, used desmodromic valve control enabling the engine to run to 9,200 rpm. These were the first bikes to use the 'Imola' desmodromic camshafts with figures of inlet opening 65° before top dead centre and closing 95° after bottom dead centre, and exhaust opening 95° before bottom dead centre and closing 60° after top dead centre. Inlet valve lift was 12 mm. Power of 84 bhp at 8,800 rpm was claimed at the rear wheel, but more importantly it was the spread of power that was so advantageous. At 7,000 rpm the engine was said to make 70 bhp. Compression was up to 10:1 and these engines still used the wide, 80° included valve angle. They also used the first versions of the new 40 mm Dell'Orto PHF concentric carburettor.

In order to keep combustion temperatures down, an oil-cooling system was fitted that cooled the oil to the cylinder heads, and dual plug ignition installed with an additional 10 mm Lodge spark-plug. This enabled ignition advance to be cut back to 34° before top dead centre. With the alternator removed from the right side of the crankshaft, total loss battery and coil ignition, still by

One of the 1972 Imola racers, this being Spaggiari's bike after it was sold to Ron Angel in Australia. The twin plug ignition and four ignition coils are easily seen. (Two Wheels)

dual points, was employed. Since his experience with electronic ignition on the 500, Fabio Taglioni was wary of employing it on the 750 for Imola, and was also worried about heat build-up inside the fairing over such a long race. Thus the condensers were mounted on the front frame down-tubes, away from the heat of the engine.

Apart from the stronger connect-ing rods machined out of solid billet, 50 gm lighter than standard, the lower end of the engine was early 750GT. There were straight cut primary drive and clutch gears (with a drilled clutch basket to save weight), but it had the same gearbox. There was no six-speed gearbox, or dry clutch, as on the 500 racers. The primary drive ratio differed from the GT and the later SS, being 31/75, or 2.419:1. Further weight was saved by completely removing the kickstart mechanism, which also served to increase ground clearance on the right side. Braking was uprated to two Lockheed front discs, and a rear 230 mm disc replacing the road bike's drum. With only left-side calipers in stock from the street bikes, these were used all round, the right-side front having an unusually long brake hose.

A high-rise exhaust pipe was on the left, but not on the right. Imola had predominantly left-hand corners, but ground clearance was still a problem because racing tyres required an 18-inch front wheel instead of a 19-inch. Total dry weight of these racers was 392 lb (178 kg), and they were reputed to pull the tallest available gearing, giving 169 mph (272 km/h).

Seven bikes were built. To ride one of them, Ducati had approached firstly Jarno Saarinen, Renzo Pasolini, and then, in February, Barry Sheene. All had declined, not feeling that the Ducati would be competitive. Ducati already had the evergreen 39-year-old Bruno Spaggiari, who had raced every factory bike since the 1950s, and knew the Imola circuit intimately. To partner Spaggiari would be the younger Ermanno Giuliano, who had raced the 500 Ducati throughout 1971. English rider Alan Dunscombe, who had already been racing a modi-fied 750GT for English importer Vic Camp, filled the third berth. Spairani now only required a top-line F750 racer to ride the last bike, and, through Vic Camp, managed to secure Paul Smart at the last minute. Originally planning to ride a Triumph Triple, the deal fell through, and

reluctantly Smart flew to Italy. While a 750 Desmo with Sport bodywork had been tested at Modena in March, with further tests by Spaggiari with revised bodywork on 6 April, it wasn't until 19 April that the Imola racers were started up for the first time at Modena, too late to correct any defects. However, Taglioni was quietly confident. Smart had equalled Agostini's lap record, set on a 500 cc MV Agusta Grand Prix bike. In their specially-constructed glass-sided transporter, all seven Ducatis – two each for Smart and Spaggiari, one each for Dunscombe and Giuliano, and one spare – were transported the 40 km (25 miles) to Imola.

On race day, 70,000 spectators crammed into Autodromo Dino Ferrari at Imola. With works machines in abundance from MV Agusta, Honda, Norton, Moto Guzzi, Triumph, and BSA, alongside works-supported Kawasaki, Laverda, Suzuki, and BMW, they had hopefully come to see the Italian factories beat the Japanese teams that had dominated Daytona. The best riders in the world were there too: Giacomo Agostini, Phil Read, Roberto Gallina, Walter Villa, Ray Pickrell, Tony Jeffries, John Cooper, Percy Tait, Ron Grant, and Daytona winner Don Emde. In prac-tice, Spaggiari, followed by Smart, had set the fastest time. With its fast sweeping curves – some smooth, others bumpy – and its up-and-down topography, Imola seemed to suit the Ducatis. Unlike Daytona this was no mere horsepower circuit. This was Imola before the advent of chicanes, a fast European circuit in the tradi-tional style.

Agostini, on a specially-prepared 750 MV, led at the start. This MV, while still with the shaft-drive of the road bikes, had a Grand Prix style frame with 500GP forks and brakes. At the end of the fourth lap Smart overtook Agostini, followed a lap later by Spaggiari. From then on the two Ducatis were untroubled out in front, and in the final five laps they were both racing for the lead. Spaggiari nipped in front, but on the final lap his bike started to misfire as he was low on fuel. He ran wide on a sweeper, allowing Smart to take a comfortable victory. It had been a

Paul Smart on his way to victory in the 1972 Imola 200. (Two Wheels)

great day for Ducati. It wasn't so bad for Paul Smart either, as he took home 7,080,000 Lire in prize money. Spairani was so excited that he donated the winning bike to Smart, who still has it on display at his shop in Paddock Wood in Kent. Spaggiari's bike ended up being sold to Ron Angel, Ducati distributor in Victoria, Australia, where it was campaigned by Kenny Blake during 1973. After spending many years in Western Australia, it also now lives in England. The race speed over 200 miles had been an astonishing 97.76 mph (157.35 km/h), with the fastest lap of 100.1 mph (161.11 km/h) being shared equally by Smart, Spaggiari, and Agostini.

After the race, Ducati promised 'Imola' replicas, but these were slow to appear. In the meantime the 750 racers were displayed at selected events around the world as part of a promotional exercise for the 750 road bikes. In June, three bikes were entered at Daytona, followed in July by the Canadian GP at Mosport, where they were raced unsuccessfully by Bruno Spaggiari and Percy Tait. Then in October, Smart won the Greek GP on the island of Corfu. Meanwhile, Smart had raced his own bike at various races in England throughout 1972, with moderate success. One was also taken to South Africa to race over the northern winter, where local rider Errol Cowan had some reasonable results in highly competitive fields that included Giacomo Agostini.

For 1973, despite the replacement of Arnaldo Milvio as general manager by Ing. de Eccher, Taglioni was given the authorization to build brand new racers, considerably removed from the street bikes. He knew that the 1972 bikes were too close to the road bikes to be competitive against the new wave of two-stroke Yamahas and Suzukis, so a completely new bike was designed, this time a real racer. As Formula 750 regulations only stipulated that the crankcases of the production bike must be retained, he designed a shorter, lighter frame, and a more powerful and compact engine. The frame featured eccentrics in the swing-arm bosses for chain adjustment, along with positions in the swing-arm to select one of three different wheelbases. The chain adjustment system ultimately found its way through to the next generation of road frames, the 860GT, yet the wheelbase selection remained peculiar to this 1973 racer. Also, to shorten the wheelbase even further, the distinctive Marzocchi leading axle forks were replaced with those of a centre-axle type after Spaggiari complained of front end instability at

Paul Smart with his Imola 750, still in completely original condition, August 1995.

the first test session at Modena. Thus, without the time to experiment further, the centre-axle Marzocchis were installed along with the flat triple clamps of the leading type. Though it meant an enormous trail increase (to nearly 6 inches), and despite reservations, it cured the wobble, and the bike subsequently handled well. Taglioni was so impressed with this suspension set-up that when the production 750SS appeared the following year it had this front end on the standard frame. Indeed, this front end geometry was fitted to the entire range of 750/900 Super Sports throughout their nine-year model life.

As he was still committed to the 90° twin, Taglioni needed more horsepower as well as a lighter, shorter bike. Here, by taking the 86 mm pistons of the 450 racer of 1970 that were readily available, he was able to shorten the stroke to 64.5 mm. This enabled revs to increase by 1,000 rpm, from the 9,200/9,500 rpm of the 1972 bike to 10,200/10,500 rpm. To take advantage of this more

oversquare bore/stroke ratio, a new head was designed with a 60° included valve angle, rather than the 80° that had been a feature of all previous Ducatis. Preparation was left to the last minute, this time due to

the endless strikes that occur in Italy from time to time. Because of delays in signing the 1972 metal-workers' contract, it wasn't until March 1973 that the strikes ended and work could begin on the new engine, barely a

The 1973 Imola racer was considerably more compact than the previous year. Here it is at Imola in 1974, again raced by Spaggiari.

month before the Imola 200. The cylinder heads, new camshafts (now giving 14 mm of intake valve lift), connecting rods, and rockers were all specially machined out of solid billets or castings, and a new vented dry clutch took the place of the previous oil-bath type. Carburettors remained the same 40 mm Dell'Ortos of the previous year, but instead of the unusual one-up, one-down exhaust system, both exhausts were now the high-rise type. Weight was down significantly, to 325 lb (147 kg). Front brakes were now forward-mounted Italian Scarab, a Lockheed pattern that would also eventually be seen on the 750 Super Sport.

On the dyno, the engine power dropped off at 9,500 rpm, yet in testing Spaggiari reported it happy to rev beyond 10,400 rpm. These problems with the Ducati dyno room meant that no one knew exactly how much power this new engine actually made, but claims in the region of 93 bhp were made. While testing at Modena, Spaggiari set an absolute record, beating Agostini's previous best on the MV 500 by 0.3 seconds, and demolishing the 750 record, set by Smart in 1972, by two seconds. With only three days to go before the race, the last engine was finished. It had to be run-in during qualifying and ended up in Spaggiari's bike.

Race day was 15 April 1973, and even without the presence of Giacomo Agostini and his MV, 100,000 people streamed in to see the second Daytona of Europe. The Ducati team consisted of three riders, Bruno Spaggiari, Bruno Kneubüller, and Mick Grant. There was also another Ducati, entered under the NCR banner for the first time, but it wasn't a short-stroke racer, and was a prototype for the production 750 Super Sport to be released later in the year. Ridden by Claudio Loigo, it finished 15th. Even without Agostini, the competition was much stronger, particularly with Jarno Saarinen on a Yamaha 351 two-stroke, and the deci-

Spaggiari at Imola in 1974. His best result this year was an eighth in the first leg.

Still mixing it with the two-strokes, Spaggiari at Imola in 1974. Number 47 is Barry Sheene.

sion to run the race in two 100-mile stages also helped the two-strokes. Still, in the first leg Kneubüller set the fastest lap at 1:49.1, almost three seconds faster than the Ducatis in 1972, and an average speed of over 103 mph (166 km/h). In the second race he crashed while catching Saarinen. Mick Grant burnt his clutch at the start of the first race, but Bruno Spaggiari again finished second overall, with a second place in the first leg, followed by a third in the second. It was a magnificent result considering the level of competition, but was to be the final race for the silver 750s as official factory bikes.

At the Imola race of 1974, Spaggiari rode one of the same bikes as in the previous year, but they were entered under his own team. With no more development they were totally outclassed and the best he could manage was an eighth in the first leg, retiring in the second. They were raced again in 1975, Spaggiari this

time electing to manage the team rather than ride. With 1972 winner Paul Smart and future 500 cc World Champion Franco Uncini riding them, the best result was Uncini's 21st overall. Smart crashed out, breaking his leg and prompting his retirement. Uncini went on to compete in the Junior Italian Championship on the Team Spaggiari 750SS, winning 15 out of 21 races. Spaggiari still has one of the bikes, which lurked forlornly behind his Fiat car workshop in Modena until his retirement two years ago. It was a pity that these bikes bowed out with such a whimper, because if they had been developed further they could have been possibly the most successful bevel-gear two-cylinder racers, and many of the engine design features may have found their way onto the production bikes. Even without that development, the short-stroke 750 racers were amongst the finest Ducatis ever built. If only they had

made a short-stroke street 750 Super Sport with the 60° valve angle in 1975.

Ducati 750 Super Sport 1974

Even more than the MV Agusta, the 1974 Ducati 750 Super Sport epitomizes the Italian sporting motorcycle of the 1970s. Whereas the production MV four-cylinder bike was intentionally designed to be as far removed from the genuine Grand Prix racers as possible (to avoid customers converting them into competition for the factory bikes), the Ducati was as close a replica to the Imola 200 winning racer of 1972 that could be built and still be street legal. Immediately after the 1972 Imola race, Spairani promised 'Imola' replicas, but in typical Ducati fashion these were slow to materialize.

A prototype emerged in late 1972 that was very much a modified GT, just like the first racer. It had the leading axle forks, wide rear sub-frame, and the distinctive fibreglass petrol tank with the instant fuel gauge clear strip. Braking was by triple Scarab discs and the engine was a detuned version of the Imola racer. Because an 18-inch front wheel was fitted to the Marzocchi forks designed for a 19-inch, the fibreglass front guard was clamped to the fork legs. The engine itself was a work of art, still with the 40 mm Dell'Ortos, desmodromic camshafts (with 11 mm of intake valve lift), and the race connecting rods milled, machined, and polished from solid chrome-molybdenum steel billet. The desmodromic system was different to that of the singles. Instead of hairpin valve springs, to provide the light pressure to seat the valves to assist starting, springs that curled around the lower rocker were fitted. The early ones tended to break, and adjustment of the closing valve clearance was now by a one-piece shim. Along with the Laverda SFC750, the 750SS pioneered the standard fitting of fairings to a production streetbike. The racing style half-fairing also had the instruments (including ammeter) and headlight mounted in it, and was supported by the steering headstem to reduce steering inertia. This proto-type had the black engine-covers of the 750 Sport. The silver bodywork was matched to a green/blue frame, quite unlike any Ducati before or since. As such, these models have earned the nickname 'The Green Frame'.

1973 came and everyone waited expectantly for the production bike. At the Milan Show at the end of the year another 750 Super Sport was displayed, now with polished engine-cases and the centre-axle Marzocchis. Earlier, a few bikes had been built and three ended up being airfreighted to the US in late-1973. Phil Schilling and Cook Neilson of *Cycle* magazine got one of them, Neilson eventually modifying his into the 'California Hot Rod' and racing it to victory in the Daytona Superbike race of 1977 (see Chapter 9). These bikes also had the black engine-cases, but with the centre-axle forks, and were basically modified 750 Sports, using Veglia instruments (now without the amme-

The desmodromic valve system of the 750SS, which used different closing springs to those on the desmo singles.

ter). They had rear-mounted Scarab front calipers and an underslung Lockheed rear caliper.

It wasn't until early-1974 that the one and only batch of round-case 750 Super Sports was produced. They were built as homologation specials for the FIM, regulations requiring 200 to be manufactured. Though there is some doubt about the number of bikes actually manufactured, as engine numbers go up to 411, Taglioni confirmed to me that 200 were built, and he supervised their production. A significant proportion (88) went to the US. Other countries were less fortunate, with the UK getting 24 and Australia 33. Germany, today the largest market for Ducati, only received 12. There were only the barest concessions made for street legality. Silencing was minimal from the Conti silencers, and the 40 mm Dell'Ortos lacked any form of air filtration. There was no provision for turn signals, let alone an electric start. Whereas the quality of the fibreglass and some of the ancillary components was dubious, the engine was a masterpiece. A special machine was installed at the factory to machine from billet each individual

con-rod, just as with the Imola racers, and all the rockers were highly polished. No other contemporary machine offered comparable performance, for while the power output of 72 bhp (at the rear wheel) was modest, the light weight – barely 397 lb (180 kg) – in combination with an extremely narrow frontal area ensured a top speed of around 130–35 mph (210–17 km/h). *Motorrad* in Germany was one of the few magazines to comprehensively test one and they achieved a top speed of 216.7 km/h (135 mph), while *Motociclismo* in Italy achieved a standing 400 metre time of 12.215 seconds at 176.47 km/h (109.7 mph).

All these 1974 bikes were identical, and they were quite different to the GTs and Sports. The engine-cases were generally drilled for an oil-cooler and had extra internal webbing, as did the side-covers. The frame dimensions too were different, as the optional high-rise exhaust system bolts on perfectly to the SS but doesn't fit a Sport. They had the higher-domed rocker covers of the 860 and later 750s, higher primary drive ratio and the same 9.5:1 Mondial pistons as the 750 Sport,

The 1974 750 Super Sport. The definitive factory cafe racer.

even though compression was listed on some brochures at 10:1. Valve sizes were standard 750, at 40 mm and 36 mm, but the desmodromic camshafts featured higher lift (11 mm) and different timing, with inlet opening 63° before top dead centre and closing 83° after bottom dead centre, and exhaust opening 80° before bottom dead centre and closing 58° after top dead centre. Despite being desmodromic these camshafts were actually slightly milder than the 750GT, with inlet duration of 326°, and valve overlap of 121°. There were lots of individually fabricated parts, like the welded steel inlet manifolds – hardly weight-saving, but indicative of a limited edition machine. These bikes had the same Marzocchi front forks and forward-mounted Scarab calipers that had been used on the 1973 Imola racers, and an overslung rear Lockheed brake caliper. The front Scarab master cylinder wasn't the best quality, and invariably leaked brake fluid over the tank. Instruments were English Smiths, and tyres were the

only V-rated ones available at the time, Metzeler C7 Racing, in identical sizes of 3.50V18 front and rear. It must be said that these tyres were not really suited to the bike, making the

steering ponderously heavy, as well as being quite slippery. They were mounted on identical Borrani WM3 18-inch rims front and rear.

For those who bought a 750 Super

Like the 1972 Imola racer, the 1974 750SS had the clear strip in the fibreglass fuel tank – an instant fuel gauge.

The 1974 750SS was the only production Ducati to use a Lockheed rear disc brake and master cylinder.

Sport, there was also the factory option of a racing uprating kit. This highly comprehensive kit contained a full fairing and brackets (patterned after the 1973 racer, not the boxier 1972 version), high-rise open megaphones, oil-cooler, 12 mm 'Imola' desmodromic camshafts, a selection of eight rear sprockets from 34 to 42 teeth and a range of main jets from 150 to 152. There was even a set of racing Lodge spark-plugs and a Renold racing chain. For engines fitted with the 'Imola' camshafts but still with Conti silencers, the maximum revs increased from 8,800 rpm to 9,000 rpm. With the megaphones, revs increased to 9,200 rpm.

However, even as the 750SS was being produced the round-case engine series was being phased out in favour of the Giugiaro-inspired square-case 860. Economics, and forthcoming legislation regarding noise and left-side gearshifting, would leave the 750SS of 1974 as the only desmodromic version of the round-case engine and the rarest and most

special of all production street Ducatis. It also represented the end of an era for production engines, the era where cost and government legislation had minimal influence on the design or execution. Where the 750 Super Sport also scored was that it was, in effect, a racing bike with lights and a horn, so it had all the hallmarks of a racing machine in handling and braking, as well as the looks of a racer. This machine is the perfect example of form following function, and successful aesthetics being not the result of stylists, but of subconscious evolution. To many it still remains the best-looking Ducati ever produced.

Ducati 860 Super Sport

After Imola in 1973, the future looked quite bleak for four-strokes in Formula 750, especially with the prospect of the Yamaha TZ700 for 1974. Endurance racing was really the only avenue left for Ducati, and as this didn't have any capacity restriction, Taglioni reasoned that he would

need a larger engine to combat the Hondas and Kawasakis. So by the simple expedient of using the 86 mm 450 racing pistons in a 74.4 mm stroke 750 Desmo, an 864 cc twin was created and first raced in the Barcelona 24 Hour race of 1973. Held at the twisting 2.25 mile (3.62 km) street circuit of Montjuich Park in July, this bike was essentially an over-bored 750SS road bike. Ridden by Salvador Canellas and Benjamin Grau it won in record time, completing 720 laps at 71 mph (114.3 km/h). So dominant were they that they beat the second place Bultaco by 16 laps. Like the Imola racers of 1972, the bike used early 750 crankcases, but had the dry clutch and centre-axle Marzocchis with Scarab brakes of the 1973 Imola bikes. Claimed power was 86 bhp at 8,200 rpm. After such success it was inevitable that a road version of the 860 prototype would appear.

The road version that was shown at the Milan Show in November 1973, however, was not the 860 Super Sport, but the 860GT (covered in Chapter 8). While the 750 Super Sport went into production, another 860 endurance bike raced at the 1974 Montjuich 24 Hour race, again ridden by Grau and Canellas and now producing around 90 bhp. Unfortunately, after 16 hours they retired with a failed gearbox while leading. In 1975, now with an 88 mm 905 cc engine with heavily-machined crankcases to allow the use of low exhausts, Canellas and Grau won yet again, at an average speed of 71.74 mph (115.45 km/h), beating their previous record by another 11 laps. By now Ducati were competing in the entire World Endurance Championship, and this is covered in Chapter 9.

In the meantime, a round-case 860 Super Sport ridden by Kenny Blake had won the 1975 Easter Bathurst Production Race in Australia. According to Ron Angel, the importer and entrant, the one-off 860SS was actually built for the Castrol Six Hour production race of October 1974, but it was declared ineligible (as was the 750 Super Sport, the organizers thinking that such a limited production race replica

Kenny Blake rode an 860 Super Sport to a stunning victory at Bathurst, Australia, in 1975. (Two Wheels)

was outside the spirit of the event). So, rather than airfreight the bike out, they sent it by sea, in time for the 1975 round of Australian production races. As raced by Kenny Blake it was visually identical to a stock 750SS, the only differences being square '860' camshaft bearing mounts on the cylinder heads and the words '860 Super Sport' on the side-covers. Carrying 750SS frame and engine numbers, this 860SS had a close-ratio gearbox and other special racing parts. To most other competitors it must have appeared as a 750SS fitted with the 86 mm pistons and barrels from a 450 single, and it was hardly a production model because it was the only one in existence. In the 20-lap race Blake completely demolished the opposition of Kawasaki 900s, and was immediately disqualified by the orga-

nizers pending confirmation from the Ducati factory that the 860SS was indeed a production bike. This duly arrived and Blake's victory reinstated. However, when the 860SS did appear as a production model, the 900SS, it was based on the square-case 860 engine, not the round-case 750.

Ducati 900 Super Sport

By taking the square-case 860 engine and placing it in the 750SS running gear the 1975 900SS was created. The 750SS continued, but was now merely a sleeved-down 860. Whereas the 860GT had been designed with US noise and left-side gearshift regulations in mind, the 1975 750/900SS continued where the 1974 bike had left off. With the right-side gearshift, small CEV tail-light, fibreglass tank (without the clear strip), open bell-

mouths, Conti silencers, and no provision for turn indicators, these bikes were still very much a limited edition factory production racer. They even had the Aprilia switch-gear and the ignition switch between the tank and seat, like the earlier 750s. Because they used the square-case engine, they had the 5 mm shorter connecting rods, with a 20 mm gudgeon pin rather than the 22 mm gudgeon of the round-case. Thus the milled connecting rods made way for regular forged items, still with a dual strengthening rib around the big-end eye, and apart from the desmodromic heads of the 1974 750SS, with polished rockers, the engine was as the 860GT, covered in the next chapter. Unfortunately this series of Super Sports inherited some of the ignition problems and poor build-quality of the 860. Also,

The Kenny Blake 860SS is still in existence. It is visually similar to a 750SS but with 860 camshaft bearing supports.

while the shorter con-rods of the square-case engine helped boost mid-range torque, the increased rod angularity put more strain on the big-end. Coupled with the abrupt ignition advance of the first series of Ducati Elettrotecnica electronic ignition, and the additional reciprocating weight of bigger pistons, the model had a reputation for poor reliability, and was prone to premature big-end failure.

All these 1975 bikes used 750SS frames and frame numbers, though they differed in detail from the earlier bike. Brakes were now Brembo 08s with larger 280 mm drilled front discs. The rear drilled disc was slightly smaller at 229 mm. The centre-axle Marzocchis with the flat triple clamps remained, as did the rear Marzocchi shock absorbers, though to help improve ground clearance they were now 5 mm longer, at 310 mm. The

tyres specified were still the Metzeler C7 Racing, and wheels were the same 40-spoke Borrani WM3 x 18. These bikes had silver frames, and silver and blue paintwork, the 750 with a silver fairing and blue stripes, and the 900 with a blue fairing and silver stripes.

Because they couldn't be sold in many countries, only 250 750SSs and 250 900SSs were made in 1975. With 198 of these 500 going to Australia, it was obvious that they were made with

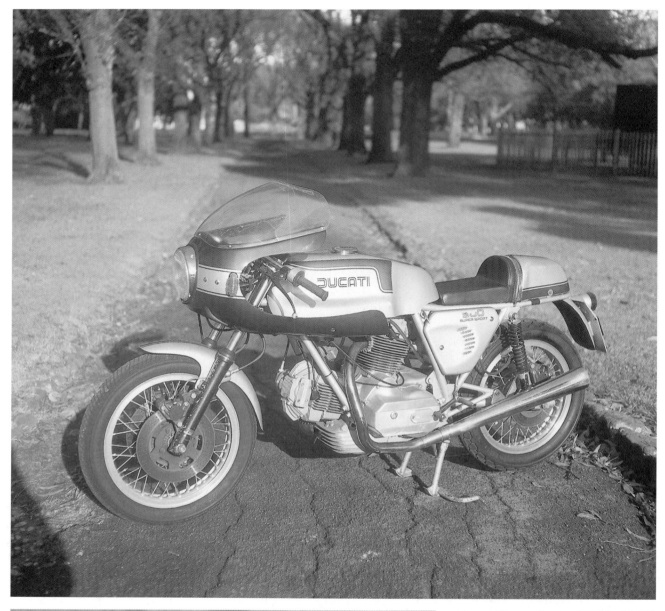

Above: *The production 900SS of 1975 had the square-case engine. Compare this to Kenny Blake's round-case prototype.*

Left: *John Warrian rode a 1975 900SS in the Australian Castrol Six Hour race for several years. Here he is on his way to winning a Three Hour support race at Surfers' Paradise in 1977. (AMCN)*

Australian production racing in mind. The Castrol Six Hour race had become the premier motorcycle event in Australia but success had eluded Ducati. Its limited edition 750SS hadn't been eligible in 1974, and it had been disqualified in previous years, so a purpose-built production racer seemed the ideal solution. This was to be the last truly raw sporting motorcycle you could buy completely uncompromised by legislation.

However, the 900SS never did manage to win the Castrol Six Hour. John Warrian's best effort in four years was a second place (shared with Terry Kelly) in 1978, still on the 1975 model bike. He had almost won in 1975 until big-end failure robbed him of victory in the final hour. While not actually winning this prestigious race, the 900SS had nevertheless established its credentials as one of the strongest-performing bikes on the market. It could certainly meet the Kawasaki Z900 and later the Z1000 head-on and not be disgraced, and combining this performance with the renowned brakes and handling of the

750SS, Ducati had created undoubtedly the best all round sports bike of its day. Unfortunately, the Six Hour race had also showed up the bike's prime weakness, reliability. Yet it would be three more years before the big-end and ignition problems were addressed.

For 1976 it was decided to put the 900 Super Sport, and its sleeved-down sister the 750, into regular production. Thus the bike needed to be modified to be acceptable for sale throughout the world. It was the next step in altering the bike and diminishing its appeal to the purist, a compromise seen at Ducati so often before and since. Now the fibreglass 'Imola'-shaped tank was replaced by a 750 Sport style steel one, and the Conti silencers by the Lafranconis of the 860. Indicators on stalks appeared from the fairing along with new Aprilia switch-gear and an ignition switch mounted on the dashboard. 32 mm Dell'Orto carburettors and air-cleaners were fitted onto the now cast aluminium inlet manifolds, and Veglia instruments replaced the

Smiths. No longer did the engine breathe directly into the atmosphere, but into a catch-tank moulded into the fibreglass seat. The gearshift was also moved to the left via the sloppy crossover shaft arrangement of the 860, the gear-selecting mechanism still residing in the right outer cover like the 750 (and the singles). The rear brake lever was thus moved to the right. It wasn't a very tidy conversion and the rubber foot-rests and levers were clumsy. While a display bike that appeared in early 1976 had a blue frame, colours for the production models were the same as for 1975, but with different graphics on the tank.

To fit a Super Sport with quiet mufflers and small carburettors really destroyed the character of the bike, but fortunately many came with the 40 mm Dell'Ortos and Contis packed in the crate. This restored the power to that of the 1975 bike, as the engine specifications were still the same. The 900SS was a strong-performing motorcycle, even if weight was up from the 750 to 414 lb (188 kg). *Cycle*

The 1976–77 900SS had a steel petrol tank and a left-side gearshift. This one has the optional Conti mufflers. (Two Wheels)

magazine, testing a 1977 (the same as 1976) bike in July 1978, achieved a standing quarter mile time of 12.91 seconds at 104.16 mph (167.6 km/h) with Lafranconis and 32 mm carburettors. The kitted bike ran 12.4 seconds at 109 mph (175 km/h). *Cycle* 'marvelled at its almost hydraulic power.' *Revs* in Australia tested both the standard and kitted versions in 1977, coming away with the conclusion that, with the 40 mm Dell'Ortos and Contis, Ducati had created an engine that was 'truly brilliant – a real credit to the Italian motorcycle industry'. They achieved a 17% overall power increase over the detuned version, with even greater gains in the mid-range. The engine was obviously designed to run in this trim. Even today, the 900SS is a brilliantly-performing motorcycle and it is no wonder that it is considered an all-time classic.

A lot of the details of the 1976–77 bikes were tidied up in 1978. The SD900 Darmah had just gone into production with a revised left-side gearshift and Bosch ignition. It also had a new big-end with a larger, 38 mm crankpin and correspondingly smaller rollers in an effort to improve reliability. These changes were now incorporated in the Super Sport, which still retained its kickstart and alloy Borrani rims. By now, with full production underway, the polished rockers disappeared, but the 1978 bikes were better than in 1976–77. The gearshift was improved, as the crossover linkages tended to develop a lot of slop with wear, and the footrests and levers neater. The engine was also smoother, with the Bosch ignition and its revised ignition advance. Unfortunately it now needed a fully-charged battery. The earlier system was notable in that it was self-generating, and if required the bike could be run without a battery at all. A dual seat was also listed as an option at this time.

In parallel with the 900SS, production of the 750SS continued, although on a much smaller scale. The 1975–77 bikes were identical to the respective 900, save for the silver fairing, smaller pistons and 750 bearing-covers on the cylinder heads. The last 750SSs appeared in 1979, with the Bosch ignition and Goldline Brembo 08 calipers. They were the last Ducatis with Borrani rims, as by now the 900SS was fitted with alloy Speedlines. Very few were made, and total production for the 750SS was only about 1,000 over five years.

During 1978 the 900SS appeared with a black and gold paint scheme along with the alloy wheels of the Darmah. This mirrored the striping of the previous year, but with gold stripes over a black petrol tank. The engine remained as before, with the option of 40 mm Dell'Ortos and Conti mufflers. The Speedline wheels were prone to cracking and soon replaced with alloy FPS ones. By now some Super Sports had the 40 mm carburettors they deserved, and the use of alloy wheels meant a 280 mm disc was now fitted at the rear. The small CEV tail-lights made way for the larger US-style ones.

The final 900SS was shown at the 1980 Bologna Show and released during 1981, now with a dual seat only, a black frame with silver bodywork, and new decals. There were lots of detail changes, but unfortunately quality control could have been better at this time. Bikes appeared with incorrect speedo drives and 'A' pistons in 'B' barrels. Some had a handle on the frame to help in putting the bike on the centre-stand, and others had early petrol tanks and front guards. Its Silentium silencers were better-looking than the Lafranconis, but still not a Conti replacement. Yet the engine and running gear remained the same, so the basic ingredients were still there. Unfortunately, the constant modernization of the Super Sport had also diminished its original appeal as a race replica. While the last bikes had better paint and fibreglass, much better electrics, cable-mounted chokes, even locking petrol caps, they lacked the raw appeal of the original, and lost a lot of the character. They also became hard to sell and in 1982 were dumped at bargain prices in markets like Australia.

So, ten years after Imola the same basic bike remained in production, but time had caught up with it. Buyers now wanted electric start and an easier bike to live with. The Super Sport had already evolved into the Mike Hailwood Replica and they both merged to become the S2. But now we are a long way from Imola. The early 750 and 900 Super Sports reflected the very best of the Italian concept of a sporting motorcycle, genuine unadulterated race replicas built irrespective of regulation and, to some extent, cost. However, the later bikes were inevitably compromised by increasing legislation, fashion, and economics, and they were no longer race replicas. The next generation of race replica Ducatis lay in another bloodline, the Pantah.

The final 900SS of 1981–82: Silentium mufflers, FPS wheels and a restyled seat.

8.

Production Mainstays

With the success of the 860 cc version of the 750 Super Sport at Barcelona in July 1973, it was obvious that the 864 cc engine would eventually make it into production. Here was an opportunity to meet increasing noise legislation and still maintain the performance levels of the 750. However, the shape of the prototype took everyone by surprise when it was displayed at the Milan Show in November 1973. Instead of entrusting the styling to Leopoldo Tartarini, who had done the rear-seat

design of the last desmodromic singles, they gave it to the car stylist Giorgetto Giugiaro, of Studio Italdesign. In the 1960s, Giugiaro had worked for Bertone and designed the beautiful 105 Series Alfa Romeo coupés, but his designs of the 1970s were less flowing, and more angular. These ideas were transported through to the 860, even to the design of the engine-cases and Lafranconi mufflers. While journalists raved about the 860 at the time (they generally assume that anything new is better than the

old), the 860 hasn't aged well, and today is considered an inferior model to the 750.

The Milan Show bike differed slightly to the eventual production models, in that it had a small bikini fairing, right-side gear-change, and Borrani 18-inch alloy rims. The frame was standard 750 Sport (with the narrower rear sub-frame). It also featured an electric start, with the starter motor between the cylinders, as it had been on the few 750GTs so fitted. When the 860 went into

The Italdesign prototype of the 860 was based around a 750GT.

The production 860GT of 1974: a departure from, but not an improvement on, the 750GT.

production it had a new frame, with bowed front down-tubes, and the eccentric adjustment at the swing-arm pivot for chain adjustment, just like the 1973 Imola racers. Steel rims and a single Brembo 11-inch disc with Ceriani forks also appeared on the production models. The style of the bike was different to the 750GT, with much higher, wider handlebars, and less of a sporting riding position. Colours were typical mid-1970s – orange, green, or blue.

It was in the engine department that most of the changes took place. Apart from the obvious external appearance, the bevel-gear camshaft drive layout was completely revised. Instead of the expensive and difficult-to-assemble train of bevel-gears of the 750, there was now a straight cut gear keyed to the crankshaft, driving two more straight cut gears mounted in ball-bearings on an alloy outrigger plate. These two gears keyed directly with a set of helical bevels matching the towershafts. The ignition contact breaker of the 750 was eliminated, so there was no longer the need for a central bevel-gear between the two

vertical shafts. While the new bevels were better-supported than in the 750, they also added considerable width to the engine. The primary advantages came through the much greater ease of assembly, because each bevel shaft could now be shimmed independently. Another advantage came with the use of a straight cut gear from the crankshaft. If, through wear, crankshaft endplay developed, this no longer affected valve timing – not a problem with constantly rebuilt racing engines, but possibly one with higher mileage street bikes. Camshafts were new, and more touring oriented than the 750, with figures of inlet opening 37° before top dead centre, and closing 74° after bottom dead centre, and exhaust opening 75° before bottom dead centre and closing 38° after top dead centre. Thus valve duration (for the same size valves) was 291° for the inlet and 293° exhaust, with valve overlap at only 75°. These milder camshafts enabled peak power to be developed at a lower, 6,900 rpm.

With the loss of the contact

breaker, there was now a space for an oil filter, still not a full flow type as it only filtered oil to the rear cylinder head, but better than no filtration at all. Although the stroke, at 74.4 mm, remained the same, the connecting rods were 5 mm shorter, giving an eye-to-eye length of 145 mm, reducing the rod/stroke ratio to 1.95:1. The cylinder barrels too were correspondingly shorter. The diameter of the small end eye was reduced to 20 mm to compensate for the increase in reciprocating weight due to the larger 86 mm pistons. These pistons were the slipper type as fitted to the 750 Sport, not the full skirt 750GT design. Compression ratio was 9.3:1. The same 36 mm crankpin and big-end bearings from the 750 were also used, as was the 750's 150 watt alternator for the first 1,683 engines, after which a 200 watt type was fitted. Ignition was now by the Ducati Elettrotecnica that had been tried on the 500 racers, with the stator being bolted onto the crankcases as had been intended on the 750. The magnetic rotor was incorporated in the flywheel on the primary drive side. Primary drive ratio was also the revised 32/70 of the 750SS. There were several revisions to the primary drive and clutch during the production of the first 860s, mainly in the type of bearings in the clutch housing. The revisions occurred at engine number 1194, with new bearings, then at number 2179, when even larger bearings were fitted into the clutch drum. There were also alterations to the clutch plates and fifth gear (after number 1194).

The valve adjustment mechanism was changed to incorporate a screw and locknut, just as with the last series of 750GTs. This aggravated the problem with the cylinder head design that only allowed for short, not particularly well-supported valve guides, and they were prone to premature wear. The cylinder head design was really designed for desmodromic valve actuation and there also wasn't much room for valve springs of a decent length. Not a problem with street bikes, but certainly one for racing.

In the electrical department the 860 was completely revamped from the 750, and not entirely successfully. New CEV switch-gear was the same as fitted to the last 750GTs and Sports. There were regulator problems, and melting switch-gear and fuse boxes, particularly on the electric start 860GTE. The instrument panel with the city/country two-level horn switch was also shared with the last 750s. To meet US Federal legislation the gearshift lever was moved to the left side via a crossover linkage behind the engine. It was a rather crude conversion and the precision of the right-side shifting bikes was lost in the process. The crossover system for the rear brake was even worse, the cross-tube being simply welded to the engine plates. The result of this was that the rear lever was set so low that the clamp severely affected ground clearance.

Despite the extra capacity, higher compression, and the use of the 750 Sports 32 mm Dell'Orto PHF32 carburettors (still with restrictive air-cleaners), the 860 didn't perform any better than the old 750GT. The weight increase to 454 lb (206 kg), or 478lb (217 kg) with electric start,

The instrument panel of the 860GT: more lights, a return to Smiths instruments, and a city/country horn switch.

more than offset any gains in maximum power. The harsh Ceriani forks and steel rimmed 18-inch wheels front and rear also didn't improve the handling over the 750, and the seat height, at 31.5 inches (800 mm), was very high. *Cycle World*, in July 1975, achieved a top speed of only 109 mph (175 km/h). The 860 didn't meet with universal approval, and there were criticisms of the riding position and the styling. Many of these were

answered with the 860GTS later in 1975.

860/900 GTS

The GTS was a successful attempt to make the 860 more appealing to European markets. It was still basically an 860GT but now had a new petrol tank design with knee indentations and a lower, wider seat. The colour was a more classical dark blue with silver stripes, and low handlebars

The 860GTS. A new petrol tank and seat, along with double front disc brakes, differentiated it from the 860GT. (AMCN)

along with a twin Brembo braking set-up at the front contributed to its more sporting emphasis. Several features from the 750s were reintroduced, notably an instrument panel modelled on the 750 Sport, with the Smiths instruments held in separate clamps on a bracket attached to the top triple clamp. The ignition key was placed on this panel along with a set of warning lights and the city/country horn switch. The headlight was mounted on the same chrome wire brackets as the earlier 750GTs, giving a lighter, more airy look, and the indicators too were the round type from the earlier bike. The electric starter was now fitted as standard, and a chrome rail was provided to aid putting the bike on the centre-stand.

New to the GTS was the choke mechanism, with a plastic lever pulling out at right angles, mounted to the left of the headlight, rather than the handlebar-mounted type of the 860GT that had been carried through from the singles. In other respects the GTS was as the 860GT – Ceriani 38 mm forks, Marzocchi 320 mm shocks, same engine and frame (except for the rear section), wheels, side-covers, and painted steel mudguards. Transfers appeared on the tank in place of badges. Initially it was sold alongside the 860GT and GTE, but by the end of 1976 both these models had gone, leaving the 860GTS as the sole V-twin besides the 750/900SS.

For 1977 the bike was essentially unchanged. From number 3670, Marzocchi forks with more offset triple clamps replaced the Cerianis, and stainless steel mudguards replaced the painted steel ones. Tank badges came back again along with new switch-gear, as fitted to the Super Sports of the same period. There was also a slightly revised instrument panel, no longer with the two-volume horn switch. Reprofiled camshafts and double valve springs were fitted after engine number 3788. The new valve timing figures, giving more duration and 97° of overlap, were inlet opening 51° before top dead centre, closing 75° after bottom dead centre, and the exhaust opening 74° before bottom dead centre, closing 46° after top dead centre. Later in the same year the 860GTS became the 900GTS with new colours, red and silver, or black and silver. The definitive 900GTS appeared in 1978 when it received the engine of the Darmah, but still had the valve spring heads. Along with this engine came an improved electric start mechanism, Bosch ignition, and a proper left-side gearshift. These improvements are detailed in the next section. The 900GTS, which was to be the last bevel-gear valve spring twin, was sold until 1979, by which time it had developed a reputation as one of the most reliable of all Ducatis. Unfortunately, it was a bit too late to save the GTS, as the problems with the very first GTs had hurt their reputation badly. The success of the desmodromic racers, along with the larger numbers of desmo engines being built, also meant that the public now associated Ducati with desmodromics, and it was time for the Darmah.

Darmah 900 Sport Desmo

While most attention has been placed by enthusiasts on the various Super Sport models, it could be argued that the Darmah was more significant. The Darmah, because it was sold in such large numbers (by Ducati standards), and at a price competitive with equivalent Japanese bikes, introduced desmodromics and the charisma of Ducati to a wider range of riders, not just the serious sporting fraternity. For the five-year period between 1977 and 1982, the Darmah formed the mainstay of Ducati production, and with its release a real attempt was made to combine traditional features with civility and reliability.

Ducati had often sent designs outside for styling and, apart from the 860GT of Giugiaro, these usually went to Leopoldo Tartarini of Italjet. Tartarini had not only restyled the last desmo singles, but also the 500 Sport Desmo in 1975. In 1976 he was also given the brief for the SD 900, or Sport Desmo 900, and he styled it along similar lines to the 500 (covered in the next section). It was to be a sport touring version of the 900SS, using an electric start 900 engine along with desmodromic

In 1978 the 860 was sold as a police bike, but with a 750GT frame, petrol tank, and side-covers.

heads, but with smaller, 32 mm Dell'Orto carburettors. The bike came out looking significantly different to previous touring Ducatis, in red and white with a ducktail seat and – what was a first for Ducati – cast alloy wheels. When first displayed, at the Bologna Show in 1976, it had FPS wheels, similar to the Moto Guzzi Le Mans, and a plexiglass screen. By the time the first production bikes appeared in August 1977 it wasn't just the styling that set the Darmah apart. There were many other changes, particularly in ignition and ancillaries. It was called the Darmah after the name of a tiger in an Italian children's story.

While the basic Darmah was really an 860GTS with desmo heads, it represented a big step forward with its electrical system. In an attempt to compete with the Japanese there were now warning lights for the side-stand and neutral, as well as indicators, generator and head and tail lights. Additionally, the electronic ignition

With the Darmah came an improved left-side gearshift, the selector mechanism no longer residing in the countershaft sprocket cover. This 1978 model has a kickstart lever.

was provided by Bosch, with transducers and coils and all associated wiring tightly squeezed under the front of the fuel tank. While the warning lights often failed, the ignition was a definite improvement over

Most 1978 Darmahs came in black and gold.

the Ducati Elettrotecnica fitted to the first square-case bikes.

The first model of 1977 came with very light five-spoke Campagnolo magnesium wheels, changing to Speedline in 1979. Both types were the cause of a serious safety scare in Australia in 1981, when various wheels started disintegrating. This initiated a nation-wide recall, and free replacement with aluminium FPS six-spoke wheels. The earliest versions also had Ceriani forks that became Marzocchis in 1978, and all had triple 280 mm Brembo discs. Later, in 1978, a black and gold version appeared with the tiger insignia on the side-panels.

The introduction of the Darmah also brought the first upgrade of the square-case engine. Not only did the ignition change to the Bosch system but the gearshift selector mechanism was moved to the left side behind the clutch housing, eliminating the need for the sloppy crossover shafts. The electric start mechanism was properly integrated into the primary drive system, greatly improving the effectiveness and reliability. Initially all Darmahs came with a kickstart as well but by 1980 this had disappeared. To endeavour to overcome the problem of big-end failure on the 900 series the crankpin was enlarged to 38 mm along with a reduction in roller diameter. This was the remedy long tried by Ducati with its singles, and in the case of the Darmah it was successful. These engines didn't suffer the premature crankshaft failure that had been a problem with the early 860s and Super Sports, but some of the increased longevity would have been due to the more gentle advance curve of the Bosch ignition. The Darmah didn't get the dual rib strengthened con-rods of the Super Sport. With the better gearshift selection and the more progressive ignition curve, coupled with instant starting and easy idle, the Darmah indeed seemed far more refined than previous Ducatis.

As longer forks and Marzocchi shocks (300 mm to bike number 989, 315 mm from bike 990) were fitted, the Darmah was quite a lot taller than a Super Sport, but did offer better ground clearance. However, it still handled in the best Ducati tradition

with rather slow steering (31° of rake and 4.3 inches of trail). A Paoli hydraulic steering damper was fitted on the right-hand side, more for cosmetic reasons than practical usefulness, as it was leaky and ineffective. This was a replacement for the equally ineffective friction damper fitted to Super Sports, which could no longer be fitted because of the new instrument console with Nippon Denso instruments. All the switchgear was Japanese too, but the headlight was an excellent Bosch halogen. In many respects the Darmah represented a departure from traditional Ducati practice. The factory had relied almost totally on Italian suppliers in the past, but there was now evidence of increased use of Japanese and German components. This would continue right through to the present day.

The Darmah created a big impression when it first appeared in 1977. Here was an electric start Super Sport, but performance was never in the same league as an SS. Despite the same desmodromic cylinder heads and 9.3:1 pistons as the 900SS, but with smaller inlet throats, even with Conti mufflers they only offered a marginal performance increase over a 750 or 860GT. 32 mm carburettors, huge air filters (with sold plastic intakes rather than the previous pleated type) and double-walled smaller diameter exhausts didn't help either. In 1979 (from number 3026)

the cylinder heads became 900SS ones, with the larger inlet ports which enabled 40 mm carburettors to bolt on easily. This allowed the engine to produce 900SS horsepower, but the size and weight (216 kg, or 475 lb, dry) of the motorcycle blunted the performance. However, the appeal of the Darmah was not as an all out sportster, more as a sport touring bike capable of covering long distances or short ones – the Italian answer to the Universal Japanese Motorcycle. The emphasis was definitely on shortish trips though, the 15-litre tank generally running onto reserve at about 180 km (112 miles), and the seat had marginal padding. They were all supplied with very low gearing (15/38 teeth sprockets for the final drive) that limited top speed. The English *Motorcycling Monthly* only achieved 112.2 mph (180.6 km/h) from their early model in July 1978, even less than a valve-spring 860GTS. *Cycle* magazine, in April 1980 – known for their editorial sympathy towards Ducatis, and 750 Super Sports in particular – liked the Darmah, but had to admit that to 'purists and owners of 750s, it wasn't a true Ducati, merely a facsimile'. Standing start quarter-mile times were close to that of a 750GT at 13.13 seconds, with a terminal speed of 101.35 mph (163.1 km/h).

In 1979 practicality took over from styling considerations, and the pretty ducktail seat was altered for more

The Darmah featured Nippon Denso instruments and integrated warning lights.

comfort. Silentium silencers replaced the ugly Lafranconis and the kickstart disappeared. Colours were still red and white, or black and gold, with most in the latter. The rear shock absorbers were now (from number 2960) the Marzocchi 315 mm oleo-pneumatic type.

At the same time the Darmah SS appeared, essentially an identical bike but with a Super Sport style half-fairing, offset clip-ons, and rear-set footrests. Other changes included three 280 mm drilled Brembo discs with six bolt mounts. This model was painted in an attractive two-tone blue, but not that many were made. It was a bike that lacked identity, not being a proper Super Sport or a sports tourer. Introduced at the Bologna Show at the end of 1978, it kept the same ducktail seat throughout its model life. Due to the improved aerodynamics, *Motor Cycle News* attained a top speed of 117.18 mph (188.6 km/h) in March 1979, still some way off the

speed of a 900SS. Not particularly popular, the 900SS Darmah only lasted until 1980.

This was now a time of diminishing motorcycle sales worldwide, and as Ducati was concentrating its efforts on developing the Pantah series, it was clear that the days of the bevel-gear engines were limited. After a peak in 1980 sales declined significantly, and to many the Darmah was still the bike it had been in 1978. By now all the bevel-gear models had been largely unchanged for several years apart from colour schemes. However, at the Bologna Show of November 1981, in an effort to broaden the appeal, Darmahs were displayed with optional fairing and panniers. It was obvious that the Darmah was near the end of its production life because the frame now appeared with an SS style swing-arm with the Seeley-type chain adjusters, as well as the eccentric adjustment at the swing-arm pivot.

Along with the last 900 Super Sports, these final Darmahs were sold off at heavily discounted prices in some markets right through until 1983. Some of the last ones were parts-bin specials, with at least one example fitted with a 900 dry clutch Mike Hailwood Replica engine.

It's important to place the Darmah in its historical perspective. Ducati had gone through some lean years previously, with some very poor managerial decisions between 1975 and 1977. The singles and round-case bikes were stopped in favour of parallel twins and the square-case 860, and only the 750 and 900SS continued to uphold their sporting tradition. Neither the 860 nor the parallel twins sold particularly well and Ducati desperately needed a mainstream bike to take over from where the 750GT had left off. With the Darmah they succeeded, but this model is generally underrated when compared to the more glamorous Super Sport models.

The 1979 900 Super Sport Darmah.

The 1982 SD900 featured a blue or burgundy paint scheme.

350/500 Parallel Twins

The history of the parallel twin Ducati went back to the 175 cc racing twin of 1957, followed by the racing 250 and 350, and finally the 500 and 700 cc prototypes of the 1960s. All of these had been completely overshadowed, both on the road and track, by the overhead camshaft singles, so Fabio Taglioni wasn't too interested when it was suggested in 1972 that the wonderful singles be replaced by a new parallel twin. He wanted nothing to do with the design – he already had designs for his Pantah with belt-driven overhead camshafts. In retrospect, the termination of the singles was a little premature when the oil crisis hit in 1974, creating an emphasis on fuel economy, but by this stage all the decisions had been made.

As with the 860 taking over from the 750, a decrease in production costs was largely the impetus behind the parallel twin. The problem was, they fitted awkwardly into the Ducati range of singles and V-twins, and as such were never a success. Because Ing. Taglioni would have nothing to

do with their initial design, the work was entrusted to Ing. Tumidei, who took the basic 1965 500 engine design and updated it. The 360° crankshaft was replaced by a 180° one, and a single overhead camshaft, driven by a chain rather than pushrods and rockers. Engine dimensions were even more oversquare than the first 500, at 78 x 52 mm. The similar 350 was 71.8 x 43.2 mm. This was the first production Ducati engine to use a forged crankshaft with plain big-end bearings (45 x 22 mm) but only two plain main bearings were used, there being no centre bearing between the cylinders. These too were large at 50 x 25 mm. Because of all these plain bearings, a real departure for Ducati, the oil pump was uprated, and two oil filters supplied. The new twin also had the revised cylinder head layout, with (for the 500) two 37 mm and 33 mm valves set at the shallower included angle of 60°, as used on the 1973 Imola racing bikes. The 350 had smaller 35 mm and 31 mm valves. Valve adjustment was by screw and locknut, and primary drive still by helical gear. To keep engine width

down, the camshaft drive sprocket was not from the crankshaft, but from a countershaft sprocket behind the cylinders, with the chain running up a narrow sleeve between the two barrels. The camshaft itself was in two pieces, coupled to the central sprocket, with valve timing, for the 500, of inlet opening 32° before top dead centre, and closing 70° after bottom dead centre, and the exhaust valve opening 68° before bottom dead centre, and closing 39° after top dead centre. The 350 had less conservative valve timing (44/85/70/27). The claimed compression ratio was 9.6:1, and the die-cast engine crankcases vertically split, with a small electric starter motor fitted in front of the engine. Carburation was by Dell'Orto as usual, PHF30 on the 500 and the older style VHB26 for the 350. Surprisingly, given the use of electronic ignition on the 860s, ignition was by battery, coil and contact breakers.

It was quite a tidy design, but when the first 350/500GTL examples were displayed during 1975 they incorporated many of the Giugiaro styling characteristics of the 860GT. In some respects the GTL sported the best quality equipment – Borrani alloy rims, 35 mm Marzocchi forks with twin Brembo 05 calipers (single on the 350) and 260 mm front discs. Yet they were not a replacement for the singles, even if they did work well as motorcycles. The single down-tube frame still used the engine as a stressed member, and the bikes were a reasonable weight at 170 kg (375 lb). Instruments and switch-gear were similar to the 860GTS, and colours were similar to the 860GT – blue, green and, later, red.

The performance of the 500 wasn't startling, and the 350 even less so. *Cycle World* only managed a standing quarter-mile of 14.92 seconds at 85.87 mph (138.2 km/h) in their test of November 1977. They found handling to be its best feature. Somehow the GTL seemed to be aimed at a different market to that of previous Ducatis, and this was its problem. In endeavouring to widen

the bike's appeal, Ducati's traditional customer-base had been neglected: they didn't want a nondescript Ducati. Fortunately, some of their misgivings were overcome with the 500 Sport.

With the adoption of desmodromic heads and a new frame with twin down-tubes, the 350/500 was sent off to Leopoldo Tartarini of Italjet for styling. His prototype featured a theme of matt black with white exhaust pipes and FPS alloy wheels (similar to the Moto Guzzi Le Mans), and was displayed at the Milan Show in November 1975. Fortunately, by the time the bike made it into production it was more tastefully styled, and altogether more satisfactory than the GTL. While the actual weight increased to 185 kg (408 lb) the desmo engine was more powerful. The desmodromic camshafts had different timing specifications, with the inlet valve opening 32° before top dead centre, and closing 75° after bottom dead centre, and the exhaust

opening 60° before bottom dead centre, and closing 45° after top dead centre. *Motorrad* had only managed a top speed of 162.2 km/h (100.8 mph) from their 500GTL in August 1976, yet their 500 Sport Desmo the following year went 180 km/h (112 mph).

The Sport Desmo was fitted with Paoli 35 mm forks with 330 mm long Marzocchi rear shocks, and FPS wheels with a rear disc brake. Certainly the engine vibrated, as you would expect of a 180° parallel twin without balance shafts, but it possessed excellent brakes and handling. Finish on the matt black-painted Lafranconi mufflers could have been better, but for a design that was intended to be economic to build, ultimately its price killed it. In England the red/white or blue/white 500 Sport Desmo was sold at the same price as the valve-spring 860GTS. The yellow/black or blue/black 350 was aimed at the Italian market.

A racing version of the Desmo Sport was also produced in 1977,

The parallel twin was tested in the running gear of a 450 Desmo. Unfortunately it didn't look this good when it went into production.

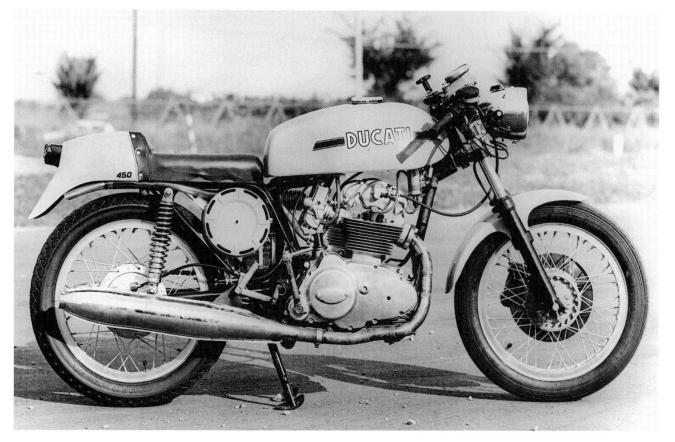

The styling of the 500GTL, strongly influenced by the 860GT.

called the 500 Super Sport. The electric starter was removed, and an oil-cooler fitted in the front of a half-fairing. With 40 mm Dell'Orto carburettors and larger valves (39 mm inlet, 35 mm exhaust), along with racing camshafts, power was up to 61 bhp at 10,500 rpm, and the weight down to 160 kg (353 lb). Claimed maximum speed was 220 km/h (137 mph).

In an effort to broaden the appeal of the parallel twin, Ducati replaced the GTL with a valve-spring version of the Sport Desmo in 1978. Called the GTV, this also came in 350 and 500 cc engine capacities and was essentially a Sport Desmo with a GTL engine. While they were sound in concept, there were too many mechanical problems with the parallel twin. Crankshaft failure and short-lived valve gear were among the problems that afflicted them all.

The GTL soldiered on until 1978, and the Sport until 1980, with only minor changes to instruments and switch-gear as with the 860/900GTS. Surprisingly, after an absence of three years, 67 500 Desmo Sports were built for the Australian market in late-

1983. They had later instruments and switch-gear, along with 600 Pantah Oscam wheels and Marzocchi forks, and were sold at a bargain price. However, they were still no match for a Pantah. By 1984 the Pantah was already a success on and off the track, and had completely eclipsed the parallel twins. While not necessarily bad motorcycles, to most Ducati enthusiasts the latter were never really the genuine article.

900/Mille S2

The early 1980s were not the best time for Ducati under the VM group. VM specialized in diesels, and much of the Ducati manufacturing plant at Borgo Panigale was taken up with diesel engine production at this time. In the lead up to 1982 there had been two failures within the motorcycle division, and two significant success stories. The successes were the Super Sport and Mike Hailwood Replica line, along with the Pantah. The parallel twins and 860s had been failures, not because they were bad designs, but because there had been reliability problems and their styling had not proved popular. The Darmah,

while a better motorcycle, had been in production for five years by now, and was being discontinued. To rationalize production, a hybrid model was created to run alongside the Super Sport line. Called the S2, it was basically a Darmah SS frame and running gear, with a restyled seat, and the fairing from the 600SL Pantah. Eventually the S2 would replace the Super Sport and became the basis of the revised Mike Hailwood Replica in 1983. The last S2s and Mike Hailwood Replicas were essentially the same, and they became the last bevel-gear twins.

The first 900S2s of 1982 had the option of either a kickstarter, as with the 900SS, or an electric start. During 1983 new alternators and regulators appeared on both versions, while earlier the shifting drum had also been modified. Either Dell'Orto PHM 40BD and BS carburettors, or Dell'Orto PHF 32AD and AS were fitted, but most S2s had the electric start and the 40 mm carburettors. The main problem with the S2 was that, while it was a motorcycle in the mould of the 900SS, it *wasn't* a 900SS, and didn't perform or handle

A few 500 Sport Desmos were made in 1983 featuring Oscam wheels and later instruments. (Two Wheels)

as well. It was taller and heavier, at 419 lb (190 kg) dry. Also, the frame wasn't as rigid, as the rear down-tubes were bowed and recessed to allow the use of the larger battery (even on the kickstart version). This meant that if you removed your hands from the handlebars at a modest 50 mph (80 kph), the bars would start oscillating disconcertingly. The same problem afflicted all the last Mike Hailwood Replicas with electric start, and was a sufficient problem for the German TüV authorities to consider a ban on these models in 1985. While not quite a 900SS, *Motor Cycle Weekly*, in 1983, achieved a best one-way speed of 123.94 mph (199.5 km/h) from a 900S2 with 40 mm carburettors and Silentiums.

The 1982 S2 was painted bronze, with yellow, orange, and red stripes, and for 1983 there was a black or red option. Oleo-pneumatic Marzocchi

shock absorbers also appeared this year, along with a red frame. The last 900 version of 1984 was largely unchanged, in red with the red frame, and tank badges rather than transfers. They all featured a new fuel cap that was particularly prone to allowing water to enter and most 900S2s have suffered rusted petrol tanks. While it was still fitted with the regular Giugiaro-inspired square-case engine, these final models had the spin-on oil filter of the last 900MHR, along with an oil-level sight glass in place of the dip-stick. The most peculiar addition to these last 900S2s was a belly pan bolted underneath the engine, and if there was ever a case of style before function, this was it. By now all bikes were electric start. Running gear for 1984 was as the MHR, with the new type 18-inch Oscam wheels that allowed the fitting of tubeless tyres.

In 1984 the 860 engine received

one last overhaul by Ing. Taglioni and his new assistant, Ing. Massimo Bordi. These changes are covered in detail in Chapter 9 with the Mike Hailwood Replicas, and this new engine was shared in 1985 by both the Mike Hailwood Replica and the Mille S2. It has to be said that while the engine was updated for the 1980s, the rest of the bike was obsolete. It was even heavier than before (at 198 kg, 436 lb, dry), and didn't steer or handle as well as the old Super Sports. This was brought home to me when I had an opportunity to ride the first 750SS of 1974 back to back with the last Mille S2 when they first came out. While the torque from the Mille engine was magnificent, carburation and smoothness were inferior. The older bike was so much more responsive, and handled better, and it was obvious that the future of the big-twin was limited in that form, and

The 1984 900S2 had a spin-on oil filter. Behind is a Mille S2 of 1985.

without a more modern chassis, the Mille wouldn't last. However, no-one expected the bevel-gear twins to disappear so quickly, and within one year the Mille was finished.

These last S2s were all black with the same red, orange, and yellow stripes, and still featured the belly pan. Engine, frame, suspension and wheels were the same as the Mille MHR detailed in the next chapter. They were not as popular as the MHR and not as many were built, and when looked at now, more than ten years later, the S2s share, with the Darmah SS, the problem of a lack of identity. They were neither Darmahs, nor real Super Sports.

9.

The Isle of Man and the Mike Hailwood Replica

While Ducati had failed at the Montjuich 24 Hour race in 1974, this didn't deter the factory from becoming involved in a serious, and almost successful, attempt at the World Endurance Championship of 1975. Benjamin Grau was teamed with Canellas as usual, but also with the 23-year-old Virginio Ferrari, and Carlo Perugini when Canellas was unavailable due to car rally commitments. These factory bikes were still very much 750SS-based, right down to the front Marzocchi forks with Scarab calipers (except Grau used Lockheeds at Montjuich and Mugello). They also had 750SS-style bodywork, and looked liked race-kitted street bikes. For Montjuich and Mugello, they used the Borrani spoked wheels, later changing to the Campagnolo magnesium type. For long races, like the Bol d'Or, the bikes had a large fairing with twin headlamps. The 1975 series started well, with Canellas and Grau winning at Montjuich on a 905 cc (88 x 74.4 mm) bike, Grau following this with a win in the Mugello 1,000 km with Virginio Ferrari. At the Bol d'Or at Le Mans, Grau crashed out on the first lap, and though he restarted he was eventually sidelined by gearbox seizure. However, Grau still went into the final round at Thruxton with a slender one-point lead over the Japauto-Honda of Ruiz and Huguet. Unfortunately, a crash saw Grau with no points for this race and he ended up third in the championship. Ferrari and Perugini also won the non-championship 1,000 km race at Misano, and Ferrari the Italian 750 cc

Championship that year on a factory-supported 750SS.

Scuderia NCR

With Ducati now under EFIM Group control and new management, economics were beginning to take precedence over prestige. Racing was deemed of secondary importance, and if it hadn't been for the persistence of an enthusiastic group of engineers and mechanics, particularly Fabio Taglioni and Franco Farnè, the endurance racers of 1975 may have been the very last racing Ducatis. Farnè had started racing Ducatis in 1956 and continued as racer, then tester, and finally chief racing mechanic. Until recently he was still involved with the World Superbike programme. So in 1976 Farnè, Mario Recchia, and Piero Cavazzi teamed up

with the Scuderia NCR of ex-factory race mechanics Giorgio Nepoti and Rino Caracchi, to create a semi-works, semi-independent racing shop. Nepoti and Caracchi had already prepared an entry of a 750 Super Sport in the 1973 Imola 200 and had raced under the NCR banner during 1975. Now, rather than compete against the two-strokes in Formula 750, they turned their efforts first to endurance racing, and later to a new Formula 1 class.

All had been involved throughout the 1960s and early 1970s with the Ducati racing team, so they collectively knew as much as anyone about the preparation of both singles and twins. NCR (or Nepoti, Caracchi Racing) now had limited access to the factory for special parts and they were conveniently located at Via

The NCR endurance racer of 1976 with a special narrow-sumped round-case engine, snail cam-chain adjustment, and spoked wheels. (Two Wheels)

Scuderia NCR, operating from Via Signorini, Bologna, until 1995.

Signorini 16, near to the factory at Borgo Panigale. So from 1976 until 1979 the factory racing Ducatis were built by Nepoti and Caracchi and officially titled the Ducati 900NCR. They were built to comply with either *Coupe d'Endurance* or Formula 1 regulations. What's more, F1 bikes were available for purchase (at the princely sum of L7,500,000 in 1978, or three times the price of a standard 900SS).

Of course the crowning glory for the 900NCR was Mike Hailwood's win at the Isle of Man in the Formula 1 race in 1978, but there had been many other notable victories at Montjuich, Mugello, and Misano in endurance races. No two of the 16 endurance racers built between 1975 and 1979 were identical. They had completely different, lightweight frames of 25Cr Mo4 (made by Daspa of Bologna, not Verlicchi), special crankcases, dry clutch, spin-on oil filter, special Marzocchi suspension units, and magnesium Campagnolo wheels with a quick release system designed by Piero Cavazzi, allowing the rear wheel to be removed leaving the disc in place. Most of the engines utilized the 750 bevel-gear layout and round-cases, but were heavily modified. Many displaced 864 cc, but some used 88 mm pistons to give 905 cc, while others used a shorter stroke of 66.5 mm with 88 mm pistons to give

a capacity of 808 cc. Desmodromic camshafts were more severe than the Imola race kit available as an option to Super Sport owners. Valve timing (inlet opening 69° before top dead centre and closing 103° after bottom dead centre, and exhaust opening 98° before bottom dead centre and closing 73° after top dead centre) and lift (11–12 mm) was to endurance specification but still not the same as for the full racing Imola bikes of 1973. The cylinder heads used the 60° valve angle and valve sizes were generally 42 and 38 mm (44 mm inlet with the largest engines). Crankshafts, rods, primary gears, and gearboxes were all special. Claimed power for the 864 cc engine was 105 bhp at 8,800 rpm, and weight was down to 325 lb (148 kg) for the short stroke endurance versions. All bikes featured the marvellous styling of Mario Recchia, though the tail and seat shape was altered several times. The 900NCR endurance bikes were impressively presented, with spectacular attention to detail. These included the highly-machined rear disc caliper carrier, and brake and gear-shift levers deeply machined to save a few more grams. Even the brake discs were sometimes radially drilled, rather than cross drilled. Giorgio Nepoti did most of the engine work, while Rino Caracchi was the master of the lathe responsible for most of the beautiful

touches that adorned these racing bikes.

Two 900NCR bikes were built in 1976, and they were favoured to win the *Coupe d'Endurance*. However, it wasn't to be a good year as the bikes were too fragile, and the budget not big enough, to compete with the Hondas and Kawasakis. In endurance trim, claimed weight was only 344 lb (156 kg), with 96 bhp at 9,000 rpm from the 905 cc engine. There were no wins, the best results being a second at Mugello with Pentti Korhonen and Christian Estrosi, and a third at Montjuich for Jose Mallol and Alejandro Tejedo (who would have more success in a few years' time).

Despite four bikes being built in 1977, this was an even leaner year for results in the *Coupe d'Endurance*, again with no wins, and only a fourth in the first round at Misano. A private 750SS ridden by Carlo Saltarelli and Arturo Venanzi finished third, beating the special 808 cc, 92 bhp, 325 lb (148 kg) NCR bike of Ermanno Giuliano and Giovanni Mariannini. With Benjamin Grau deserting Ducati for a Honda in 1977, there was no success for Ducati at Montjuich Park either. NCR bikes were still raced in

Giorgio Nepoti balancing a crankshaft in his workshop, 1993.

Rino Caracchi preparing a 450 for a customer in 1993.

back with Ducati after a poor year with Honda – teamed up with Victor Palomo (1976 F750 World Championship winner) to come sixth at Montjuich. Carlo Perugini, and future 500 cc World Champion and Ducati team manager Marco Lucchinelli, also rode the NCRs that year. Some of the bikes had duplex chain final drive, and others tried out the Campagnolo hydraulic conical rear brake, as used by Walter Villa on his 250 and 350 cc AMF Harley-Davidson World Championship winning machines of 1976. A significant result in 1978, but almost completely overshadowed by Mike Hailwood's Isle of Man success, was Canellas and Grau's win in the Silhouette class at the 24 Hour race at Le Mans, on an almost standard 900SS.

Results were much better in 1979. The five bikes, now with 90 mm pistons giving 947 cc, had engines that were more or less at the peak of their development. These still used a highly-modified round-case, with the electronic ignition mounted exter-

endurance events throughout 1978 and 1979, but a new racing class had now appeared, more suited to the Bologna twins – the TT Formula One World Championship. Before considering this it's worth first taking a look at some of the successes and details of

the final 900NCR endurance bikes.

Again with four bikes, results in 1978 were equally lean except for Misano and Montjuich. Sauro Pazzaglia and Giovanni Mariannini came third at Misano on their 864 cc NCR, while Benjamin Grau – now

A 1979 900NCR endurance racer. This one has a left-side gearshift conversion through the swing-arm pivot.

The same 1979 bike. Very few engine parts were shared with the production bikes.

Grau, with Canellas, came third at Montjuich in 1979. Still using the special narrow-sumped round-case engine, the swing-arm was now box-section.

nally on the right side of the engine, that had appeared on the endurance bikes in 1978. The swing-arm was box section, and there was a revised fairing and seat arrangement. Victor Palomo and Mario Lega came second at Assen and third at Nürburgring, while Canellas and Grau came third at Montjuich.

Except for Montjuich 1979 was really the end of regular factory involvement in the Coupe d'Endurance. One of the most amazing results of all was the win by Jose Mallol and Alejandro Tejedo in 1980 on a 900SS modified for the Silhouette class. Entered by local importer Ricardo Fargas, they only raced because the event was also the final round of the Spanish Endurance Championship. After all the big names either crashed or broke down, the Spaniards took a Ducati to victory for the first time in five years. They had covered 757 laps at 74.12 mph (119.3 km/h), 26 more laps than Grau and Canellas in 1975. In 1981, Mallol and Tejedo were slowed by breakages of their Campagnolo wheels, but Benjamin Grau and Enrique de Juan, on a 950 Ducati, covered 771 laps to take second place. This bike was a factory-modified square-case 900SS with a two-into-one exhaust and lacking many of the special individual features of the NCR bikes. Amazingly, with the addition of Carlos Cardus, Grau came

fourth at Montjuich in 1982, the 900 Ducati's final fling in endurance racing, for it was truly outclassed by now. Fortunately, Ducati had a new generation bike, and the next year saw Benjamin Grau in the winners' circle again (see Chapter 11).

The TT Formula One Championship was created in 1976 in order to save the Isle of Man races that had been boycotted by leading Grand Prix riders that year. For 1977 there would be one event, the Isle of Man TT only, and the rules suited Ducati. 1,000 examples of an engine needed to have been manufactured and the crankcases, cylinder heads, and barrels needed to have a similar external appearance. Stroke must remain the same, but there was no restriction on any engine modifications. The regulations were much freer than those of modern day World Superbike racing, as any frame, brakes, wheels or suspension could be used. Exhaust systems too could be anything, as long as they were 115dB(A) measured at 11 metres.

In the production race at the Isle of Man in 1976, Roger Nicholls and Steve Tonkin, on a modified Sports Motorcycles-entered 750SS (with 860 pistons), had given some indication of the Ducati's suitability to the Island. Nicholls set a best lap of 103.13 mph (165.96 km/h) before retiring. The following year Steve Wynne of Sports Motorcycles managed to obtain a used 900NCR endurance racer for Nicholls to ride, and he almost won the race from Phil Read on a Honda, but for a controversial shortening of the race that saw the Honda go without their final fuel stop. When Steve Wynne managed to persuade Mike Hailwood to race a

Mike Hailwood won the 750 class on a 750SS in the 1977 Castrol Six Hour race for production motorcycles, held in Australia. (AMCN)

Ducati as part of his Isle of Man return of 1978, Ducati agreed to supply new F1 900NCRs. In October 1977, a few months prior to the TT, Hailwood had ridden a square-case 750SS in the Australian Castrol Six Hour production race at Amaroo Park, Sydney, where he and team-mate Jim Scaysbrook managed an impressive sixth overall.

The Formula One bikes, like that made for Mike Hailwood, used Daspa frames (weighing only 25 lb, and with extra bracing between the down-tubes and the steering head) and narrow crankcases with the spin-on oil filter. They lacked such detail touches of the endurance bikes as the quick release wheel, or even the special magnesium-bodied Marzocchi suspension. Eight complete F1 bikes, along with 20 engines displacing 864 cc, were built in 1978, and they continued to be built for several more years. According to Rino Caracchi a total of 18 customer bikes were made, and 70 of the special Daspa frames. While some of the later customer bikes used engines based on the square-case, for 1978 the engines were part 900SS and part 750SS, using 900 heads and barrels on a 750 cam gear train. They even had the 750 ignition points, replaced by an electronic Lucas Rita by Wynne. The narrower sump allowed the use of low pipes rather than the high 'Imola' type, and a spin-on oil filter, and all these engines had a dry clutch and external oil-cooler mounted on the steering head. The NCR bikes came with the gearshift on the right side (via a 750 selector box) and the brake on the left, but Hailwood had a conversion, with the gearshift cross-over shaft going through the swing-arm pivot. (This was because he could no longer shift gears with his right foot as a result of injuries caused in a horrific Formula 2 car crash at the Nürburgring in 1974.) They also featured the one-piece tank/fairing unit of the endurance bikes.

Two NCR Formula One bikes were sold to Sports Motorcycles, but they were shipped very late, still residing in Bologna in April. As soon as he got them, Steve Wynne completely stripped and reassembled the bikes, installing US Venolia teflon-coated

Hailwood testing the 900NCR at Oulton Park in May 1978.

11:1 pistons (as used by Cook Neilson at Daytona in 1977 – see next section), machining additional key-ways in the bevel-gears to fine tune the valve timing, and drilling most of the internal components to save weight. Girling shocks replaced the Marzocchis. An important modification was the replacement of the normal six-dog gearbox by one having only three engagement dogs, which was to become standard on all Ducatis four years later. In race trim for Hailwood, the bike weighed in at only 360 lb (163 kg). When *Motor Cycle Mechanic* put it on their dyno in October 1978, maximum power at the rear wheel was 80.5 bhp at 8,500 rpm. Sports Motorcycles entered three bikes at the TT. Besides Hailwood, Roger Nicholls rode one, and Mike's mate from

The victorious Sports Motorcycles-prepared Isle of Man Ducati was later bought by Wolfgang Reiss in Hannover. Here it is on display in his garage in 1988.

Australia, Jim Scaysbrook, the other.

The TT F1 race itself, on 3 June 1978, was one of the greatest days ever for Ducati. 38-year-old Hailwood had not raced on the island for 11 years, but on a bike giving away at least 20 bhp to the Hondas and Kawasakis he demonstrated not only his superiority, but also that of a tractable, good-handling two-cylinder motorcycle on a road circuit. In the process he demolished Phil Read's previous lap record by 9 mph, achieving 110.62 mph (178 km/h), and completed the race at an average speed of 108.51 mph (174.6 km/h). In his own words, it 'was the easiest TT I can remember'. His speed had been such that he would have finished fifth in the Classic TT against TZ750 Yamahas. If he had maintained his practice speed of 111 mph (178.6 km/h), he could have finished third. It had been a fairy-tale comeback, and Hailwood's success did a lot to ensure the continuation of the Isle of Man as a racing event. His success on a Ducati was to be of similar promo-tional benefit to the factory as the Imola victory of 1972 had been.

One week later, on 11 June, at the traditional Mallory Park post-TT event, Hailwood again won the F1 race on the Ducati, averaging 93.18 mph (150 km/h). Here he convincingly beat John Cowie (980 Kawasaki) and Phil Read (888 Honda) on a traditional British short circuit. The large crowd was spellbound. There were two more outings that year on the Sports Motorcycles Ducati, Donington and Silverstone. At Donington a broken piston ring caused Hailwood to ride harder than the Dunlop tyres would allow, to make up for a 500 rpm shortfall, and he crashed. For Silverstone a wider, 3.5-inch Campagnolo wheel was fitted to increase the tyre's effective radius, which, along with a front slick to replace the intermediate, caused some problems with the Marzocchi suspension. Out-powered by the Kawasakis and Hondas on the super-fast circuit, Hailwood still managed a 110 mph (177 km/h) lap and third place.

After these F1 races Hailwood returned to New Zealand, where he was living at that time. He teamed up with Jim Scaysbrook again in the Australian Castrol Six Hour production race to ride a 750SS, but this time Scaysbrook crashed while they were in the lead of the 750 class. Scaysbrook took his 900NCR back to Australia, where it was campaigned for several years, most notably by future World 500 cc Champion Wayne Gardner in the inaugural Coca Cola Eight Hour race at Oran Park in 1980.

As had happened after Imola, Ducati, elated with this success, promised Mike Hailwood Replicas. These were slow in appearing and, unlike the original 'Imola' replica 750SSs, bore only a superficial resemblance to the genuine Mike Hailwood Ducati when they were eventually put into production late in 1979. Hailwood also agreed to ride a Ducati at the 1979 TT, but this time Ducati were to provide the bikes themselves. Hailwood tested the new F1 and

Hailwood rode the Sports Motorcycles Ducati to a spectacular victory in the F1 race at the Isle of Man in 1978. (Two Wheels)

Future 500 cc World Champion Wayne Gardner rode a 900NCR at the Coca Cola 800 endurance race in Sydney in 1980. Here he leads in the early stages.

endurance bikes at Misano, but he crashed before any improvements could be tested. The bikes had the square section swing-arm and a re-routed exhaust pipe behind the rear sub-frame.

Problems with EFIM management almost meant that there would be no factory bike for Hailwood, but at the last moment Ducati agreed to provide the bikes and factory mechanics. When the factory F1 bikes eventually arrived in May 1979 they were only modified wet clutch square-case 900SSs. The Classic TT bike was the latest type NCR endurance racer with the square section swing-arm and revised exhaust system. The factory also sent Franco Farnè, Rino Caracchi, and Nani Nero along with the 860 cc F1 and 950 cc Classic TT machines. Initial testing at Oulton Park showed both bikes to be inferior to the previous year, so Steve Wynne replaced the swing-arms with an earlier type, and even tried the 1978 frame. The 950 cc bike handled so

poorly that Hailwood elected to ride a Suzuki in the Classic. Even his F1 bike was no match for the previous year, his best practice lap being only 105.88 mph (170.4 km/h). The production-based 900SS engine didn't produce enough power, but unfortunately the special narrow sump NCR crankcases were no longer legal for F1, and the best he could manage was fifth, with a loose battery and cracked exhaust pipe. In the Classic TT, George Fogarty crashed his 950 cc bike badly at Signpost Corner, but he still finished seventh on an 860 in the F1 race.

It was an unfortunate follow up to the magnificent 1978 result, and Hailwood declined to ride the F1 Ducati in the post-TT events of 1979. George Fogarty and others campaigned Sports Motorcycles 900s in F1 events for a couple more years, and Fogarty's son, Carl, went on to achieve greater things for Ducati 15 years later.

Ducati continued to make Formula

About to test the 1979 F1 bike at Misano in April 1979, Hailwood talks to Pat Slinn, Sports Motorcycles' race manager. (Two Wheels)

Hailwood crashed during the test session at Misano, cracking two ribs. (Two Wheels)

One bikes in 1980, but primarily for the Italian series. Wanes Francini won the 1980 Italian Regions Trophy Championship on this final version, that now had fully floating discs, new wheels, and a revised exhaust system. The bevel-gear bikes were, by now, quite outclassed in international events. However, in 1981 Carlo Perugini and Mauro Ricci won the Italian Endurance Championship on a 900NCR. To celebrate this victory a 1982-version 900 TT1/*Coupe d'Endurance* bike was displayed at the Milan Show at the end of 1981 alongside the new TT2 600. With the square-case engine and electric start,

it had the twin-filler caps of so many NCR bikes but was little changed externally.

The 'California Hot Rod'

Before looking at the production bikes that resulted from Mike Hailwood's magnificent success at the Isle of Man in 1978, it is important to outline one more significant victory for Ducati that had occurred over 12 months prior to the Isle of Man of 1978. This was Cook Neilson's victory at the 1977 Daytona Superbike race on a privately prepared 750SS, with no factory support.

Cook Neilson was then editor of the now defunct *Cycle* magazine, and along with fellow journalist and Ducati enthusiast Phil Schilling had been racing a 750SS throughout 1975. For 1976 they decided to attempt the newly-created AMA Superbike series against factory-supported BMWs and Kawasakis. The bike had been very successful as a 750 throughout the 1975 season running 'Imola' race kit camshafts and high-rise Conti mufflers, so the next step was to fit 87 mm Venolia pistons (with Yamaha XT500 rings) for a capacity of 883 cc, Harley-Davidson 42 mm inlet valves, BMW exhausts, Toyota gudgeon pins, and K-Mart ignition coils. They called it the 'California Hot Rod'. Weight was paired off significantly using a magnesium Fontana rear brake caliper and mounting plate, along with Harry Hunt plasma-coated aluminium front discs and Morris magnesium wheels, to get the weight down to 398 lb (180 kg). Neilson only managed third at Daytona in 1976, but still set the fastest trap speed of 145.2 mph (233.7 km/h). Wherever they raced, Schilling always took a picture of Fabio Taglioni, poor results occurring only when they forgot Doctor T's picture!

For the next year they had a new gearbox made by Marvin Webster, and a re-worked Jerry Branch cylinder head, now with 44 mm Harley-Davidson XR inlet valves. Standard Ducati 750SS crankshafts were used, but replaced regularly, and the 883 cc engine put out 90.4 bhp at 8,300 rpm.

The factory-prepared F1 bike of 1979, now with a square-case engine, was inferior to that of the previous year. (Two Wheels)

Hailwood still managed to finish fifth in the F1 race on the Isle of Man in 1979.

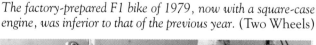

Steve Wynne prepared the successful Hailwood Ducatis. Here he is with the 1979 F1 bike in February 1994.

The 1980 F1 bike that Wanes Francini used to win the 1980 Italian Regions Trophy. (Two Wheels)

Phil Schilling astride the 'California Hot Rod' at Laguna Seca in 1977. (Art Friedman)

Cook Neilson competed in the AMA Superbike series throughout 1977. Here he is at Sears Point. (Art Friedman)

At Daytona, Neilson won the 1977 Superbike race at an average speed of 100.982 mph (162.51 km/h), with a timed trap speed of 149.50 mph (240.6 km/h).

Other Americans subsequently prepared and raced Ducatis in AMA Superbike events. Reno Leoni imported a 900NCR racer for Mike Baldwin in 1978, but he was disqualified after finishing a close second to Wes Cooley's Yoshimura Suzuki at Pocono; the AMA didn't consider the NCR a genuine production bike. Paul Ritter raced a 905 cc Ducati to success at Sears Point, and then bought the Cook Neilson bike. Others who rode for Reno Leoni included Richard Schlachter (who won several AMA Superbike races), Freddie Spencer (who almost won the Daytona 200 in 1979), and Jimmy Adamo (tragically killed at Daytona in 1993). However, by 1981 Ducatis were no longer contenders for the AMA Superbike Championship, being relegated to the Battle of the Twins class. Here they were virtually unbeatable, Jimmy Adamo, on Reno

Leoni's bike, winning the US Battle of the Twins class three years in a row in 1981–83. Even in AMA Superbike events Adamo, on Reno Leoni's 947 cc 110 bhp bevel-gear twin, was a top ten finisher right through until 1984, and one of the fastest bevel-gear twins ever with a recorded trap speed of 161.7 mph (260.2 km/h) at Daytona in 1982. For 1985 Leoni and Adamo campaigned a Pantah-based Cagiva Alazzurra before reverting to a Mille-based racer in 1986.

The Mike Hailwood Replica

It was more than a year after Hailwood's victory at the Isle of Man before the first production Mike Hailwood Replica appeared on display at the London Show. The styling was based on the unsuccessful 1979 bike, and was very much a cosmetic alteration of a 900SS. They had a one-piece fibreglass fairing and a fibreglass cover over the ordinary steel SS petrol tank to appease British regulations. There were no side-covers, so the rear 40 mm Dell'Orto carburettor and battery were clearly

visible. While the tank and seat design was modelled on the 900NCR – the colours being the red/white/green of Hailwood's winning bike over a red frame – there was provision for a pillion with a removable cowling over the seat. Along with Darmah Nippon Denso instruments and switch-gear, these first models of MHR also had Conti exhausts, Campagnolo or Speedline magnesium wheels, and Brembo Gold-Line 08 brake calipers front and rear. They also differed from the 900SS in having a closer-fitting left-side exhaust pipe, 330 mm long Marzocchi rear shock absorbers, and polished alloy Marzocchi forks rather than black-painted ones. In addition performance was restored due to the fitting of 40 mm carburettors and Contis, and these first MHRs were excellent-performing machines, just like the first 900SSs. Despite a weight increase to 444 lb (201 kg), *Motor Cycle Weekly* reached 129 mph (208 km/h) in their test of October 1979.

It wasn't long before two of the problems of these very first models

The 1979 Mike Hailwood Replica had a one-piece fairing. This example has Campagnolo wheels. (Two Wheels)

were rectified. In 1980 the petrol tank became a sculptured steel one, and the wheels FPS aluminium. With the release of the revised 900SS in 1981, the MHR also came in for an update, with a two-piece fairing, and side-covers (now covering the battery and rear carburettor). The two-piece fairing made maintenance tasks, like oil changes, much simpler, but the MHR was even closer to the standard 900SS with black-painted forks, regular Brembo brake calipers, and Silentium mufflers.

The MHR featured the same engine specifications as the 900SS, but with only 40 mm PHM Dell'Ortos. Still with 9.3:1 compression, power was a claimed to be 63 bhp at 7,400 rpm, whereas the 900SS with 32 mm carburettors produced a claimed 57 bhp at the same rpm, both with Silentium silencers. The MHR had higher final drive gearing with 15/33 teeth sprockets giving 2.2:1 (900SSs at this time had 16/38, or 2.375:1). Weight was up again to 463 lb (210 kg) dry. Instruments were still Nippon Denso, whereas the 900SS

had Veglia. An important modification that occurred in 1982, from engine 2919 (and to all 900 SS and S2 engines), was the replacement of the six-dog gearbox with one using only three dogs, as used on the original Hailwood bike of 1978. This dramatically improved the reliability of the gearbox and reduced any tendency to jump out of gear.

During 1983 the Mike Hailwood Replica went through a major redesign, coinciding with the end of the 900SS and its replacement with the 900S2. The Replica now used the inferior S2 frame to accommodate an electric start, and this caused some problems, as mentioned in the previous chapter. Wheels were Oscam type to enable the use of tubeless tyres, there was a new, narrower two-piece fairing, and a new instrument panel with revised warning lights. Other styling changes included different, slotted side-covers, and new graphics. The Brembo brake calipers were mounted behind the 38 mm Marzocchi fork legs and the clip-on bars offset, as with the S2. A first for

Ducati were electromagnetic fuel taps, and air caps on the fork legs. Some of these MHRs came with a Conti two-into-one exhaust system; however, most had the usual Silentiums and air cleaners. New Marzocchi gas rear shock absorbers, indicators and tail-light, and a larger 120/90V18 rear Michelin M48 tyre completed the specifications.

While some of the 1983 MHR 900s retained the old square-case engine, this year also saw a new engine introduced, which incorporated the first major revisions since the Darmah of 1977. The engine-case was completely restyled to accommodate a much more compact Nippon Denso starter motor, a new alternator, and a hydraulically operated, dry clutch. A spin-on oil filter replaced the previous cartridge type, and now an oil-level sight glass appeared in the left-side crankcase. The kickstart had completely disappeared and couldn't even be retro-fitted, but fortunately the new electric start was very reliable – at least on the 900. Within the engine, everything was as before, except for Cermetal – the Italian equivalent of Nikasil – lined bores. The crankshaft was still the pressed-up roller bearing type and all internal gear ratios were as before. There was a slight reduction in ignition advance from the Bosch W7B electronic ignition system, now a maximum 28°, from 32° the previous year. (Ignition advance had gradually been reduced over the years from the 38° of the original 750GT.)

While not the final development of the bevel-gear engine, in some ways these 1983–84 MHR900 engines were the best of all. Smoothness approached 750 levels, and they were very tractable over a wide power band, more so than the later Mille MHR with its altered gear ratios. They were fast, particularly in top speed, but ground clearance with the fairing fitted was very poor. *Motor Cycle News* ran their test bike to 129 mph (208 km/h) in October 1983, with Silentium mufflers. The basic problem with this model was that while the engine was an improvement, the use of S2 frame and chassis components was a retrograde step. The higher-mounted engine contributed to a top heavy feel, and the bike was physically much larger than before. The dry weight was up yet again, to 467 lb (212 kg). I bought one of these bikes in 1984, but sold it two years later, continually frustrated with its handling when compared to the older Ducatis.

The 1983 900MHR was really only a stop-gap prior to the appearance of the final version of the bevel-gear engine, the Mille, and as soon as it was released there was talk of an even newer, V4, engine. When the development of a the V4 was dropped, Taglioni and Bordi turned their attention to the bevel-gear twin. The first change was to the crankshaft, now a Pantah-style forged one-piece item with plain big-end bearings. Crankpin diameter went up from 38 to 45 mm, with a huge increase in rigidity. Like the Pantah, but unlike the parallel twins, the high-speed angular ball-bearings for the mains were still retained, but with extra webbing in the cases to cope with extra stress. Along with this new crankshaft, the stroke was lengthened

The last MHR, the Mille of 1985, virtually indistinguishable from the 900 of 1984.

to 80 mm. However, to keep the engine the same height as the 900, the new pistons had their gudgeons closer to the top of the piston and the standard 860 con-rod length was maintained. Thus the rod to stroke ratio was lowered even more to 1.81:1. This had the effect of increasing low-speed torque, but at the cost of higher piston acceleration and more side-thrust, not really a problem on a street engine with an 8,000 rpm limit. Rather than use the 90 mm pistons of the last 950 cc NCR racers, the 88 mm pistons of the earlier 905 cc bikes were used to give a capacity of 972 cc.

The oil filtration was modified to provide a full-flow filter (a larger filter in the same location) and larger capacity oil pump. All the developments of the final 900 were also included, notably the revised engine covers, Nippon Denso starter motor, and dry clutch. Unfortunately the larger engine taxed the starter motor to the limit and cold-starting was a significant problem, even with a fully-charged battery. The extra friction of the plain big-end bearings coupled with 108 cc meant that many a Mille MHR or S2 had to be push-started on a cold morning. The cylinder heads

still didn't utilize the 60° cylinder heads of the Pantah, but the 80° heads had larger valves, now 42 mm inlet and 38 mm exhaust. All the gear ratios were altered for this larger engine. The primary drive was raised yet again to 39/69, or 1.769:1, and the internal ratios were different, with much wider ratios between first and fifth. While fourth and fifth gears remained unchanged, first was now 2.720:1 rather than 2.237:1, second was 1.761:1 as opposed to 1.562:1, and third was now 1.250:1, where previously it was 1.204:1. With a very low 15/41 final drive ratio, a Mille would easily run to its 8,000 rpm red-line in top gear. Claimed power for the Mille was up slightly from the 900, to 76 bhp at 7,500 rpm.

This Mille engine was placed in the identical 900 MHR running gear. The earlier bikes had black-painted forks, but these were painted red on final examples, along with a red front guard. As it had the S2 frame and suspension it suffered from the same deficiencies. The first examples appeared in mid-1984, and when tested by *Motorrad* in November they achieved 214 km/h (133 mph). The bike also weighed in

at 240 kg (529 lb) wet. When compared to their test of the 1974 750SS, which achieved 216.7 km/h (135 mph) and weighed 202 kg (445 lb) wet, one must wonder at the progress over ten years.

With the Cagiva take-over, the days of expensive bevel-gear engines were numbered, and by the end of 1985 the Mille was finished. This year saw a prototype built using a 16-inch front wheel and M1R Marzocchi forks, and Massimo Tamburini, formerly of Bimota, developed a new frame of square-section tubing, with a single shock rear end and 16-inch wheels, for the Mille engine. However, nothing ever came of these. I saw a Mille MHR with the new Cagiva-inspired Ducati lettering at the factory at the end of 1985, but by now production had ended. It was unfortunate, because, with development, this engine had potential. All it really needed was more up-to-date running gear, but economics had forced its hand. It was a difficult time for Ducati with Cagiva taking control, and production was at an all-time low. Some remained unsold into 1986, and they were to be the last of the illustrious line of bevel-gear Ducatis.

10

The Pantah: 500SL and 600SL

The story goes that in 1976, when the management of Ducati finally realized that the parallel twins were a commercial disaster, Ing. Taglioni smiled, reached into his bottom draw, and presented them with the full technical drawings for a 500 cc V-twin engine. The origins of the Pantah went back to the Armaroli 500 cc Grand Prix racer of 1973, and many of the features tried on this racing engine were incorporated in the first production models of 1979. The Pantah could have gone into production much earlier, but the EFIM management was in turmoil. During 1977–78 motorcycle production at Borgo Panigale was at an all-time low, partly due to the decline in the US market, but also because of the unsatisfactory model range, and in July 1978 control of Ducati passed to another conglomerate, the VM Group. VM were heavily involved in diesel engines, so they used the Ducati plant in Bologna for their production and development of industrial diesels. Under the control of the company in Rome, industrial diesel engine production was increased, while that of motorcycles was decreased. Finally, in 1979, after a two-year delay, Fabio Taglioni was allowed to put his new engine and motorcycle into production, an engine so successful that it continues to form the basis of the entire range of modern Ducatis.

While the range of production bevel-gear twins remained strongly influenced by the singles throughout their lifespan, the Pantah was a combination of the past and present. The prototype 500 cc Pantah had its

The only example of the Armaroli-designed 500 cc double overhead camshaft racer of 1973. This still used the Seeley frame but had a rear-exiting exhaust.

roots very much in the 1971–73 racers. It used the same bore and stroke of 74 mm and 58 mm, and, like the final 500 racer of 1973, used toothed belts to drive the double overhead camshafts. When asked in 1977, by Dennis Noyes of *Motor Cycle*, why he chose to change to toothed belts over bevel-gears and shafts, Taglioni replied: 'It is no more precise but it lowers mechanical noise and will cut assembly costs. Our big V-twins are expensive to build because of the materials, and they have to be built with great care because of shimming and setting up clearances. With the belt drive we get the same accuracy without the complexity'. Taglioni also went on to say that several aspects of the design of the Pantah were compromised by the necessity to use many components from the parallel twin.

While not actually built by Ducati,

the 1973 500 cc double overhead camshaft, eight-valve racing engine pioneered quite a few features that would eventually find their way to the production engines. The engine came from another Bolognese company, Armaroli, and was based on the 500 cc bevel-gear crankcases. It still had the gearshift on the right side, and primary drive and dry multi-plate clutch on the left. The exposed toothed belts were driven from the crankshaft inside the primary gears, so the drive moved from the right side of the engine to the left. Ignition was by a set of contact breakers mounted on the external reduction gear. In a move pre-empting the Paso 13 years later, the rear cylinder head was reversed so that both Dell'Orto carburettors faced forward between the cylinders, with a rear exiting exhaust pipe. Unlike the bevel-gear 500 racing engine, the front cylinder

had radial finning, similar to the Moto Guzzi racing singles of the 1950s. Power was 74 bhp at 12,000 rpm, not up significantly from the bevel-gear engines. Mounted in one of the Seeley frames with triple Lockheed discs and leading axle Marzocchis, it was raced occasionally by Spaggiari in 1973 without success.

Initial development versions of the new Pantah engine still used needle roller big-end bearings, Ing. Taglioni being reluctant to accept plain bearings. However, experience with the parallel twins had some effect on his thinking. By the time the first prototype was displayed at the Milan Show of November 1977, it had full-flow oil filtration, with a spin-on oil filter, and a one-piece forged crankshaft. This show model also featured a full fairing in the style of the race-kit 750/900SS fairing, and Campagnolo hydroconical brakes. Belt-covers on these early

The prototype 500 Pantah of 1977, with Campagnolo hydroconical brakes.

engines mimicked the cylinder head finning. Not much development happened throughout 1978, and for the Cologne Show in October another version was exhibited, now with polished aluminium cam belt covers. One month later, at Milan, the Pantah had the Speedlines replaced by six-spoke FPS wheels. Production was announced to begin in March the following year, but it would be several months after that before the first series was built. The pre-production bikes were painted two-tone blue and white, but the first series of 250 bikes, when they finally appeared after the summer break of 1979, were red and silver.

The Pantah deviated considerably in design from the 750/860 bevel-gear twins. It was intended for desmodromic valves only, and was much more compact. While using the 90° twin cylinder layout with vertically split crankcases, the swing-arm was also pivoted on bearings within the gearbox casing. This was done to bring the pivot as close as possible to the countershaft sprocket, reducing chain snatch. In many ways the Pantah was a mirror image of the bigger twin and earlier 500 racers. The crankshaft was still supported by axial thrust ball main bearings, Taglioni being wary of the plain main bearings as fitted to the parallel twin, with the helical primary drive gears on the right side, and the alternator on the left. Whereas the cylinders were offset with the horizontal cylinder to the left on the 750/860, in the interests of keeping the exhaust pipes more compact, this was also reversed on the Pantah. Also, unlike the big twin, the flywheel with ignition trigger sat inside the 200 watt alternator. The Bosch BTZ ignition system was new, and was adapted from the same system used on the Darmah SD900. As it was designed to be electric start only, the starter motor was neatly fitted under the front cylinder and drove through reduction gearing to a sprag clutch screwed to the back of the flywheel. The toothed belts and valve gear were driven off a jackshaft running between the cylinders and geared from the crankshaft on the left side. This enabled the engine to be kept much narrower (at only 14.8

inches or 376 mm) than the bigger engines that needed to fit the geared camshaft drive inside the alternator rotor.

The primary drive, with a ratio of 31/69 or 2.226:1, drove a standard Ducati-style wet multi-plate clutch, something which has been under continued refinement by the factory. It is beyond the scope of this book to detail every modification to Ducati clutches over the years, but generally they occur at almost annual intervals. If there has been an Achilles heel to Ducati engines over the years, it has been the clutch, and as the engines get successively more powerful, the clutch slipping problem is exacerbated. The Pantah clutch too was the reverse of the 860, in that the six springs clamped the driving and driven plates from the inside outward of the alloy clutch drum and hub. The forged one-piece crankshaft necessitated the change to two-piece connecting rods with plain bearing big-ends, and a corresponding increase in oil pressure. Whereas the old engines, with all their ball and roller bearings, could run with only 15 psi from its geared pump, the Pantah flow rate was regulated to 70 psi. The geared oil pump resided in the same location as the earlier engines, but was now driven by the helical primary drive gear.

Unlike the larger twin, maintaining a short wheelbase wasn't such a problem, so the gearbox was the indirect type, with separate input and output shafts. Consequently the engine rotated forward, not backward as the 750/860. As with the 860, though, the first engines (to engine number 3245), used gearboxes with six engagement dogs. Following racing 860 practice, these became the stronger three-dog type in 1982. Much of the reason for making the Pantah a mirror image of the earlier twin was so that the gearshift could be properly incorporated on the left side. The cylinder barrels were also Gilnisil (an Italian Nikasil), a plating incorporating silicon and carbon particles that was much harder than iron, lighter, harder-wearing, and offered better heat transfer. The only down side was that the cylinders couldn't be rebored. The two-valve cylinder

heads used the 60° included valve angle of the 1973 racing bikes and parallel twins, with 37.5 mm inlet and 33.5 mm exhaust valves. The desmodromic valve actuation system mirrored Taglioni's design for the parallel twin 500 Sport, but with the different timing figures of inlet opening 50° before top dead centre and closing 80° after bottom dead centre. The exhaust opened 75° before bottom dead centre, closing 45° after top dead centre. Feeding these cylinder heads were 36 mm Dell'Orto PHF carburettors, restricted by a large air-filter on top of the engine, under the fuel tank. Compression ratio was 9.5:1, and claimed power was 52 bhp at 9,050 rpm.

Supporting this engine was a trellis-type frame, also designed by Taglioni. Two pairs of parallel tubes running from the rear cylinder to the steering head met another pair of tubes running up from the rear of the crankcases. This was braced for extra rigidity. The engine hung below the trellis and was bolted to it at six points. It wasn't the most compact frame, as the wheelbase was still 57 inches (1,450 mm), but it was considerably shorter than the larger twins. Suspension was by Marzocchi front and rear, with 35 mm diameter forks and 310 mm shock absorbers. With clip-on handlebars, and a half-fairing, the 180 kg (396 lb) Pantah 500SL was still very much a sporting motorcycle. The Nippon Denso instruments and the switch-gear were the same as on the Darmah.

When the first production models finally appeared during 1980 they were painted a pale blue, with red and dark blue stripes. The styling didn't meet with universal acclaim, and the first 500SLs were unlike other V-twin Ducatis in that they had very little bottom end and mid-range power. As delivered, the Pantah was an extremely quiet bike with its toothed belt camshaft drive, rubber plugs in between the cylinder fins, and quiet Contis. The engine liked to rev, but unfortunately the gearing was so high at 2.533:1 that performance was limited, and the bike wouldn't run near to its power peak in top gear. *Motor Cycle Weekly* managed 114.34 mph (184 km/h) in October 1980,

Left and right profiles of a 1957 double overhead-camshaft 125 cc Grand Prix Bialbero.

Above: *One of the two 350 cc racing twins built in 1960. Later they were sold to John Surtees, who commissioned this Reynolds frame with leading-link forks.*

Right: *The first production sporting 250 was the four-speed Diana, or Daytona, of 1962.*

The 450 Desmo of 1972, affectionately titled 'the Silver Shotgun'. (Two Wheels)

Top right: *Leopoldo Tartarini restyled the Desmo single for the 1973 season to mirror the 750 Sport.*

Bottom right: *The 750GT of 1971 heralded the range of 90º V-twins.*

The classic round-case 750 engine, here in a 750 Sport.

A 1974 750 Sport, with the optional half-fairing.

The definitive factory production racer, the 1974 750 Super Sport.

A year later, the square-case 750 Super Sport of 1975.

Above: *The 900SS was restyled for 1979. This example has non-standard wire-spoked wheels.*

Top right: *1984 was the last year for the 900 Mike Hailwood Replica.*

Bottom right: *The final 600SL Pantah of 1984 was painted in MHR colours.*

Virginio Ferrari won the Italian Formula One Championship on a factory TT1 in 1985.

The 750 Santa Monica of 1988, the final limited edition F1.

1988 saw the tricolore 851, followed in1989 by the all-red 851 Strada.

The 851 soon became an 888, the fastest being the Sport Production series. From the left are an SP3, 4 and 5 of 1991,1992, and 1993.

Another limited production model was the 900 Superlight, based on a 900SS. This is the first version, dating to 1992.

A small number of Supermono racers have been built since 1993, incorporating many innovative design features. The water pump is driven by the exhaust camshaft, and inside the left engine-cover sits a dry alternator.

1994 brought the 916 with a completely new frame, and styling similar to the Supermono. Following the 888 Sport Production, there was also this 916 SP.

Carl Fogarty won his first World Superbike Championship in 1994 on the 916 racer.

Despite being a new design, the engine of the 916 was still similar to the 888. Compare this to the Supermono.

The 748 Sport Production became available for 600 Super Sport racing in 1995.

Troy Corser rode for the Promotor team in 1995 and 1996, finishing second in the 1995 World Superbike Championship.

Carl Fogarty was the only rider for the Gia.Ca.Moto. Ducati Performance factory team of 1998.

The 1999 996SPS incorporated new decals, black Marchesini wheels and new front brake discs while the class-leading engine and chassis remained unchanged.

The author on a 1982 500SL.

running to only 8,500 rpm in top gear. Contemporary tests were extremely complimentary about the handling of the Pantah. With a 30.5° steering-head angle, the Pantah was a stable motorcycle, and the frame more than sufficient for the modest weight and power of the 500 cc engine. My experience with 500 Pantahs was that they handled well enough, and steered slowly and predictably, yet did exhibit signs of looseness somewhere between the rear wheel and steering head over bumpy roads. The 35 mm forks were lacking in rigidity too, especially by modern standards. The engines, though, while lacking in torque compared to an 860, were thoroughly reliable and oil-tight. However, a small practical problem with Pantahs was the slow discharge of the 12-volt 14Ah battery if they weren't used regularly.

In line with past Ducati practice, it was obvious that a simple overbore would be the first step in the development of the Pantah. Already, early in 1980, a 600 Pantah with a Mike Hailwood Replica-style full fairing had been seen at the factory, and a factory racing kit that included larger pistons was marketed for the 500, just as the first production bikes became available. The new 600SL was displayed late in 1980 along with a prototype turbocharged Pantah engine. Nothing came of the

turbocharged version, but the 600SL became available in early 1981, with silver paintwork, a new fairing, and a hydraulically-actuated wet clutch with stronger springs. Paoli 35 mm forks were fitted on the earliest versions, and throughout 1981 and 1982 either Marzocchi or Paoli forks and shock absorbers appeared on the production bikes. These also had larger 08 Brembo front brake calipers, mounted behind the fork legs, and a larger 400H18 rear tyre. The 600SL

was unchanged throughout 1982 except for a black plastic front guard. Claimed dry weight was up to 187 kg (411 lb).

The 500 Pantah continued alongside the 600, and in 1981 received the 600-style fairing, but not the hydraulic clutch. The engine cases were standardized as they had been with the square-case 750/900SS in 1975, so that, in effect, from number 1654 the 500 was a sleeved-down 600 (for some reason 290 engines after this had the earlier cases). The extra capacity for the 600 was gained in exactly the same way as the 750 had become an 860, by a 6 mm cylinder bore increase. With an 80 mm bore and the 58 mm stroke, capacity was 583 cc, with compression still 9.5:1. Valve sizes, valve timing, and carburettors were shared by both models. Claimed power was 58 bhp at 8,500, but by 1982 it had risen to 61 bhp at 9,100 rpm, with compression now 10.4:1. For the 500 the power went down to 45 bhp in 1982, with no change in specification. There were many aberrations between claimed power and weight figures for various models at this time, but it is difficult to believe that a simple 17% capacity increase would equate to a 35% power boost. The 600SL was even more highly-geared than the 500 at

The 1980 prototype 600SL with a MHR fairing.

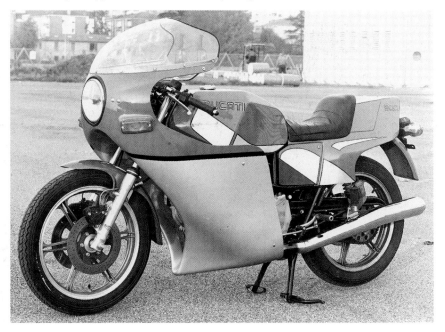

The 1982 500SL with its restyled fairing. In the background is a 1981 600SL.

2.4:1, and also wouldn't run to the red-line in top gear. The English *Motor Cycle News* in April 1982 could only manage 117.29 mph (188.8 km/h), in fourth gear. It was five mph slower in top!

Both the 500 and 600SL Pantahs were listed through to 1984, by which time the 600 was painted in the Mike Hailwood Replica colours of red, with green and white stripes, with a red frame. These last 600s had also reverted to a cable-operated clutch and now had a larger, steel clutch basket. The last 500SLs were white with red stripes. For the Italian market, a 350SL appeared in 1983, also in the MHR colours, but with silver FPS wheels. The 349 cc engine, with a 66 x 51 mm bore and stroke, 10.3:1 compression, and 30 mm Dell'Orto carburettors, produced 40 bhp at 9,600 rpm.

Pantah 600TL and 350XL

To complement the sporting 500/600SLs, the 600TL debuted at the Milan Show of 1981. The TL had the same chassis and desmo engine as

the 600SL, but with a small fairing, square headlight, new tank and seat, and a new instrument panel incorporating a fuel gauge. Other features that distinguished it from the SLs were electromagnetic fuel taps, a side stand, and smaller, Brembo 05 brake

calipers. The production version was released in April the following year, along with the 350XL for the Italian market. Both these bikes were touring oriented, with higher handlebars than the 600SL. The 350 was a more appealingly-styled bike in black and

By 1983 the 600SL was painted in MHR colours.

red, but the 600TL was one of those unfortunate styling exercises that Ducati have tried from time to time. It was a bike that rivalled the 860GT for ugliness, but under the bodywork was a competent motorcycle. The 350 engine of the XL was the same as the later 350SL detailed in the previous section, but whereas the 600TL had the foot-rests mounted on large alloy plates, the 350XL still had the rear-set controls. For the German market and their specific insurance categories, a 27 PS version of the 350XL was also built. Claimed weight for these models was less than that of the SLs, both being 177 kg (390 lb). *Motociclismo* tested a 350XL in February 1983 and achieved a top speed of 165.2 km/h (102.6 mph) from their 187 kg (412 lb) test bike.

Also displayed at the 1981 Milan Show was an unusual bike called the 500 Pantah Speedway. A joint Ducati/Alfa Romeo project, this bike was intended for 'Ice Trophy' racing, and was fitted with spiked tyres and no brakes. There were 190 spikes on the front and 235 on the rear, and the basis of the bike was a 500SL Pantah. It was raced in 1982 by the Austrian rider Hans Maier but was not a hugely successful project. Only ten bikes were built.

The 1982 600TL was white with red and yellow stripes, but was a poor seller, due to its styling. Like the SL, a combination of either Paoli or Marzocchi suspension was used. Production continued through 1983, now painted metallic grey, and fitted with the Oscam wheels of other models of that time and Silentium silencers. There was also a 350TL version available for the Italian market during 1983, and by 1984 the 600TL was being heavily discounted on the UK market. Cagiva, who had just taken over Ducati, already had their 650 Alazurra as a replacement and there was no longer any need for the TL. My experience with these later 600TLs confirmed that they were underrated bikes, condemned by their styling. The 58 bhp 600 engine was smooth, and torquier than the 500, but the bikes were still very overgeared, limiting top end performance.

When *Motociclismo* tested a 600TL in September 1983, they achieved

The 1982 600TL wasn't one of Ducati's styling successes.

179.85 km/h (111.8 mph). Producing 52.7 bhp at 8,500 rpm, and weighing 188 kg (414 lb), the 600TL's performance data was surprisingly similar to that of the earlier 750GT. A blue and white police version was also built, with a number being sold to the Bologna police department. Called the 600 Polizia Urbana, claimed top speed was 165 km/h (102.5 mph) with full police specification that included a radio and loud-

hailer. Ultimately the TL failed because, as in the past, Ducati didn't understand that their traditional market wanted good-looking, sporting motorcycles.

Pantah 650SL

To homologate the 750TT1, Ducati needed to stroke the Pantah engine, and as an interim way of getting this stroke homologated the 650SL was created. While most aspects of the

A more successfully styled bike was the 350XL.

Some of the 60 bhp 500 Pantah Speedway bikes survive. This one was for sale at the Imola market in 1995.

The Bologna police display their 600 Polizie Urbane at the Piazza Nettuno in 1982.

The final Pantah was the 650SL of 1984–86.

motorcycle and engine could be altered for the TT Formula racing classes, the road-going crankcases, cylinder-head castings, and stroke of the engine had to remain unchanged. By boring and stroking the 600, the 650 emerged, but it could easily have been a full 750. Also, for 1984 the World Endurance Championship saw a drop in the capacity limit from 1,000 cc to 750, so a 750 cc Pantah-based racer could once again mean that Ducati could be competitive in this class. By lengthening the stroke 3.5 mm to 61.5 mm, a moderate 2 mm overbore, to 82 mm, created the 649 cc engine. Valve sizes remained as for the 500 and 600, 37.5 mm inlet

and 33.5 mm exhaust. Compression ratio was down slightly to 10:1, and power only up slightly to 62 bhp at 8,500 rpm. The most noticeable improvement with the 650 engine was some more mid-range torque.

Painted in the red/yellow colours of the factory F2 bikes, the 650SL was virtually identical to the final 600SL. They both shared the wheels, large indicators and tail-light of the 1983 MHR and 900S2, but the 650SL had the instrument panel of the 600TL with the large plastic surround, its electromagnetic fuel taps, and the new type of fuel cap that was notorious for allowing water, as well as petrol, into the tank. The 650SL

continued in production after the Cagiva take-over, even though the same engine was sent to Varese for the 650 Alazzurra. Despite being available through to 1986, they are a less common model than the earlier 500 and 600SL.

With the factory racing full 750 cc engines by the time the 650SL was available, it was overshadowed by the prospect of the street version of the 750TT1. When the 750F1 finally appeared in 1985, the 650SL was immediately superseded. It offered no real advance over the 500SL of 1979, yet the 750F1 was potentially a race replica in the very best Ducati tradition.

11.

Racing Pantahs and the 750F1

As the racing success of the 900NCR waned, the Pantah took over, and during 1980 two 600 cc race-kitted Pantahs were prepared by Franco Farnè. These were campaigned successfully in the Italian national junior championship by Wanes Francini, Paolo Menchini, and Guido Del Piano, and were based on the standard SL frame but with Marzocchi racing suspension. The red and yellow bodywork was similar in style to that of the 900NCR, and power from the 583 cc engines was up to 70 bhp at 9,800 rpm. Then, for the 1981 season, Fabio Taglioni released his *tour de force*, the TT2.

The prototype TT2 was tested in Spain over the winter by Angel Nieto (14 times World 50 cc and 125 cc Champion) and successful Ducati endurance racer Salvador Canellas. So good was its design that, at its debut race meeting on 29 March 1981, the TT2, in the hands of Sauro Pazzaglia, won the opening round of the Italian TTF2 series at Misano. However, even as the TT2 was making its presence felt on Italian circuits, Sports Motorcycles' Steve

The first factory racing Pantah was this 600 of 1980.

Wynne and Pat Slinn had prepared a modified 500SL Pantah for Tony Rutter to race in the Isle of Man Formula 2 event in June 1981. Originally promised two factory bikes that didn't materialise, they had found an insurance write-off, installed a factory race kit, sent the frame off to Ron Williams of Maxton for some extra bracing, and signed up Isle of Man veteran Tony Rutter. Rutter won at an average of 101.91 mph (164 km/h), with a fastest lap of 103.51 mph (166.58 km/h). Ducati were pleased enough with this victory to offer Rutter a TT2 factory bike for the next round at Ulster on August 22. In atrocious conditions, Rutter finished second to secure the 1981 World Formula Two Championship.

The TT2 marked the return of the factory to official competition after an absence since 1975. By using an 81 mm bore capacity was increased to 597 cc, almost the class limit, and a completely new frame was designed by Taglioni and made by Verlicchi.

Weighing only 7 kg (16 lb), rear suspension was by a cantilever and single Paoli shock absorber. This frame was exceedingly compact and strong, being heavily triangulated around the steering head, and comprising essentially straight tubes. It bolted to the engine in four places, still using the latter as a stressed member, with butt-fitted bosses rather than flat tabs as on the SL. The 18-litre fibreglass petrol tank was encased by this frame. Fitted with 35 mm Marzocchi racing forks with magnesium sliders and 280 mm Brembo front discs, the racer weighed in at a mere 270 lb (122 kg). It was also extremely compact, with only a 55-inch (1,395 mm) wheelbase. The 18-inch Campagnolo wheels were 2.15 inches wide on the front, and 3.00 inches on the rear.

In the engine department, the TT2 was pure factory racer. The 81 mm Borgo pistons only had moderate compression of 10:1, but valves were larger at 41 mm inlet and 35 mm

exhaust. These valves were operated by desmodromic camshafts giving 12 mm of intake lift and 10 mm of exhaust. Italian regulations permitted the use of 40 mm Dell'Orto carburettors, but for the TT World Championship, standard 36 mm carburettors needed to be retained. Claimed power was 76 bhp at 10,750 rpm. There was much evidence of weight saving – exposed camshaft drive belts, a magnesium primary drive cover, and hydraulically operated dry clutch. A lightweight two-into-one exhaust system was also used. Internally most gears were drilled for lightness and ignition was still by electronic Bosch BTZ, with the small battery mounted in the rear tailpiece. Because Italian regulations required an electric starter, both this and the 200 watt alternator were retained.

The TT2 was a very effective racing machine, in the best Taglioni tradition of achieving maximum results through a balance of power

The TT2 was unveiled for the 1981 season, one of the all-time classic racing Ducatis.

and weight. It was light, athletic, slim, had a wide power-band, and Taglioni was especially proud of the specific fuel consumption figures of 187 gr/HP/hr – less than a diesel! Just how effective it was as a racer was displayed by Massimo Broccoli in October 1981 at the final round of the Italian 500 series at Mugello. On a TT2 sleeved down to 500 cc, he finished seventh in a field of 500GP Suzukis and Yamahas. Broccoli had already secured the Italian TT2 championship ahead of the Kawasaki-powered Bimota KB2s. In its first full year the TT2 had won the two championship series that it had contested.

The TT2 was even more successful in 1982. In the Italian TT2 championship Walter Cussigh won every round on his factory TT2, and the now 40-year-old Tony Rutter again won the World TT2 Championship. For the Italian events power was up to 78 bhp at 10,500 rpm using 41 mm Malossi Dell'Orto carburettors, and Cussigh favoured a 16-inch Campagnolo front wheel with a 3.25–4.50 Michelin front tyre. Rutter still used the 18-inch wheels, preferring them to the 16-inch type on the bumpier street circuits. At the Isle of Man he was considerably faster than the previous year, winning the Formula 2 race on the factory bike at an average speed of 108.50 mph (174.61 km/h), with a fastest lap of 109.27 mph (175.85 km/h). He was timed at 144 mph (232 km/h) at a speed trap at the Highlander. With the World Championship now extended to three rounds, Rutter scored perfect points on his factory bike. He won at Vila Real in Portugal at an average speed of 86.69 mph (139.51 km/h), following it at Ulster with a win at 100.73 mph (162.1 kph).

During 1982 a limited number of production TT2 replicas were built for privateers. These were very close to the factory bikes but lacked items such as the magnesium primary drive cover and hydraulically-operated dry clutch. They still had the racing magnesium Marzocchi forks and 18-inch Campagnolo wheels. The engine had the same valve sizes as the factory racer, and valve timing figures of inlet opening 74° before top dead

centre and closing 92° after bottom dead centre, and exhaust opening 100° before bottom dead centre and closing 64° after top dead centre. Still only using 36 mm Dell'Ortos, power was a claimed 76 bhp at 10,750 rpm. The TT2 also had straight cut primary gears, with a higher ratio than the street bikes. 36/70 teeth gave a ratio of 1.94:1. The five-speed gearbox had the same ratios as the street bike, except for fifth gear being moved closer to fourth. The final drive was considerably lower, at 3.15:1, with 13 and 41 teeth sprockets. Like the factory racer, an oil-cooler was mounted in the fairing, cooling oil to the cylinder heads in a similar system to that of the Imola racers a decade earlier. Because it still had the electric starting mechanism, weight was 130 kg (286 lb). Rear suspension was not Paoli as in 1981, but a Marzocchi PVS 1 remote reservoir gas shock absorber. Only about 20 of these bikes were made in 1982.

Racing results for the TT2 in 1983 weren't quite as spectacular as the previous year. Tony Rutter again won the World TT2 Championship, but not quite as convincingly. At the Isle of Man he headed a Ducati one-two with Graeme McGregor, at an average speed of 108.20 mph (174.13 km/h), with a fastest lap of 109.44 mph (176.12 km/h). At the other two rounds at Ulster and Assen he could only manage second, but it was enough to win the championship again. Another batch of TT2 replicas was built for 1983, virtually identical to the previous year, but now with a Campagnolo 3.50 x 16 inch front wheel to complement a rear 3.50 x 18 inch. Malossi modified 41 mm smooth bore Dell'Orto carburettors were fitted, and power was up to a claimed 78 bhp at 10,500 rpm.

750TT1

With the possibility of the World Championship TT2 class disappearing completely, Ducati hastened development of a 750 cc TT1 version of the Pantah for 1984. As previously mentioned, both TT1 and World Endurance were becoming limited to 750 cc, so a longer 61.5 mm stroked crankshaft was homologated with the 650SL Pantah. Even as far back as

March 1982 a 750 cc version of the TT2 had been raced by Jimmy Adamo for Reno Leoni at the Daytona 200, finishing 13th overall. This bike had produced nearly 95 bhp at 10,250 rpm, with a top speed of almost 155 mph (250 km/h). The following year at Daytona, this time in the Battle of the Twins race, Tony Rutter took the 750 TT1 to third place. Then, in July 1983, at Ducati's happy hunting ground, Montjuich Park, a TT1 won the now non-championship 24 Hour race with Benjamin Grau, Enrique de Juan, and Luis Reyes. Prepared by Franco Farnè, the 135 kg (298 lb) racer produced 86 bhp at 9,000 rpm, but the riders limited this to 8,000 rpm during the race, and 83–4 bhp. In front of 250,000 spectators they completed 708 laps, compared to the second-place French Kawasaki's 690.

While Tony Rutter still raced the 600TT2 in 1984, and won the Formula 2 World Championship for the fourth successive year, he also campaigned a 750 cc version of the same bike in Formula 1. He failed to win the Isle of Man F2 race, coming second, but won at Vila Real (at 90.81 mph, or 146.14 km/h). Trevor Nation, also on a 600TT2, came second in the championship. In Formula 1, Rutter managed third overall on the new Ducati during the 1984 season, and the 750 had limited success in endurance racing. At the non-championship Le Mans 24 Hour race in April, a 750 TT1 ridden by Marc Granie, Philippe Guichon, and Didier Vuillemin finished fourth; there were only 18 finishers from a field of 54. They followed this up with a fourth at the Österreichring 1,000 km race, third in the Liège 24 Hours at Spa, and fourth at the Mugello Six Hours. They finished fifth in the final placings. The works bike of Walter Villa and Walter Cussigh came fourth at the ADAC Eight Hour race at the Nürburgring, but was plagued with problems throughout the season.

The TT1 differed slightly from the TT2. It still had the cantilever swing-arm, but this was wider to accommodate wider wheels, and was painted red and blue, rather than red and yellow. The countershaft sprocket was offset for the larger section rear tyre,

As well as winning four TT2 World Championships, Tony Rutter finished third in the TT F1 race on the Isle of Man in 1984.

and the wheel now included a quick-change assembly in which the disc and caliper stayed in the swing-arm as the wheel and sprocket were removed. A 16-inch front wheel was specified, but most were raced with an 18-inch front. The 35 mm magnesium Marzocchi forks were retained. 88 mm pistons and the longer 61.5 mm stroke gave 748 cc. It no longer had the wet clutch, but a mechanically-operated dry clutch housed in an NCR primary drive cover. With the same valve sizes as the TT2, claimed power was only up to 80 bhp at the rear wheel.

The factory racer used by Walter Villa differed considerably from the customer TT1. The steering-head angle was reduced to 24°, and a rising rate suspension system was used, similar to the Suzuki full-floater, along with a box-section swing-arm. The bikes immediately suffered suspension problems, with retirement at Le Mans. During 1984, 41.7 mm Kayaba front forks with hydraulic anti-dive were tried, from a Suzuki RG500, before settling on new 42 mm

aluminium slider Marzocchis. Brakes were the new type of quickly-detachable four piston Brembos with larger, 300 mm discs, and a small, 230 mm disc at the rear. Marvic three-spoke 16-inch front wheels were used, along with 16-, 17- or 18-inch rears. Rim widths ranged from 3.5 inches on the front to 5.5 inches on the rear. By the end of the season a 16-inch front and 17-inch rear wheel were fitted, along with the new series of Michelin radial. The claimed dry weight was 287 lb (130 kg).

The engine was considerably developed from the TT2. Larger valves (44 mm and 38 mm) were operated by camshafts with intake lift of 11.45 mm and exhaust lift of 10.35 mm. Timing figures were inlet opening 75° before top dead centre, and closing 90° after bottom dead centre, and exhaust opening 102° before bottom dead centre, and closing 61° after top dead centre. Stronger, American-made Carillo con-rods were used on a standard, polished crankshaft. The 10.3:1 pistons were the cause of one failure during the

season, as were problems with valve seats, but the engine still produced 94 bhp at 10,000 rpm with the 41 mm Dell'Orto-Malossi carburettors, reduced slightly to 90 bhp for 24-hour events. The Bosch ignition rotor and alternator were now fitted in the magnesium left-side case, away from engine oil, and a mechanically-operated dry clutch replaced the previous hydraulic one. The factory TT1 was by now significantly removed from the TT2, and ready for another assault on the World Endurance Championship, and Italian F1, in 1985.

Before detailing the F1 events, it must be mentioned that 1985 was also the final year for the TT2. Tony Rutter, riding a factory TT1 with the rising rate rear suspension, but fitted with a 600 cc engine, again won the Formula 2 race at the Isle of Man, but at the slower speed of 107.79 mph (173.47 km/h). He followed this with a second at Vila Real, and a third at Montjuich Park. Unfortunately a serious accident in the F1 race at Montjuich, on a Suzuki GSXR 750,

Walter Villa on a TT1 at the Bol d'Or 24 Hour race in 1984.

tragically ended Rutter's career, and he was lucky to survive, having been initially pronounced dead. Despite not completing the season, Rutter still managed to finish second in the World TT F2 Championship that year. His record of four World Championships had been amongst the most significant racing results ever achieved by Ducati.

Despite all the development on the TT1 by Taglioni, Franco Farnè, and Walter Villa, the 1985 Endurance season was even less successful than the previous year. The only placings were a fifth and sixth at the opening round at Monza with Walter Cussigh/Oscar la Ferla, and Virginio Ferrari/Marco Lucchinelli. In the Formula 1 World Championship, Dieter Rechtenbach managed sixth overall, by virtue of finishing second

Tony Rutter's last win on the Isle of Man was in 1985, on a factory TT2 with 16-inch wheels and rising rate rear suspension.

at Montjuich, always Ducati's most successful venue. Another significant result for the TT1 was Marco Lucchinelli's sixth place in the Daytona Formula 1 race in March. It was a different story in the Italian Formula 1 Championship. Here TT1 Ducatis filled the first seven places, with Virginio Ferrari taking the title from Marco Lucchinelli.

1986 started well, with Marco Lucchinelli winning the Battle of the Twins race at Daytona in March on an experimental 851 cc (92 x 64 mm) 750F1-based racer at just over 104 mph (167 km/h). Lucchinelli raced in both the Formula 1 and Battle of the Twins, and later went on to win the Battle of the Twins race at Laguna Seca. He also won the opening round of the World TT Formula 1 Championship at the Autodromo Santa Monica, at Misano, on 6 April, at an average speed of 90.14 mph (145.06 km/h). Unfortunately he couldn't repeat this performance in other rounds. Graeme McGregor eventually came sixth overall in the championship on a non-factory TT1. There was no factory involvement in the Endurance World Championship until the debut of the new water-cooled eight-valve 748 at the Bol d'Or in September, but that is the beginning of a new generation, and belongs in Chapter 13. However, at the Jerez Eight Hour race on 28 September, Juan Garriga and Marco Lucchinelli were teamed together on a four-valve 750TT1. They had pole position and initially led the race, eventually finishing second. Later, at the Barcelona 24 Hour race on 26 October 1986 (a non-championship event) Juan Garriga, Carlos Cardus, and the steadfast Benjamin Grau won using the 851 cc version of the TT1, proving the reliability of the larger engine. An 818 cc (92 x 61.5 mm) version of the engine was also tried during 1986, notably by Jimmy Adamo at the Battle of the Twins race at Daytona.

The final outing for the factory air-cooled racer was at the Pro Twins race at Laguna Seca in 1987. Marco Lucchinelli again rode, and his 851 cc bike featured revised inlet ports and ducting and metal shrouding around the rear cylinder to keep it cool. The

Virginio Ferrari rode this TT1 to victory in the 1985 Italian Formula 1 Championship. He now manages the Ducati Corse World Superbike racing team.

standard TT1 chassis was fitted with a new type of upside-down White Power fork with a single, centrally-located spring damper unit. At the rear, a lightweight GSG Roma shock absorber was used. Wheels were Marvic 17-inch front and rear.

Besides the factory bikes, which were undoubtedly the most spectacular, TT1 replicas were widely raced with some success throughout the world. In Spain, Antonio Cobas built a frame for the F1, and Kenny Roberts tested this bike at Misano in August

1985 along with the Cagiva C10V 500 cc Grand Prix bike. Juan Garriga had raced it at the Montjuich round of the World Formula 1 championship (the same race where Tony Rutter was injured), and had actually led at one stage before crashing. In Australia, future GP rider Kevin Magee rode local tuner Bob Brown's home-built 750 TT1 to some amazing results throughout 1984 and 1985 against 1,000 cc Hondas and Suzukis. Later the bike was enlarged to 850 cc and raced by Robert Holden and Aaron Slight with considerable success in the emerging Superbike class. In Battle of the Twins classes around the world, replicas of the TT1 took over where the bigger twins left off, but as a competitor to the Japanese head-on the TT1 was now outdated. The two-valve Pantah heads had reached the limit of their development, and a new cylinder-head design was needed.

Ducati 750F1

As expected, there were plans to produce a street version of the TT1 racing bike, and, typically, it took a

The final version of the TT1, with experimental upside-down White Power front fork, was tested by Raymond Roche at Misano in April 1987. Franco Farnè is making some final adjustments.

The same bike with mechanics Giuliano Pedretti and Primo Forasassi. The ducting to the rear cylinder can be clearly seen.

while in coming. While replica frame kits made by Harris were available in England for the Pantah engine, at Ducati the original Pantah soldiered on. The TT2 and TT1 had brought them track success, but there was still a question over the reliability of the Pantah crankcases when the engine was enlarged to 750 cc. 1983 was also the time of negotiations regarding the Cagiva takeover, so both production and development were limited. Also, because a new oil-cooled V-four 1,000 cc engine was being developed at the same time, resources were stretched, and this delayed the introduction of the 750F1. However, the commencement of Cagiva control saw the V-four project cancelled, and by mid-1984 a prototype 750F1 was displayed. This bike used a replica of the Verlicchi racing TT2 frame with a steel cantilever swing-arm, and provision for a centre-stand. A square headlight was fitted in the full fairing,

and it had 16-inch gold-painted Oscam wheels. Claimed power was 70 bhp at 9,000 rpm, with dry weight at 165 kg (364 lb). Other features were a hydraulic clutch and a two-into-one exhaust system. 36 or 40 mm Dell'Orto carburettors were specified, and the compression ratio was a high 10.4:1.

In mid-November 1984, photographs of mock production bikes appeared, now with an 18-inch rear wheel, and in February 1985 the 750F1 was premiered at the Sydney Motorcycle Exhibition. It still didn't have the fully-floating Brembo 280 mm front discs and 260 mm rear, but the engine was painted black and had a Conti two-into-one exhaust system, claimed to meet all noise regulations. The red frame, sourced from the TT2/TT1, had been widened to accommodate the camshaft belt covers and an adjustable steering damper fitted to complement the

16-inch front wheel. Even before the bike had gone into production there was controversy surrounding the fitting of a 16-inch front wheel.

When the first production models appeared during 1985 they were a confusing mixture of good and bad. The engine was only an over-bored 650 Pantah, still with the 37.5 and 33.5 mm valves of the 500. The oil-cooler lines were cheap rubber hoses crimped into place, yet the brake discs were full-floating iron Brembos. Basic air-assisted Marzocchi 38 mm suspension was used at the front and a Marzocchi adjustable shock absorber at the rear (which was still a cantilever rather than rising rate), yet an aluminium petrol tank was fitted. It was also the very last Ducati to feature the old Giugiaro graphics that had first appeared on the 860 in 1975. The rear seat and tail section was much larger and uglier than on the TT1 and TT2, designed to locate the

A 1985 F1 at rest at the Piazzale Michelangelo, Florence.

14Ah battery, and a dual seat at a later stage.

While still using the 36 mm PHF Dell'Orto carburettors of the Pantah, the 750F1 received new camshafts along with 9.3:1 88 mm pistons. Valve timing was now inlet opening 29° before top dead centre, closing 90° after bottom dead centre, and exhaust opening 70° before bottom dead centre, closing 48° after top dead centre, and power was only a claimed 62.5 bhp at 7,500 rpm. The primary drive ratio was altered, more in line to that of the TT2, to 36/71, or 1.97:1, and the 750F1 also received the fifth gear ratio of the TT2 at 0.97:1. A 300 watt alternator provided electrical power. Weight was up to 175 kg (386 lb), but it was still a much more compact motorcycle than the preceding Pantah. The wheelbase was only 1,400 mm (55 inches), and a far cry from the older bevel-gear bikes with their 60-inch wheelbase. Compared to the racer, steering rake was increased to 28°, with corresponding trail of 5.2 inches, making the F1 a relatively slow steerer in the traditional Ducati fashion. Performance wasn't particularly outstanding for its day, and didn't even match the 750SS of over ten years earlier. *Motorrad* tested the two bikes back to back in November 1985 and found the older bike accelerated faster and had a higher top speed. The 750F1 managed 206 km/h (128 mph) but was considerably punchier in the mid-range. I rode one of the first examples and, after the heavy feel of the last Mike Hailwood Replicas, was pleasantly surprised by the light weight and responsiveness of the F1. The F1 was a generation ahead when it came to steering and handling. Despite only a cantilever rear suspension system, the light weight and short wheelbase made the F1 a surprisingly quick road bike for its power output. Just like the magnificent TT1 and TT2 racers, it managed to match much more powerful bikes with its better balance and power characteristics. The only problem with the F1 was that, because it was derived from the TT2, it was a very small motorcycle and the riding position was consequently cramped for larger riders.

By late-1985 F1s were being displayed with the new Cagiva graphics and logo. Some of these were silver and red, but they were all interim models before the arrival of the significantly improved 750F1 for 1986. Following racing experience with the TT1, the original 500 type crankcase, which had always cracked around the drive side main bearing under the stress of racing, was finally strengthened, with extra webbing between it and the gearbox mainshaft bearing. Straight cut primary gears now took power to a hydraulically-operated dry clutch and a new, stronger gearbox was fitted with 30° wider gears. The crankshaft was strengthened around the big-end journal with new connecting rods. The oil-cooling was now full-flow, rather than just a cylinder head bypass, and, in keeping with the larger capacity, valve sizes were increased to the 41 and 35 mm of the TT2, necessitating a move to smaller 12 mm spark-plugs. Along with slightly revised camshafts (about 8° retarded), and an increase in compression to 10:1 using higher-domed pistons, power went up to a claimed 75 bhp at 9,000 rpm. The new camshaft timing was, inlet opening 39° before top dead centre, and closing 80° after bottom dead centre, and exhaust opening 80° before bottom dead centre, and closing 38°

after top dead centre. The same Dell'Orto PHF36 carburettors were used, with small foam air-filters.

The engine was certainly an improvement, and so was the front suspension. 40 mm Forcella-Italia forks, with provision for a wide range of adjustment in damping and preload, were vastly superior to the non-adjustable 38 mm Marzocchis. Also, the rear 260 mm disc was no longer the fully-floating type, and the 22-litre aluminium petrol tank became an 18-litre steel one. As has often been the case at Ducati, some things improve, but other details exhibit cost-cutting when models are revised. However, the instrument layout with the white-faced Veglias was a welcome relief from the Nippon Densos that had by now become dated, and still carries through to today on the Super Sport line. The styling of the rear seat was improved, but it still looked awkward from some angles, and the red Oscam wheels mirrored the racing TT1.

Cycle magazine summed up the 750F1 succinctly in February 1987 when it said 'the F1 allows a very competent street rider to understand how a race bike feels because the engine will help him rather than intimidate him'. For the F1 still didn't possess exceptional horsepower. When *Cycle* tested an F1 in June 1988, it only achieved a standing

The 1986 750F1 was a better motorcycle than the 1985 version. (Two Wheels)

The attractive layout of the 1986 750F1 instrument panel featured white-faced Veglias.

quarter-mile time of 12.70 seconds at 103.1 mph (166 km/h). Perhaps the most disappointing aspect of the new 750 engine was the vibration, which

after a long ride would leave you with numbed wrists. Somehow, the short-stroke 750 engine never managed to feel as smooth and relaxed as the earlier bevel-gear examples.

For 1987 and 1988 the 750F1 continued to be marketed in small numbers beside the new range of Cagiva-inspired Ducatis. From bike number 1505 the Japanese Kokusan ignition, that had first appeared on the limited edition 750 Montjuich, replaced the Bosch system. Also, the last versions had a locking fuel cap and a dual seat. However, by now the F1 was an anachronism within a Ducati range that was becoming increasingly Cagiva-influenced. To quote *Cycle* magazine again, the 750F1 was 'the last true fundamentalist Ducati'.

750 Montjuich, Laguna Seca and Santa Monica

To celebrate the win by Grau, de Juan, and Reyes in the 24 Hour race

at Montjuich Park in 1983, a limited edition race replica F1 in the finest Ducati tradition was announced at the end of 1985, and displayed at the Milan Show. As usual it had taken long enough to appear, but like the first 750SS of 1974 many thought it worth the wait. Though essentially a 750F1, the Montjuich was tuned considerably with hotter camshafts, Dell'Orto PHM40ND carburettors, and a less restrictive Verlicchi two-into-one *Riservato Competizione* exhaust system. Even though it still only had the cantilever rear end, the swing-arm was Verlicchi aluminium, and in a carry-over from the 750TT1 both front and rear wheels were 16-inch. The wheels were lightweight composite Marvic with magnesium hubs and spokes, and Akront aluminium rims. Rim sizes were much wider than the standard F1 at 3.50 x 16 and 4.25 x 16, and shod with Michelin 120/60V16 and 180/60V16 tyres. Other detail differences

The final 750F1 of 1988 had a dual seat.

included a 22-litre aluminium fuel tank like the first 750F1, four-piston Brembo 'Gold Line' racing calipers with fully-floating discs all round (280 mm at the front and 260 mm rear), a vented dry clutch, and different front guard. While the prototype featured a centre-stand, the production models saved a few kilos by only specifying a side-stand. The relationship between the Montjuich and F1 was similar to that which existed between the original 750SS and 750 Sport: a limited production bike that offered higher performance through engine modifications, better brakes, and less weight.

However, this is where the concept of the two bikes differs. The Montjuich was created and sold as a limited edition item, each of the 200 bikes having a numbered plaque on the petrol tank. It was only several years later that anyone realized how rare the original 750SS was, and by that stage many had been raced and ruined. Still, there were many detail differences to the Montjuich, and it was both lighter and significantly more powerful than the standard F1. Starting with the engine, the Montjuich received new camshafts with timing figures of inlet opening 67° before top dead centre, and closing 99° after bottom dead centre, and exhaust opening 93° before bottom dead centre and closing 70° after top dead centre. With 137° of valve overlap, these camshafts had more than the racing TT1, and inlet duration of 346° was also slightly more than the TT1. These were the fiercest camshafts ever fitted to a street Ducati, and as such the Montjuich was peakier than expected. Along with the larger carburettors and racing exhaust system, the camshafts lifted claimed power for the Montjuich to 95 bhp at 10,000 rpm. Unlike the earlier 750SS, the lower half of the engine was standard 750F1. There were no polished crank-shafts or con-rods, and the 10:1 pistons and barrels were identical to the F1. The Montjuich had an aluminium clutch drum and slightly different gearbox internals, to accommodate the outboard countershaft sprocket. Rather than the Bosch ignition that had been used since 1977, a Kokusan system was used for the first time.

To compensate for the 16-inch rear wheel, the final-drive gearing was altered to 15/43, or 2.87:1, and a narrower, 5/8 x 1/4 inch chain was used. The Montjuich also used a better-quality Marzocchi rear shock absorber, but tests still criticized it for being underdamped. Claimed dry weight was a mere 155 kg (342 lb), but *Motorrad* weighed their test bike in at 178 kg (392 lb) fully wet, still much less than any other two-cylinder street Ducati. *Moto Sprint*, in April 1986, managed 221 km/h (137.3 mph), with 75 bhp at 10,000 rpm. *Cycle World* also put

The 1986 750F1 Montjuich was a true race replica in the best Ducati tradition.

theirs through a standing quarter-mile in 11.87 seconds, at 113.52 mph (182.7 km/h).

By now the Cagiva take-over was well in effect, and the new management was anxious to promote both Cagiva and Ducati in the US. It was this that led to Lucchinelli racing in and winning the Battle of the Twins at the Californian track of Laguna Seca. Though hardly as prestigious a win as that at Montjuich, it was considered momentous enough to name the 1987 series of F1 race replicas after it. Each of these 200 bikes had a replica Marco Lucchinelli signature on its petrol tank.

There were numerous differences between the Montjuich and Laguna Seca. Historically, Ducati have often lowered the specification of successive models. This was true of the 750/900SSs that in 1976 acquired indicators, smaller carburettors, and Lafranconi silencers, and a similar situation occurred in 1987 with the Laguna Seca. Most noticeable was the replacement of the lightweight Marvic wheels and fully-floating discs, with 16-inch Oscam wheels and 280 and 270 mm discs straight off the 750 Paso. Some Laguna Secas came with a dual seat option, detracting from its race replica status, and the alloy petrol tank became a standard

The 750 Laguna Seca of 1987 shared its wheels and brakes with the Paso.

Each Laguna Seca came with this Marco Lucchinelli signature on the petrol tank.

steel F1 item. However, the engine specification was unchanged, and the Laguna Seca still offered significant performance gains over a standard 750F1, despite a noticeable weight increase. The exhaust system was either the Conti two-into-one of the 750F1, which hurt the power, or one with a less restrictive aluminium silencer. Claimed power was down slightly to 91 bhp at 10,000 rpm, and weight up to 165 kg (364 lb). The Laguna Seca came with a plastic mudguard over the rear wheel, attached to the aluminium swing-arm, and like the Montjuich it was painted red and silver.

Performance of the Laguna Seca was similar to that of the Montjuich. In October 1987, with the less restrictive exhaust, *La Moto* achieved a top speed of 221 km/h (137 mph), the same as the Montjuich. *Motorcyclist* in the US, testing a Laguna Seca with the Conti exhaust system, could only get a best standing quarter-mile time of 12.53 seconds at 105.7 mph (170 km/h). Their bike also weighed in at 418 lb (190 kg) wet, up considerably on the Montjuich.

Despite the factory's commitment to the Paso and the new 851, the limited edition 750F1 continued into 1988 with the Santa Monica. Named after the circuit at Misano where Marco Lucchinelli won the Formula 1 World Championship race in 1986, this bike was a hybrid of the

Montjuich and Laguna Seca. The composite Marvic wheels and fully-floating disc rotors returned, but with street-legal four-piston Brembo brake calipers, rather than the Gold Line racing versions (although the prototype was fitted with Gold Line brakes and a Verlicchi exhaust). The dual seat was standard, as was the Laguna Seca silencer with the aluminium can, along with the steel fuel tank. Colour was red and white. When *Moto Sprint* tested the Santa Monica in August 1988 it went 219.715 km/h (136.5 mph) and weighed 173 kg (381 lb) wet. It also made 73.63 bhp at 9,250 rpm.

As such, the entire 750F1 line, and in particular the three models of limited edition replicas, represented the end of an era for Ducati. It started with one of the most successful Ducati racing bikes ever, the 600 TT2, and ended with a series of race replicas totally in keeping with the spirit and essence of Ducati. They were the last bikes with unfiltered 40 mm Dell'Orto carburettors breathing directly into the atmosphere, and, along with the smaller 350/400F3, the last Ducatis with symmetrical cylinder heads, those with both exhaust ports facing forwards.

350/400F3

The anomalies of both the Italian and Japanese markets have led to a range of smaller-engined Ducatis over the

The final batch of 400F3s at the factory in January 1989. They had a six-speed gearbox.

years. By the mid-1980s Japan was the largest market for Ducati, and their market requirements dictated a 400. The Italian market had always required a 350, and there had been 350 parallel twins such as the 350GTL, 350GTV, and 350 Desmo Sport, along with the 350XL Pantah especially for this. It seemed logical to capitalize on the success of the 750F1 by creating virtually identical bikes with smaller motors, and this is a practice that Ducati still continues today. Both the 350 and 400F3s of 1986 onwards were essentially 750F1s, but they continued in production until 1989, whereas the 750F1 was discontinued in 1988. The Italian market 350 had the engine of the 350XL. With a bore and stroke of 66 x 51 mm, and valve sizes of 33.5 mm and 30.5 mm, the 350 engine produced 42 bhp at 9,700 rpm. Carburation was by two Dell'Orto PHF30s and even the valve timing was different for the smaller engine, with the inlet opening 40° before top dead centre, and closing 80° after bottom dead centre, and the exhaust opening 57° before bottom dead centre, and closing 43° after top dead centre. The 400F3 was a bored 350, with engine dimensions of 70.5 x 51 mm to give 398 cc. Power was up slightly to 45 bhp at 10,000 rpm.

Much more basic suspension than the F1 was fitted, with 35 mm Marzocchi forks, and smaller, 260 mm dual discs were fitted along with 05 Brembo calipers. The paint scheme for both the 350 and 400 was a very attractive red and white. Instruments on some 400s were the Mille MHR Nippon Denso type, while the 350 had the white-faced Veglias of the 750F1. Claimed weight was only 165 kg (364 lb). As tested by *Motociclismo* in November 1986, the 350F3 went 178.3 km/h (110.8 mph). The final version of the 400F3 had a six-speed gearbox and a dual seat, and was still being shipped to Japan in early 1989.

12.

The Cagiva Take-over

During the period of the early 1980s, when Ducati was under the VM Group of industries, only about 3,000 motorcycles a year were being built, and the plant was very unprofitable. By 1983 the situation was so bad that the future of Ducati motorcycle production looked very bleak, then in a surprise move the managers of the VM Group started negotiations with the relatively unknown Cagiva company from Varese. On 1 June a press statement was released in Milan announcing a joint venture.

Cagiva had been built in 1978 out of the ashes of AMF-Harley Davidson (formerly Aermacchi) by the two Castiglioni brothers, Claudio and Gianfranco. Their move from manufacturing combination locks for briefcases and a wide range of fasteners and electrical hardware to motorcycles was a brave one. However, within four years they were producing 40,000 motorcycles a year from their converted aircraft hangars on the foreshore of the Lago di Varese, north of Milan. These motorcycles were predominantly of small capacity (less than 350cc), so in order to expand their range into larger varieties it was easier to buy engines from outside than develop new ones. The initial agreement called for Ducati to supply engines for a range of Cagiva-badged motorcycles for seven years, with an option for automatic renewal. There were to be 6,000 engines for 1984, 10,000 in 1985, and 14,000 in the following years, with production of all Ducati motorcycles to cease by the end of 1984.

Production of the Cagiva range of Ducati-powered motorcycles was initially very slow, so Ducati persuaded their parent group, VM, to allow the continuation of motorcycle production for another year. Then, during 1985, Cagiva bought Ducati, and with it pledged to maintain the Ducati name with a completely new range of bikes. Later they also bought Husqvarna and Moto Morini, and today the Cagiva group is the largest manufacturer of motorcycles in Italy.

750 and 906 Paso

When Cagiva acquired Ducati in 1985, they also inherited a production line-up with an uncertain future. The Mille engine had reached the limit of its development, but there was still development life in the Pantah range of engines. The biggest problem facing Ducati at this time was that they were not profitable, and there was no new investment, a scenario similar to that which had afflicted the British motorcycle industry in the 1970s. Even before the Castiglionis bought Ducati, the bevel-gear engines had been considered too expensive to produce. Taglioni had indicated as much back in 1977, but the future seemed to be with smaller-capacity motorcycles at that stage, so the bevel-gear engine continued for a few more years. Cagiva immediately decided to concentrate on the Pantah, which by that time had only been developed to a maximum of 750cc. The initial contract had called for Ducati motors to be installed in Cagiva motorcycles, and several models appeared under this agreement, notably the 650

Alazzurra and the Elefant off-road bike. The 750 Pantah motor had made it to the F1, but the Castiglionis were determined to develop a completely new type of Ducati. The future of the Ducati marque lay in the radical Paso of 1986, not the traditional-style 750F1.

To the traditionalist, the announcement and display of the 750 Paso at the Milan Show of 1985 was a surprise – it was such a huge departure from the hard-edged, sporting F1 style. However, underneath all the bodywork was a vastly more modern motorcycle. It may not have been a race replica, but it promised to be the first Ducati that was a complete package. While the 750F1 was an excellent sporting motorcycle, as delivered from the factory it had poor rear suspension and inferior Michelin A48/M48 tyres, as was traditionally the case with Ducatis, even the race replicas, and the Paso was the first to break with this tradition.

The origins of the Paso only went back to 1984. When Cagiva entered into the agreement with Ducati, they also approached Bimota in Rimini to develop a new motorcycle around the Pantah engine. Massimo Tamburini (the 'ta' in 'Bimota') had broken with Giuseppe Morri (the 'mo' in the name) and set up on his own with Roberto Gallina, the former Italian racing champion and manager of the Suzuki HB Grand Prix team. He had been involved with the design of the TGA1 Suzuki Grand Prix with which both Marco Lucchinelli and Franco Uncini had won the 1981 and 1982 500 cc World Championships, and was approached by Cagiva to design a new chassis for the Mille (outlined in Chapter 9). Soon Tamburini was to become head of the Cagiva research and development department, and when he considered the Bimota Pantah, later the DB1, too impractical for mass-production, he began work on a completely new frame for the Pantah engine (Bimota later put the DB1 into limited production). Tamburini called his new design the Paso, in memory of his friend and Grand Prix racer Renzo Pasolini, tragically killed in an accident at Monza in 1973.

Departing from more recent Ducati practice, Massimo Tamburini's cradle for the 750 Pantah engine did not use the engine as a stressed member. It was closely modelled on the frame that Bimota had designed for Yamaha, which had eventually become the FJ1100. Built from square-section tubing, but with an aluminium swing-arm with eccentric chain adjustment, both the wheelbase and steering geometry were altered from the 750F1. The swing-arm was lengthened by 60 mm, and the steering head angle pulled in to 25°, to give a wheelbase of 1,450 mm (57 inches). Trail was much less than the F1, at 103 mm (4 inches) rather than 133 mm (5.24 inches). The lower cradle unbolted to ease engine removal, but more importantly the new frame allowed access to the rear cylinder head to aid servicing of the desmodromic valve gear. There was no attempt to make the engine and frame visually appealing as they were to be completely covered by bodywork, but unclothed the Paso was one of the messiest looking Ducatis.

With the latest Marzocchi 42 mm M1R forks, and Öhlins CA 2508 rear shock absorber operating through a 'Soft Damp' rising rate linkage, the Paso had much more sophisticated suspension than any previous street Ducati. The Marzocchi forks were unusual in that the right fork leg controlled the rebound damping only, while the left fork leg looked after the compression stroke. Adjustment for rebound damping was provided by an external four-position knob on the right leg, which had initially appeared on the TT1 and TT2, and also on the Cagiva 500 cc Grand Prix bike. The

rear Öhlins featured hydraulically adjustable spring preload. The wheel sizes were also a considerable break with tradition, with 3.75 x 16 and 5.00 x 16 inch Oscam wheels shod with the first new-generation low-profile Pirelli MP7 series radial tyres. The use of such wide tyres also required the engine to be offset to the left for the chain to clear the rear tyre.

There were also many changes to the engine. In a departure seen on the Cagiva Elefant a year earlier, the rear cylinder was rotated so that both inlet manifolds faced each other between the cylinders. The advantage of this was that both inlet tracts could now be of equal length, and straighter. They would also lend themselves to downdraught carburettors. Unfortunately, the choice of carburettors available for such a layout was limited, and Cagiva chose to adapt a Weber automotive type. This 44DCNF 107 twin-barrel carburettor, 44 mm wide at the throttle and 36 mm at the venturi, was problematic and the cause of many complaints and factory jetting revisions. Despite problems with an off idle and mid-range flat spot, backfiring when hot, and throttle hesitations, the factory persevered with the Weber until 1991, seemingly oblivious to these problems. Finally they got the

new engine right when they fitted the Mikuni carburettors for the 1991 season.

In other respects the engine was much the same as the 1986 750F1. It had the larger valves and slightly retarded valve timing (39/80/80/38), together with the stronger engine cases and gearbox, and a hydraulically operated dry clutch. All Pasos had the Kokusan ignition with the coils mounted on the left side of the frame, and there were two oil-coolers, one on each side of the fairing. Considering that the engine was now effectively silenced by the Silentium mufflers, the claimed power of 72.5 bhp at 7,900 rpm was very respectable. Where the Paso really did suffer in comparison with the F1 was in its weight. The claimed dry weight was 195 kg (430 lb), but *Cycle* weighed their test bike at 495 lb (224 kg) wet, a full 69 lb (31 kg) heavier than the F1. The top speed achieved by *Motociclismo* in December 1986 was only 204.2 km/h (127 mph). However, sheer performance was not what the Paso was about. This was a refined sports tourer aimed at appealing to a broader range of riders than traditional Ducatis. The press loved it. *Motorcyclist* in the US in February 1987 said that 'the Paso represents a truly streetable version of the exotic Italian sport bike'.

The 750 Paso, with its full coverage bodywork, was a significant departure from the 750F1.

There were many other changes incorporated in the Paso. A fuel pump kept the Weber supplied, and features like a fuel level gauge and much more modern switchgear put the Paso on a par with Japanese bikes. The styling, with totally enclosed bodywork and no clear fairing screen, was original, and eye-catching. However, while in many respects the Paso did bring Ducati up to date, as a sporting bike it still could not match a 750F1. I had the opportunity to test one of the first 750 Pasos in company with an F1, and the Paso was a disappointment. It understeered badly, and throttle response was vastly inferior to that provided by the 750F1's Dell'Orto PHM36s.

By 1987 the Öhlins rear shock absorber had been replaced by a much harsher Marzocchi unit, but in 1988 only small changes occurred. The triple clamps and handlebars were now painted black, and a fold-out handle was fitted to help in putting the bike on the centre-stand. In addition to red, there was now also the option of blue or white paintwork. The 750 Paso continued through until 1990, by which time it had the revised silencers from the new model 900SS, and the Weber had received numerous jetting modifications.

The importance of the Paso lay not in whether or not it was a superior motorcycle to the Ducatis of the past, but in the incorporation of new ideas within the traditional framework. For the first time since 1980, when the entire range had desmodromic valve gear, there was a genuine commitment to aid servicing. The new frame design not only aided access to the rear cylinder head for valve adjustment, but Massimo Bordi's assistant, Luigi Mengoli, also simplified the rocker layout by incorporating a spring clip on the opening rocker shaft so that the rocker could be moved sideways to allow shim removal. No longer did the opening rockers and pins need to be removed. Unfortunately the 750 Paso still did not appeal to the traditional Ducati buyer, and ultimately suffered a similar fate to that of the 600TL and 900 Darmah. It was sold off at heavily discounted prices in 1990, by which time it had been superseded. Still, it provided a strong basis for further development during 1988, and by 1989 had evolved into the 906 Paso.

Most of the changes between the 750 and the 906 occurred in the engine, which was now based on the new 851 'large crankcase' eight-valve engine detailed in the next chapter. With a six-speed gearbox rather than the 750's five-speed, the new bike was called the 906, the '6' indicating the six speeds. Actual capacity of the new engine was 904cc, for while the bore of 92 mm was shared with the 851, an extra 4 mm of stroke, to 68 mm, gave additional displacement. With an extra 6.5 mm of stroke over the 750, con-rod length also grew, from 124 mm to 130 mm. The con-rod length to stroke ratio was still 1.9:1, despite the necessity to keep the cylinder and head as short as possible. Big-end bearing size increased to 42 mm from the 40 mm on the 750. In other respects, too, the 906 was a marriage of the 750 and 851: the water cooling for the cylinders and heads of the 851 was coupled with the two-valve desmodromic heads of the 750 and similar Weber 44DCNF 116 twin-choke downdraught carburettor with slightly revised jetting (160 rather than 150 main jet). The dual oil-coolers of the 750 went, to be replaced by a single radiator. Valve sizes were up to 43 mm inlet and 38 mm exhaust, and in the search for more performance there were new camshafts yet again. These featured steeper ramps and higher lift, but less overlap. Valve timing was now inlet opening 20° before top dead centre and closing 60° after bottom dead centre, and exhaust opening 58° before bottom dead centre and closing 20° after top dead centre. Valve lift was increased considerably from the 750, to 11.1 mm for the inlet (9.35 mm on the 750) and 10.56 mm for the exhaust (8.50 mm on the 750). Despite a slight reduction in the compression ratio to 9.2:1, the claimed power went up to 88 bhp at 8,000 rpm. The combustion chamber also came in for some redesign at this stage, to become the 'tri-spherical' type.

The 750's Kokusan ignition with progressive advance was replaced by a Marelli Digiplex inductive discharge type, powered by a new 350-watt alternator, up from the 750's 300-watt type. The clutch and all the gearbox and primary drive ratios were shared with the 851, as were the water pump,

The 906 Paso appeared in 1988, with different colours to the 750 but offering no real improvement.

thermostat and radiator. Despite the very similar external appearance of the 750 and 906 Paso, there were a few changes to the frame and suspension. To prevent the front wheel hitting the longer front cylinder, a 20 mm-longer Marzocchi M1R 42 mm fork was fitted, with 15 mm less travel, and revised fork offset brought the trail back to 96 mm (3.8 inches). The rear suspension was identical to the later 750 Paso, with a Marzocchi shock absorber connected to the 'Soft Damp' rising rate system. The 16-inch Oscam wheels were the same as the 750, as were the Brembo brakes. Unfortunately, despite the power increase the downside to all this extra engine sophistication was in the claimed increased weight of 10 kg, to 205 kg (452 lb).

In many ways the 906 represented an even greater departure from the traditional Ducati philosophy of reducing power and weight to achieve a balanced motorcycle. This was demonstrated clearly in contemporary road tests of the 906, for while the new, larger engine produced more mid-range torque, overall performance was not improved on the 750 Paso. In November 1989 *Cycle* magazine managed 60.64 bhp at 7,000 rpm (only 6 bhp up on the 750), and the bike weighed in at a massive 235 kg (518 lb) wet. Drag strip performance was also slightly slower than the 750, at 12.79 seconds at 102 mph (164 km/h) for the standing quarter mile. On the other side of the Atlantic, performance of the 906 also failed to meet expectations. *Motorrad*, in January 1989, could only coax a maximum speed of 191 km/h (119 mph) from their test bike. However, testers welcomed the Cagiva influence on improved fit and finish, and though the Weber now carburetted better than it had two years earlier, it was still not perfect. The 906 lasted until 1990, by which time the new model 900SS had an oil-cooled version of the same motor, and the clutch actuation assembly had moved to the left-hand side of the engine. It was not one of the most memorable Ducatis, having less than a two-year production run, but it was to become one of their better sport-touring models when developed further for

the 1991 season as the fuel-injected 907 IE.

Indiana

As soon as Cagiva bought Ducati in 1985 they were looking for ways to use the production capabilities of the Bologna factory more effectively. By broadening the appeal of the range of Ducatis, especially for the US market, they hoped to expand production of the desmodromic Pantah engine. There had already been the Elefant enduro bike and the Cagiva Alazzurra

of 1984, and in 1985 a prototype 900 bevel-gear-powered cruiser-style bike was built. This fortunately never made it out of Varese, but from it emerged the Indiana in 1986.

While based on the Alazzurra, the Indiana followed the Paso and Elefant lead in that it had the reversed rear cylinder head. There were two versions, a 350 for the Italian market and a 650 for elsewhere. A departure from other models was in the carburation. While the 350 Indiana had 30 mm Dell'Ortos, those of the 650 came

The brochure of the 1986 Indiana indicated that it was intended for the US market.

fitted with 36 mm Bing constant vacuum carburettors. They had more conservative valve timing than the Elefant and Alazzurra, but still a high 10:1 compression ratio. Because of the vertical cylinder's rear-facing exhaust, the exhaust pipe snaked around the right side of the engine to maintain the symmetrical cruiser look. Claimed power for the 350 was 38 bhp at 9,250 rpm, and for the 650 53 bhp at 7,000 rpm, so for this type of motorcycle they were not sluggish performers. To finish the styling of the engine the cam-belt covers, dry hydraulic clutch cover (650), and left-side engine cover were chromed. The 350 had a cable-operated wet clutch.

The frame followed that of the Elefant rather than the Alazzurra. Built from square-section steel tubing, it was also a full cradle with a removable bolt on the right front down-tube to allow easy access to the camshaft belt covers. While the cast aluminium box-section swing-arm still pivoted in the rear of the engine crankcase, the engine itself was rigidly mounted at four points. However, because it was designed for a ladder-type frame, alloy arms from the engine to the frame bolted to the front engine mounts. A hollow pressed-steel backbone formed the basis of the structure, and also funnelled air into the airbox and filter beneath the seat. Generous 40 mm Marzocchi leading axle forks (a reminder of the early 750GT) were fitted. If it had not been for the cruiser-style rake of 33°, and the same wheelbase as the old 750GT (1,530 mm or 60.2 inches), the Indiana would probably have been quite a snappy handler. Twin Marzocchi shocks graced the rear end and braking was by a single 260 mm front disc and a larger, 280 mm, rear disc. The front brake calliper was one of the first four-piston Brembo types.

The Indiana did not receive particularly good press reports. *Cycle* wrote that the 'suspension compliance and handling are areas where the Italians are clearly one, perhaps two generations behind the latest Japanese-style cruisers'. The model was not successful, and in many export markets not even sold at all. Like the 600TL, the Indiana grew into a police bike, and also into a 750 cc version with 55 bhp and 32 mm Bing carburettors. By 1988 it was no longer offered as a 650, but the 350 continued for the Italian market. Even though sales were poor, both the 750 and 350 continued until 1990. Of all the less successful Ducati models, the Indiana was possibly the one that most completely missed the target. In retrospect it seems ludicrous that Taglioni's magnificent engine, one that had won four World TT2 Championships, should end up in this style of bike. When its target market is considered, it is not surprising that buyers did not take to a cruiser with desmodromic valve gear.

While the Indiana was directed at the American market, it is worth noting too that the Cagiva Elefant enduro bike, in 900 cc Mikuni carburetted form, was marketed as a Ducati in the US from 1993. Called the Ducati E-900, this was just a re-badged Elefant in the hope that sales would benefit from the association with the Ducati name, rather than that of the lesser-known Cagiva. The racing versions had also had success in the Paris–Dakar race of 1994. Using the air-cooled engine from the 900SS, de-tuned to produce 68 bhp, in the Elefant full-cradle square-section frame, this was a large trail bike. Dry weight was 185 kg (408 lb), but the wet weight was 224 kg (494 lb) as tested by *Motorcyclist* in September 1993. The bike was fitted with 45 mm Showa inverted forks, and rear suspension was by a Boge shock absorber operating through the Cagiva 'Soft Damp' linkage. Braking was by two 282 mm front discs with single-action twin piston Brembo callipers, with a 240 mm disc at the rear. Not really a dirt bike because of its size, and not really a street bike, the Ducati E-900 was the two-wheeled Range Rover.

750 Sport/900 Super Sport (Weber models)

While the Paso, and to a lesser extent the Indiana, Alazzurra and Elefant, signified the path that Cagiva intended for Ducati, the 750F1 continued in production alongside them during 1986 and 1987. The 750F1, despite being an older design, continued to sell well, but was still an expensive motorcycle to produce, with its Forcella Italia forks and fully floating Brembo brakes. It was therefore decided to replace it with a similarly styled, Paso-derived model.

The Castiglionis were well aware of the historical significance of certain models of Ducati and also conscious of the importance of this to the Ducati enthusiast. With the release of the 750 Sport a deliberate attempt was made to appeal to those enthusiasts who could remember the superb 750 Sport of 1972–74. By combining ingredients from both the Paso and 750F1, Ducati hoped to recreate a classic, and lure back their traditional customers.

This *nuovo* 750 Sport was basically the engine of the Paso in the chassis of a modified 750F1. With the Paso there had been a new commitment to engines with reversed rear cylinder heads enabling the Weber 44DCNF 113 carburettor to be used. Consequently the F1 trellis frame, which was a descendent of the quadruple World Championship-winning Verlicchi F2 type, needed some modification so that the large air filter could be fitted. The steel swing-arm of the F1 and F2 made way for an aluminium item (still a cantilever), similar in type to that on the limited edition Montjuich and Laguna Seca 750 F1s, but the 16-inch Oscam wheels and Brembo brakes were straight off the Paso. The aluminium swing-arm would be a constant problem, suffering from cracks and breakages, and warranty replacement in some countries.

The engine, including the intake and exhaust system, was identical to the 750 Paso but for the use of one oil-cooler rather than two. While the wheels and brakes were also the same, much more basic suspension was used to keep costs down. Non-adjustable 40 mm Marzocchi M1BB forks, and a Marzocchi PBS1R rear shock, were fitted. Like the F1, 28° of rake was used. Combined with 4.5 inches (114 mm) of trail, the steering of the 750 Sport was slow, more like a traditional Ducati. The wheelbase, at 1,450 mm (57 inches), was up slightly on the

A 1989 750 Sport at speed. (Two Wheels)

short 750F1, and the weight was a claimed 180 kg (397 lb).

As far as performance went, the 750 Sport was similar to the F1. *Motor Cycle News*, in September 1988, achieved a creditable best top speed of 132.6 mph (213.4 km/h), and in December 1989 *Cycle World* put their test bike through a standing quarter mile at 12.44 seconds at 107.27 mph (172.6 km/h). Most test reports were guarded in their praise for the bike. In many respects it was a step backwards from the Paso, which handled better, and it did not possess the symmetry and breeding of the 750F1. There were still carburettor problems with the Weber, and, being so obviously a cost-conscious entry-level Ducati, it lacked identity.

Released in mid-1988, these new Sports were initially painted bright red and blue. It was not the most attractive styling, and only a few months later, at the IFMA Cologne Show, the 1989 model was displayed in red and silver. The motor was also now air- and oil-cooled, with jackets around the bore liners circulating oil and supplementing normal airflow around the finned cylinders. An alternative colour scheme of silver and black was also offered at this time, but there were far fewer made in these colours. The 750 Sport failed to recreate the legend of

its earlier namesake. With its 16-inch wheels the proportions were wrong, and it lacked the character of the older bike. By 1990 it had finished, but was already being developed into a superior design.

With the introduction of the water-cooled 906 Paso during 1989, it seemed logical to put this larger engine in the 750 Sport chassis, and in the process hopefully resurrect another classic Ducati, the 900SS. However, wanting to maintain the light and functional concept that set the 750 Sport apart from the Paso, the 904 cc engine that was installed in this traditional Ducati-style space frame eschewed the water cooling of the 906 Paso. Following an example set by the Paris–Dakar Cagiva Elefants of 1988 and 1989, and incorporated in the 750 Sport, the new engine used oil-cooled cylinders and heads. As with the 906, the crankcases and six-speed gearbox were shared with the 851, but the 900SS had the longer-stroked 68 mm crankshaft of the 906. It also used the same two-valve cylinder head with the 'tri-spherical' combustion chamber, the 43 mm and 38 mm valves, and 9.2:1 compression. The camshafts were similar to those of the 906, the valve overlap of only 40° being very moderate by Ducati standards. The valve lift was more like

that of the older 'Imola' camshafts, 11.76 mm for the inlet valve, and 10.56 mm for the exhaust. New camshaft belt covers appeared on these larger engines, allowing for belt tension adjustment without removing the entire cover.

Carburation was still by the Weber 44DCNF carburettor, and ignition by the Marelli Digiplex of the 906, but power was down slightly from the 906 to 83 bhp at 8,400 rpm. This would not be a handicap because the 900SS was considerably lighter than the 906 (180 kg versus 205 kg). The frame was that of the 750 Sport, but for some extra bracing around the steering head, and slightly less steering head angle at 27°, giving 122 mm (4.8 inches) of trail. The wheelbase was the same 1,450 mm (57 inches). However, the wheels, brakes and suspension were considerably upgraded from the smaller model. Instead of the 16-inch Oscams from the Paso, the white-painted 17-inch wheels came off the 1989 model 851, and their rim widths were a thoroughly modern 3.50 x 17, and 5.50 x 17. New 40 mm Marzocchi forks were fitted with the normal Marzocchi shock absorber operated by the aluminium swing-arm, still with no linkage. The brakes, too, were now from the 851, with four-piston 32 mm Brembo brake callipers, but operating slightly smaller 300 mm steel discs. At the rear was a 245 mm disc and Brembo twin-piston calliper. While the styling drew very much on the 750 Sport, the exhaust system mirrored that of the 851.

In grafting the larger wheels on to the 750 Sport, Ducati had created a much taller motorcycle, and with weight distribution heavily biased towards the rear, handling was less than perfect. They seemed to have made the same mistake as when they built the second generation of Mike Hailwood Replicas in 1983. By raising the centre of gravity and putting the rider too high, they took away the agility of the earlier model. The steering was still very slow and there was too much trail, so the bike was unwilling to turn quickly. Also, despite four years of development, the Weber carburettor was still not right. In October 1989 *Performance Bikes*

Two generations of 900SS: a 1989 model in the foreground with a 1978 model behind.

complained of the 'imperfect carburation . . . when you really whack the throttle open at 4,000 rpm'. However, the bike performed considerably more strongly than previous two-valve twins. The Italian magazine *Moto Sprint* in November 1989 ran their test bike, weighing in at a modest wet weight of 192.9 kg (425 lb), to 219.369 km/h (136 mph).

Comparisons were inevitably drawn between the old and new 900SS. On paper the new bike was lighter, shorter, had vastly superior brakes and tyres, and, but for the Weber carburettor, was easier to live with. Like the 750 Sport, there were still problems with cracking of the aluminium swing-arm. Performance was up on the older model, but not dramatically so. The styling lacked the raw good looks of the earlier bike, and sales were not as good as expected. This would all be changed for the 1991 season when the 900SS came in for a dramatic

revision, and in the process Ducati built a real successor to its earlier namesake.

907IE

At the Cologne Motorcycle Show in September 1990, not only was the revised 900SS displayed, but the Paso was also updated and considerably improved. This final version of the Paso was called the 907IE. The Paso name went, and so did many of the peculiarities that had afflicted it. After years of complaints, the Weber carburettor was finally laid to rest, and replaced on the 907 with the Weber Marelli electronic fuel injection system from the 851, hence the initials 'IE', *iniezione elettronica*. The fitting of 17-inch wheels also eliminated the idiosyncratic handling of the Pasos. For 1991 the entire range of 851 and 900 engines featured stronger crankcases. After a series of crankcase cracking problems experienced by the factory while racing, and

winning, the World Superbike Championship during 1990, the new crankcases had more extensive webbing and ribbing around the cylinder support base.

While the engine was essentially the water-cooled 904 cc two-valve unit of the 906, power was up to a claimed 90 bhp at 8,500 rpm. Sharing the same throttle sensors and computer with the 851, the 907 used smaller 42 mm throttle bodies rather than the 851's 50 mm examples. The camshafts of the 1989 900SS, together with the injection system and the higher-volume black-chromed cylindrical mufflers, translated into vastly improved engine performance over the 906. On *Cycle* magazine's dyno in February 1991 the 907 made 70.0 bhp at 8,500 rpm, nearly 10 more than the 906. On the road this produced a standing quarter mile time of 11.74 seconds at 112.24 mph (180.6 km/h). Top speed was up too, with *Cycle World*, in their test of

The 907IE addressed many of the criticisms of the earlier Paso.

June 1991, managing a measured top speed of 136 mph (219 km/h).

The chassis also came in for revision. Tamburini's box-section, full-cradle frame was retained, along with the Marzocchi Duo-Shock and 41.7 mm M1R fork. As with the 900SS of the previous year, the same 17-inch wheels were fitted. The new front wheel was about 40 mm taller than that of the original Paso, and this necessitated reducing the fork travel slightly to 125 mm (4.9 inches), and lengthening the fork legs by 10 mm. Still with a steep 25° fork rake, trail went up to 107 mm (4.2 inches), and with a new 851-style swing-arm, wheelbase grew to 1,490 mm (58.7 inches). Claimed dry weight was 215 kg (474 lb), but the bike actually weighed around 230 kg (507 lb) wet, still a few pounds less than its predecessor. The brakes were also an upgrade from the 906, with the same 300 mm steel discs and four-piston Brembo P4.32d callipers

that had been fitted to the 1989 900SS.

The fairing was slightly revised from the earlier Pasos, with a NACA duct incorporated on the solid windscreen in an effort to reduce turbulence at the rider's helmet. Ducati also wanted the 907 to appeal to a wider range of riders by having the valve adjustment intervals extended to 6,000 miles (10,000 km). This was an attempt to compete head-on with Honda's VFR750, a sport touring motorcycle with a similar concept. For the first time Ducati had a machine that could actually meet the Japanese, not only in performance terms but also in practicality. Only in terms of price did the 907IE suffer in comparison with the Honda, but then it did offer electronic fuel injection. *Cycle* magazine successfully summed up the 907 by saying that 'the 907 has an engine that responds crisply straight from the box, and has handling on par with some of the best

The 907 cockpit, with full instrumentation and a solid windscreen.

sport bikes – yet it's still comfortable and civil, and hasn't lost any Latin character.'

Surprisingly, the 907IE failed to sell as well as expected. Offered again in 1992, with the option of metallic black paint, it finished that year, although unsold stock continued to be sold in the US in 1993. The front brake disc size went up to 320 mm along with the new type of gold Brembo P4.30-34 callipers. The 907 had finally become the bike that the Paso should have been originally. Reliability and finish were much improved, it was a superb sports touring motorcycle, and once again Ducati buyers had demonstrated their preference for sporting motorcycles. But those looking for a 907 replacement had to wait until the release of the Sport Touring ST2 in 1997.

350/400/600/750/900 Super Sport

Just as the 750F1 had existed in both 350 and 400 versions for the Italian and Japanese markets, the superseded 750 Sport was transformed into a unique Japanese market 400 Super Sport Junior for the 1990 season. First displayed at the Tokyo Show in late 1989, this bike was essentially a 900 Super Sport with the smaller 400 cc engine of the 400F3, but with the rear cylinder head reversed, as was the pattern now throughout the range. However, there were a number of interesting features that were peculiar to this particular model. In many ways it seemed to be a way to use up superseded spare parts, and in others to try out new ones. Thus it had the 16-inch composite Marvics that had been fitted to the 750 Montjuich, Santa Monica and 1988 851 Strada, together with the same 280 mm fully floating Brembo front discs, and 260 mm rear disc. The bodywork, frame (with the 27° steering head angle) and aluminium swing-arm were 900 Super Sport, but this bike did not have the troublesome Weber carburettor, which was replaced by a pair of Mikuni CVK V36 constant-velocity type, and these worked so well that Mikunis found their way into the entire range of Super Sports within a year.

Like the final 400F3, the Super Sport Junior had a six-speed gearbox and cable-operated wet clutch. The exhaust system, with cylindrical mufflers, was from the 1989 900SS. Weight was less, at 174 kg (384 lb), and the bikes were painted red over a white frame. Claimed power was 50 bhp at 11,000 rpm for the 398 cc engine. This unusual bike continued until 1991, by which time a new 400SS Junior had appeared, based on the new model Super Sport. The older models were still being advertised in Japan as late as August 1991, alongside the new one.

In 1989 Massimo Bordi took the deliberate step of creating two distinct but complementary Ducati production lines. On one side there was the new-technology 851 series backed up with a successful racing programme in World Superbike, and on the other was the development and refinement of the F2 Pantah racing bike that had first appeared in 1981. As there was no longer any use for a racing version of the two-valve Pantah, the air-cooled line was to remain a street bike with all the racing duties going to the water-cooled eight-valve series, which was marketed to appeal to the traditional Ducati owner who wanted a less complex motorcycle than the water-cooled and electronically fuel-injected eight-valve 851.

The 1989 900SS had shown promise but was still a flawed motorcycle. The revision that occurred during 1990 was not major, but was enough to create one of Ducati's modern classics. The desmodromic 904 cc air- and oil-cooled engine remained essentially the same but for the stronger crankcases that were standardised throughout the range

that year. The biggest change was in the use of Mikuni 38 mm B67 (B73 for the US) constant-velocity carburettors, matched to equal-length inlet manifolds, a first for carburetted Ducatis. While not vastly improving the power output, throttle response almost matched that of the fuel-injected 907IE. The new 900SS also saw the return of the Kokusan ignition rather than the Marelli Digiplex.

While the frame was still similar, in order to quicken the steering the rake was reduced from 27° to 25°, with much less trail at 103 mm (4.1 inches). A new aluminium swing-arm reduced the wheelbase to 1,410 mm (55.5 inches) and was attached to a slightly longer Showa GD 022-007-OX shock absorber that raised the rear end and provided 65 mm (2.56 inches) of travel, still without any linkage. The Marzocchi M1R front forks went, and were replaced by a set of multi-adjustable 41 mm Showa GD 011 upside-down forks. The 17-inch Brembo wheels were same as the previous year, but larger 320 mm front disc brakes were now fitted, together with the 245 mm rear disc. In a further concession towards ease of

In 1992 all the new bikes were still tested at the small track at the Borgo Panigale factory. Here a 900SS is being tested prior to shipment.

maintenance, the newly styled steel fuel tank flipped up to allow access to the battery and air-cleaner. The oil-cooler was no longer mounted in the fairing, but on a bracket cast into the front cylinder head exhaust valve rocker cover; this was a very vulnerable position, right behind the front wheel. While the new aluminium swing-arm did not resolve all the previous cracking problems, the chain adjustment bolt also proved to be a weak point on the new model and was modified the following year.

The riding position was also completely revised, with higher clip-on handlebars and lower footpegs. A newly styled petrol tank, fairing and seat completed the redesign, which was first exhibited at the Cologne Show in September 1990. Two versions were offered, one with a half fairing clearly showing the engine and exposed oil-cooler, and one with full fairing. While the 900SS still had basically a traditional air-cooled engine, this engine was not the aesthetic delight that the earlier engines had been. However, it was a Ducati that carried on the tradition of the earlier 900SS by generating impressive performance through low weight and high torque. It lacked the high horsepower and technological complexity of even the 851, let alone Japanese four-cylinder motorcycles, but on the road it almost matched them and was easier to ride.

From 1991, power was now stated as at the rear wheel, rather than the crankshaft, so the claimed power for the 900SS was 73 bhp at 7,000 rpm. The claimed weight for the half-faired version was 180 kg (397 lb), but the on-the-road weight was about 200 kg (440 lb). The fully faired version weighed slightly more, at 183 kg (403 lb). Performance was similar to the 1989 900SS. In January 1991 *Motociclismo* put their test bike through the speed trap at 219.0 km/h (136 mph), and *Cycle*, in September 1991, managed a standing quarter mile time of 11.64 seconds at 114.72 mph (184.6 km/h), faster than a 907IE and not too far short of the 851. *Cycle* summed up the 900SS with the comment, '. . . this is the superlative sport bike that the Ducati faithful knew was at the heart of the

The 900SS has continued essentially unchanged until 1997. This 1995 model has an underslung rear brake calliper and upgraded front forks.

original Pantah, the TT2, and the F1'. So good was the 1991 900SS that it continued as the mainstay of the Ducati range, virtually unchanged, until the end of 1997.

For 1992 only minor graphics changes, a passenger rear seat cowling, black-painted wheels, revised footrests brackets, and gold Brembo P4.30-34 front brake callipers (though these were fitted to 1991 bikes from no 1601) differentiated the two models. For the US, a black option with white wheels was available. There were even fewer changes for 1993. The frame was now bronze, and there was a new set of graphics, with a gold rather than black-bordered Ducati logo, and 'Desmodue' being termed for the Super Sport line. In 1994 the wheels also became bronze, the fork was an uprated Showa, also fitted to the Superlight, and the clutch and brake reservoirs were remotely mounted. A larger-diameter front axle stiffened up the front end, and the foot controls and supports were now black. These changes lifted the claimed dry weight to 186 kg (410 lb). The 1995 model had an oil temperature gauge added to the instrument panel, the rear brake calliper was underslung, and there was a new windshield. These minimal differences from year to year show that the basic motorcycle was

right when it was released in 1991. During 1995 7,195 Super Sports were manufactured, down slightly on the 7,597 of 1994, and considerably less than the peak year of 1992, when 8,545 Super Sports were built.

In November 1990 at the Bologna Show, two months after the new 900SS was displayed at Cologne, a smaller 750SS was shown, to be released during 1991. Using the five-speed 750 engine of the 750 Sport, it also featured a hydraulically operated dry clutch with the actuating system of the earlier 750, rather than the 900 type that operated from the left-side crankcase. While still using the Mikuni carburettor, they were the slightly different 38-B70 type. The 750SS used what Massimo Bordi termed the 'small crankcase', or the Pantah crankcase. This was used for all engines of 750 cc and less, and thus could not accommodate the six-speed gearbox of the newer 'big crankcase' family unless it was for the 350 cc or 400 cc versions that used narrower gears. The 750SS did not have the external oil-cooler of the 900, and had completely different valve timing. These new desmodromic camshafts would be standardised throughout the entire small crankcase family, including the 350, 400 and 600 Super Sport, as well as the later 600 Monster. The inlet valve opened at 31° before top dead centre, and closed 88° after bottom dead centre, while the exhaust valve opened at 72° before bottom dead centre and closed at 46° after top dead centre. Valve overlap, at 77°, was more like the Ducatis of the past, and the valve lift for the 41 mm and 35 mm valves much less than the 900, at 9.35 mm and 8.50 mm. Claimed power was 60 bhp at 8,500 rpm (at the rear wheel).

The 1991 750SS was only fitted with a single front 320 mm disc brake, and was the first Ducati to use the new gold Brembo P4 30/34 calliper. Following the practice of the racing Brembos, the new calliper used four pistons, but with the leading piston being of a smaller (30 mm) diameter than the trailing one (34 mm). The 750SS also used a smaller Brembo rear wheel, at 4.50 x 17. The front forks were still 41 mm upside-down Showas, but the non-adjustable GD 031 type. Weight was down to 173 kg

(381 lb) and, like the 900, the 750 was offered with a choice of full or half fairings. With the full fairing, weight went up to 176 kg (388 lb), while the on-the-road weight (half-faired) was still a very light 417 lb (189 kg) as tested by *Motorcyclist* in April 1992, making the 750SS easily the lightest 750 cc bike on the market. A month earlier, in March 1992, *Cycle World* had put their test 750SS through the standing quarter mile at 12.10 seconds and 108.17 mph (174 km/h), noticeably faster than both the 750 Sport and earlier 750F1 that shared a similar engine. In the US the half-faired 750SS was sold as an entry level Ducati for a bargain $7,350 in 1992, but was less attractively priced in other markets. Top speed was, however, down on the 900SS, with *Moto Sprint* managing 208 km/h (129 mph).

The next year saw the 750SS receive the oil-cooler of the 900SS, together with the black-painted

wheels; as with the 900SS, there was also the option of metallic black and white wheels. The engine was unchanged but for the clutch, which now became a hydraulically operated wet type, a modification that would find its way to all the small crankcase models. 1993 saw that year's revised colours and graphics of the 900SS, and for 1994 the 750SS received double 320 mm front discs, a steel swing-arm instead of the 900SS's aluminium type, along with the bronze wheels and larger-diameter front axle. The 750SS continued largely unchanged for 1995, but for the replacement of the Showa GD 031 forks by a new type of upside-down Marzocchi. There was no 750SS for the US market after 1994, and a hybrid model was marketed; called the 900CR, it was essentially a 900SS engine mounted in the more basic running gear of the 750SS.

Alongside the 750SS in 1991 there was a new model 400 Super Sport

The 750SS for 1994 had twin front disc brakes and a steel swing-arm.

Junior, replacing the unusual 1990 Japanese market version. There was also a 350 Sport for the Italian market. These bikes used identical running gear to the 750, and also came with the option of half or full fairing. The 66 x 51 mm 350 had 10.7:1 compression and produced 36 bhp at 10,500 rpm, while the 70.5 x 51 mm 400 with 10:1 compression made 46 bhp, also at 10,500 rpm. Both engines still used the large 38 mm Mikuni carburettors of the larger bikes, but they produced flat spots under full throttle, not unlike the Weber-carburetted models. The exhaust system was a two-into-one, exiting on the right side, and, unlike the previous 400SS, the wet clutch was now hydraulically operated. The colour scheme of the SS Junior

seemed to be a year behind the larger bikes, with the black-painted wheels coming in 1993, together with the bronze frame and steel swing-arm.

For 1994 the 350 was discontinued and replaced by a 27 bhp version of the 400 for the German market. The various changes to the 750SS that year also appeared on the Junior, and the almost identical 600SS was added to the range, in 33 and 53 bhp versions. While building the SS Junior was undoubtedly a useful method for the factory to increase sales, the physical proportions of the bike were that of the 750SS, so it really ended up being a considerably underpowered motorcycle. MO magazine in Germany, testing a 1993 400 cc model in March of that year, still managed a respectable top speed

of 175 km/h (108.7 mph), but the bike weighed in at 190 kg (419 lb). Coupled with the general lack of mid-range power that the small engine provided, testers were not over-enthusiastic about the Junior. Also, by this time the Japanese market was becoming less important for Ducati, being overtaken by Germany, and the sales of the 400 slowed. For 1995 the 400SS Junior was no longer offered, but reappeared in 1996 and 1997 for the Italian market.

The last 600 Ducati had been the 600SL of 1984, and the 600SS released for the 1994 season resur-rected the same 80 x 58 mm, 583cc, five-speed engine. With the valve timing and Mikuni carburettors of the 350/400/750SS, the new 600 made 53 bhp at 8,250 rpm (at the rear wheel). While it seemed that the 600SS was merely an update of a ten-year-old design, it was actually a significant improvement, reflecting ten years of subsequent development of the Pantah engine. Also offered as a 33 bhp for some markets, in 53 bhp form it was a superior model to the asth-matic 350 and 400SSs from which it was derived. This was shown in the performance. MO magazine, in December 1994, managed 197 km/h (122.4 mph) from their 182 kg (401 lb) wet test bike. The 600SS contin-ued virtually unchanged in 1995, but for the use of new 41 mm upside-down Marzocchi forks, the right leg no longer having the provision to mount an additional brake calliper.

900 Superlight

Following the success of the numbered series of 851 (888) Sport Production bikes in 1990 and 1991, a

The 600SS of 1994 resurrected the 600SL of ten years earlier.

The 1992 900 Superlight came with a numbered plaque.

numbered series of 900 Super Sports was planned for 1992. To be called the 900SL, or 900 Superlight, originally 500 bikes were to be made, but this eventually became 1,317, with 300 bright yellow ones going to the USA. However, unlike the 888SPs, the Superlight had the standard 73 bhp 900SS engine, frame and suspension. The lightweight parts on the bike took the form of carbon-fibre mudguards, vented clutch cover, and 17-inch Marvic composite wheels of the type fitted to the 750 Montjuich, Santa Monica, 851 Strada of 1988, and Japanese market 400SS of 1989. Other main differences were a single seat (with minimal padding), high-rise exhausts, and fully floating 320 mm Brembo front discs. The Superlight was only offered with a full fairing, and with a claimed weight of 176 kg (388 lb) it was indeed a light bike, being significantly lighter than any comparable bike in its class.

Performance was similar to the regular 900SS. However, *Motorrad*, testing Superlight No 537 in June 1992, only managed a top speed of 204 km/h (126.7 mph). *Cycle World*, in August 1992, put their test bike No 253 through a standing quarter mile at 11.74 seconds and 113.78 mph (183.1 km/h), almost identical to their 1991-test 900SS. On the scales the Superlight failed to match the factory claim of being 7 kg less than the 900SS. *Cycle World*'s example weighed in at just 5 lb (2.3 kg) less, 409 lb (185 kg) dry, or 436 lb (198 kg) wet. Also, despite the presence of a numbered plate on the triple clamp, too many Superlights were built for them to benefit from any rarity value. They also offered few advantages over a standard 900SS except for the wheels and carbon-fibre guards.

The next year saw the release of Superlight II, but this model was unfortunately a step backwards. Repeating a scenario so often typical of Ducati, the first model was the best, with subsequent versions losing many of the special detail touches. First to go were the Marvic wheels, replaced by the regular Brembo type, now painted bronze to match the frame. There was no longer a vented clutch cover, and even the fully floating Brembo front discs were replaced by the normal steel variety. The only concession made to differentiate the Superlight II from the normal 900SS was the use of a fully floating rear brake linkage, with a carbon-fibre torque arm; breakages of this on some early models of both the Superlight II and 888SP5 saw its replacement by an alloy item. All these changes pushed the claimed weight up to 179 kg (395 lb), though *PS* weighed in their 1993 test bike at 200.5 kg (442 lb) wet, only 3 kg up on the 1992 model. Massimo Bordi admitted to me in 1993 that the Superlight of that year had been a mistake, and many details were rectified for 1994.

While cosmetically the 1994 Superlight III was very similar to the Superlight II, there were quite a few changes. First, the fully floating Brembo front discs returned and, instead of the regular clutch cover, a carbon-fibre one appeared. There was a new, stronger swing-arm, and the suspension was uprated through the use of the 41 mm higher-specification

The 1992 900 Superlight, while not especially fast, was still a magnificent riding machine.

Two yellow Superlight IVs of 1995.

upside-down Showa forks that had appeared on the 1993 888SP5. The brake and clutch fluid reservoirs were remotely mounted, and the colours were now red or yellow. Weight was up yet again, to 182 kg (401 lb) dry, but the Superlight III was a more attractive proposition than the II had been. The Superlight IV of 1995 was almost identical, but for the addition of an oil temperature gauge and the new windshield, both shared with the 900SS. Each year production was reduced, and only 578 Superlights were produced in 1995.

The Superlight was no longer offered for the US market in 1994. In its place was the 900SS Sport Production, a Superlight III with a dual seat and low exhaust pipes. These 175 bikes also came with a serialised plate, and they were again offered in 1995. The lack of any passenger accommodation was one of the limitations of the Superlight, and in many markets they had to be discounted. While the sporting purist preferred the single seat, most buyers required a pillion, and for that reason the regular 900SS consistently outsold its more expensive and glamorous partner. If the Superlight had been a genuine limited edition bike, like the 888 Sport Production series, offering improved engine performance with better-quality suspension, it might have been more successful.

As it was, for most buyers there were few benefits over a standard Super Sport to justify the additional cost.

M600/900 Monster

By the end of 1992, with the end of the 907IE, the entire Ducati range was one of sporting motorcycles. These were the successful lines of the Super Sport Desmodue, and Desmoquattro, so there was some surprise when a completely different Ducati was released at the Cologne

Show in October 1992. Called the M900, and nicknamed *Il Mostro* ('the Monster'), it was the brainchild of Miguel Galluzzi, and was neither a sporting nor touring motorcycle. Neither was it a cruiser like the unsuccessful Indiana, but underneath its minimalist styling lay a truly competent sporting motorcycle in the best Ducati tradition. The Monster was probably the first successor to the original 750GT, a light motorcycle with a race-bred frame, torquey engine, and an upright riding position. It was also released at exactly the right time, and was immediately successful, though production was delayed until mid-1993 because of component supply problems. The Monster became a fashion statement, even being bought by such notables as Barry Sheene and Damon Hill.

The Monster seemed to be a 'parts bin special'. The engine was the identical 73 bhp air/oil-cooled unit of the 900SS, but the oil cooler was now mounted above the front cylinder. The frame was a modified 851/888 with 24° of fork rake and 104 mm (4 inches) of trail, and the same rear suspension linkage (without ride height adjustment). As this was the same frame that had been used to win three consecutive World Superbike Championships, it was obviously understressed by the 900SS motor.

A 1993 900M, or Monster. Underneath the unique styling lay a competent motor-cycle.

The non-adjustable 41 mm inverted Showa forks of the 750SS and a Boge rear unit were fitted, but the front brakes were the same dual 320 mm Brembos of the 900SS, as were the 17-inch Brembo wheels. The M900 was a curious mixture. There was no tachometer on the basic instrument panel, but parts of the bodywork (like the side panels) were carbon-fibre. The low weight of 184 kg (406 lb), and the low seat height of 770 mm (30.3 inches), contributed to a compact and manoeuvrable package. The US magazine *Motorcyclist*, testing a Monster in October 1993, put their example through a standing quarter mile in 11.78 seconds, at 112.0 mph (180 km/h). Their measured top speed, despite the poor aerodynamics, was 128 mph (206 km/h). This was with the same (15/37) final drive gearing as the 900SS, but there was also the option of a 39-tooth rear wheel sprocket. Even fully wet, the Monster only weighed 199 kg (439 lb), and certainly performed much more strongly than the old 750GT or any of its derivatives such as the 860GT, GTS or 900SD Darmah. Despite

limited ground clearance due to the low mufflers, it also handled considerably more adeptly on its shorter, 1,430 mm (56.3-inch) wheelbase.

The M900 continued unchanged through 1994 except for the addition of black as well as red paintwork. For 1995 it mirrored the rest of the range by gaining the bronze frame and wheels, together with grey timing belt covers and rear sprocket cover. The mufflers now featured a chamfer to increase ground clearance.

During 1995 a small number (30) of special M900s, called the 'Club Italia', were manufactured for members of this exclusive club at the instigation of the Castiglioni brothers. Members included Piero Ferrari, Michele Alboreto and Clay Regazzoni. Not for sale, they were fitted with many higher-specification components such as an Öhlins rear shock absorber, fully floating iron Brembo discs, a leather seat, and fully adjustable Showa forks.

So successful was the Monster concept that in 1994 a 600 version, in red or yellow, was released. Using the same motor as the 600SS, but with

the 900M two-into-two exhaust system, and the same single 320 mm disc front brake, the 600M was also made in 33 bhp as well as 53 bhp versions. Dry weight was 174 kg (384 lb), and the 600M tested by *Motociclismo* in September 1994 managed a top speed of 176.0 km/h (109.4 mph). With a standing 400-metre time of 13.592 seconds, at 156.36 km/h (97 mph), the 600M performed very similarly to the 750GT of more than 20 years earlier. In 1995 the 600M received the minor changes of the 900M, and at the 1995 Milan Show the only new Ducati model displayed was the 750 Monster, identical to the 600 but for the larger engine and an oil-cooler.

The Monster soon established itself as an important model in the Ducati line-up, and 6,023 units were sold during 1995. While it has been undoubtedly successful in the short time it has been in production, it remains to be seen how long the Monster's appeal will last; previous Ducatis that have not had a totally sporting focus have always suffered falling sales after a couple of years.

13.

The 851:
Four Valves and Water-cooling

At Daytona in March 1987 the Desmoquattro Ducati 851 created a sensation by matching the speed of the four-cylinder Japanese bikes. It would have qualified sixth in the field for the Daytona 200, had it been eligible for the Superbike class, and recorded a trap speed of 165.44 mph (266 km/h). A few months earlier the 748 cc prototype, at its debut outing at the Bol d'Or 24 Hour endurance race, had also impressed with its speed, if not its reliability. For the first time a 750 cc twin had the speed to match a 750 cc four. Over the ensuing eight years this same basic motorcycle has almost completely dominated the World Superbike series. From its inception in 1988 until the end of 1999, the Ducati Desmoquattro in its various incarnations, from 851 to 996 cc, has won 159 races out of a total of 286. The 851, and its descendants, had become the most successful racing Ducati ever.

Following the positive reception for the Paso after the Milan Show of 1985, the Castiglionis were enthusiastic to develop a more modern, new four-valve engine, and Ing. Massimo Bordi was given the task of developing it. Bordi was an excellent choice, having completed his degree in mechanical engineering with a thesis on a four-valve cylinder head with desmodromically actuated valves. Over a period of six months many designs were investigated, including regular valve spring, four-valve heads, heads with five and even six valves, and desmodromic four-valve heads. The British firm Cosworth was consulted regarding the design of a

four-valve cylinder head, but they wanted nothing to do with desmodromics. A partnership of Mike Costin and Keith Duckworth, Cosworth had created one of the most successful Formula 1 car engines ever in the Ford DFV V8. However, their brief flirtation with desmodromics had not been successful. As the Castiglionis wanted the new engine to be desmodromic, Bordi therefore had to do much of the development himself.

As with Taglioni's first design, the Gran Sport, the new engine was not to be compromised by the limitations of production engineering, and from the outset was designed for maximum performance. Water-cooling enabled full advantage to be taken of four-valve heads with a narrower included

valve angle. Previous experimentation with four-valve heads on the air-cooled 500 twin in 1971–73 had yielded little benefit because it was impossible to get a sufficiently shallow combustion chamber. This new cylinder head was closely modelled on the Cosworth FVA Formula 2 car engine with an included valve angle of 40°, and was effectively a full race system to start with. While an even narrower valve angle may have been desirable in terms of thermal efficiency (more recent Cosworth designs such as the DVF and DFY had included valve angles of 38° and 22°), this was not possible with the mechanical layout of the head. The benefits of the desmodromic layout would have been diminished through

Ing. Massimo Bordi was responsible for the design of the 851. Today he is the general manager of Ducati Motor S.p.A.

compromising the working angle of the rockers on the valve stems. As it was, the inlet ports were very straight, and the compression ratio could still be kept at a high 11:1. The desmodromic layout used two belt-driven overhead camshafts per cylinder. These four-lobed camshafts slipped through tunnels in the heads, supported by ball bearings on the right side, and bushings on the left. Two lobes opened the inlet valves through straight rockers, while the other two closed the valves with 'L'-shaped rockers.

Six months of thought and discussion were followed by only a week of drawing, and in April 1986 blueprints appeared in order for new engine parts to be manufactured. Using modified Pantah crankcases, but with more widely spaced cylinder studs, the prototype engine shared the dimensions of the 750F1 at 88 x 61.5 mm, giving 748 cc. This enabled it to be run in the World Endurance Championship, but with the air-cooled Pantah being raced concurrently in 851 cc form, it was obvious that development of the new engine would include a larger capacity. The prototype had 34 mm and 30 mm valves, and besides the water-cooling was the first Ducati to use open-loop computerised electronic fuel injection. Derived from experience in Ferrari Formula 1 racing cars, the Weber-Marelli IAW fuel injection system used sensors to monitor coolant temperature, engine revs, throttle position, air temperature and barometric pressure. These sensors were common components used on a range of Lancia and Fiat cars, and were sometimes of dubious quality. The computer memory contained a number of maps and, depending on the information from the sensors, plotted the timing of the two injectors together with the ignition advance. These EPROMs (erasable programmable read-only memory) were loaded into the computer with fixed instructions regarding specific fuel and ignition requirements derived from actual dyno tests. Known as an 'alpha/N' system, the computer responded to information from 'alpha' (throttle position), and 'N' (number of rpm). Ignition signals

originated with a magnetic reluctor in the left engine case, triggering four tabs spaced at 90° on an alternator flywheel splined to the crankshaft. A second reluctor read a pulse from the camshaft drive pinion, allowing the computer to distinguish which piston was at top dead centre. The fuel was supplied by an electric pump at a pressure of 43.5psi (3 bar) to two injectors inside 50 mm intakes narrowing to 46 mm at the cylinder inlet. Originally designed for cars with multi-point injection, the same basic system with a 'P8' central processor unit is still used today on those engines with twin injectors.

The adoption of water-cooled cylinders and heads required a water pump to be fitted on the left side of the engine, driven off the left end of the camshaft belt drive shaft running between the cylinders. There was also a radiator, and part of the frame was used as a coolant pipe. Water from the pump surrounded the cylinders first, cooling the cylinder heads. At 10,000 rpm the pump circulated coolant at a modest 26 litres per minute.

By 13 September 1986, five months after the initial drawings appeared, an engine had been tested and installed in a modified 750F1 frame. Amazingly, five days later, on

18 September, the bike was racing at the Paul Ricard circuit in the South of France at the Bol d'Or 24 Hour endurance race. Ridden by Marco Lucchinelli, Juan Garriga and Virginio Ferrari, after 15 hours the new 748 was in seventh place before retiring with a broken con-rod. Still, it had been an impressive debut, especially as at 170 kg (375 lb) it was considerably overweight.

The next meeting for the new motorcycle was at the Daytona Battle of the Twins race in March 1987. Now in 851 cc form, it produced a claimed 120 bhp at 11,500 rpm at the rear wheel, and Marco Lucchinelli won easily. The larger engine used 92 mm three-ring pistons with a 64 mm stroke. The titanium Carillo-style con-rods were made by the Austrian firm of Pankl, and were the same 124 mm eye-to-eye length as the 750, giving a still respectable rod-to-stroke ratio of 1.93:1. The prototype of 1986 had 40 mm con-rod big-end bearings, but these were increased to 42 mm for the larger engine. Now with a six-speed gearbox fitted into larger crankcases, 1987 was a time of constant development. Initially valve timing mirrored the long duration and wide overlap that had been Ducati's trademark over the years with their two-valve engines. The

Marco Lucchinelli on his way to victory on the 851 prototype in the Daytona Battle of the Twins race of 1987.

Daytona 851 cc bike used camshafts with the inlet valve opening 69° before top dead centre and closing 97° after bottom dead centre, and the exhaust valve opening 100° before bottom dead centre and closing 64° after top dead centre. With 346° of inlet valve duration and 133° of valve overlap, they were not yet of the shorter-duration, high-valve-lift type that was generally used in four-valve engines. The valve lift was 10 mm on the inlet, and 9 mm on the exhaust, for an inlet valve lift of 0.32 times the valve-head diameter. Other racing four-valve engines were using camshafts with lifts of up to 0.45 times the valve-head diameter. The valve sizes were down to 32 mm and 28 mm on the 851 prototype.

The chassis was based on the 750TT1-style multi-tube steel space frame with a braced aluminium swing-arm and a similar full-floater-type rising rate rear suspension. Like the Pantah, the swing-arm pivoted on the rear of the crankcases. While the engine was technologically advanced, the use of the steel frame was a link with the past, as were some of the dimensions. The steering head angle of 27½° was similar to past Ducatis, but in other respects the 851 was state of the art. The Marvic wheels were 3.50 x 17 and 5.50 x 17, and the front brakes dual 320 mm Brembos with four-piston callipers. The rear brake was a tiny 230 mm item. Front forks were Marzocchi 41.7 mm M1R and the rear shock absorber the same GSG Roma type that was being used on the final version of the TT1 air-cooled racer, also being raced in 1987. Wheelbase was a moderate 1,430 mm (56 inches), but the main problem with the bike was its weight. At around 150 kg (330 lb), the 851 cc racer was a long way from the minimum 140 kg (309 lb) allowed by European Superbike regulations.

This early 851 still had room for development. The engine looked messy with pipes everywhere and the computer just strapped on the right-hand side. Twenty-five replica racers were promised by mid-1987, and a prototype street version displayed by June, but it would be well into 1988 before these became a reality. That was also to be the first year of the

Lucchinelli's 851 Daytona racer in the pits.

World Superbike Championship, and Ducati needed to build 200 bikes in order for the 851 to be homologated for that series. It could race because the regulations allowed for 1,000 cc two-cylinder bikes to compete against 750 cc fours.

1988

The factory racing 851 had a dream debut when Marco Lucchinelli won the opening round of the new World Superbike Championship at Donington, England, on 3 April. However, he only managed to win one more race that year, the first leg at Zeltweg, Austria, in July. The bike was plagued with a series of crankcase and electrical problems and in order to prepare for the 1989 season Ducati decided not to contest the final two rounds in Australia and New Zealand. In retrospect this was a mistake, because series leader Davide Tardozzi

Lucchinelli about to take to the track for practice at Zeltweg in 1988. On the right is long-time factory mechanic Giuliano Pedretti.

and his Bimota suffered a loss of form, allowing Fred Merkel to win the title. If Ducati had raced, Lucchinelli could well have won the inaugural series, but he ended up fifth.

Throughout 1988 the racing 851 was constantly developed. Initially 851 cc, soon it had grown to 888 cc by a 2 mm overbore to 94 mm. There were claims from competitors that the engine was even bigger, so fast was it for a twin. With the slightly larger valve sizes of 33 mm and 29 mm, along with a revised EPROM chip and airbox, the power was up to 125 bhp at 11,000 rpm at the rear wheel. The original Marzocchi M1R forks were replaced by a new Marzocchi upside-down type, and the swing-arm more heavily braced by the end of the season. The engine was tidied cosmetically with neater coolant plumbing, and the computer was now mounted behind the seat. It was still a heavy bike, though, at 148 kg (326 lb) dry, or 162 kg (357 lb) wet.

Three versions were offered to prospective customers, comprising 20 Lucchinelli Replicas, 200 851 Superbikes, and 300 851 Stradas. The Stradas were the *tricolore* models, and they were largely hand-built because full-scale production had not yet been implemented. The all-red Lucchinelli Replica was 888 cc, just like the factory racer, and with its 11.2:1 compression claimed power (at the crankshaft) of 130 bhp at 10,500 rpm. The frame, with 27$\frac{1}{2}$° rake and 105 mm (4.1 inches) of trail, 17-inch Marvic wheels, and Marzocchi 41.7 mm M1R forks and rear Supermono shocks, was the same as the 851 Superbike. The front brake discs were in between the factory racer and the Superbike at 300 mm, with street-type Brembo four-piston callipers. These 888s were the first in an annual series of factory replicas sold to selected customers to race in super-bike events, but initially most priva-teer bikes failed to achieve significant results. The bikes were too slow and heavy as they came from the factory, and the new technology of the Weber-Marelli fuel injection limited the ease of tuning until alternative EPROM chips became available from non-factory sources.

Most of those who wanted to race

an 851 had no access to the Lucchinelli Replica, but could purchase an 851 Superbike. Purely a homologation special, these were an unusual mixture of street and racing bike. In red, white and green, with a silver frame, they came with Michelin 12/60V17 and 18/67V17 racing slicks mounted on magnesium 3.50 x 17 and 5.50 x 17 Marvic wheels, electric starter, a side stand, and head and tail lights. The engine was 851 cc (92 x 64 mm) with the 32 mm and 28 mm valves of the 1987 prototype racer. Valve timing, however, was different, with the inlet opening at 44° before top dead centre, closing 73° after bottom dead centre, and the exhaust opening 77° before bottom dead centre and closing 42° after top dead centre. These camshafts still opened the nimonic valves 10 mm and 9 mm. With a modest 10.6:1 compression ratio, claimed power was 120 bhp at 10,000 rpm at the crankshaft.

The brakes were two 280 mm fully floating Brembo discs on the front, and a 260 mm on the rear, with street-type Brembo P4.32B and P2.T08N callipers. In other respects the 851 Superbike was the same as the Lucchinelli Replica, and also had the braced aluminium swing-arm. Wheelbase was up slightly to 1,460 mm (57.5 inches) and claimed weight

was 165 kg (364 lb) dry, but this was very optimistic. *Cycle World*, testing an 851 Superbike in April 1988, weighed their bike at 417 lb (189 kg) dry, and 445 lb (202 kg) wet – too much for a racing bike. Still, they managed a top speed of 154 mph (249 km/h).

Alongside the 851 Superbike was the 851 Strada. Using the same frame (without the reinforced swing-arm) and similar bodywork (with Paso-style mirrors), the Strada differed in the use of the 16-inch Marvic/Akront composite wheels, and a de-tuned engine. With the same 32 mm and 28 mm valve sizes, camshaft timing used less duration and overlap, and there was less valve lift. The inlet valve opened 11° before top dead centre, closing 70° after bottom dead centre, and the exhaust valve opened 62° before bottom dead centre, closing 18° after top dead centre. Inlet valve lift was 9.60 mm and exhaust valve lift 8.74 mm. With slightly less compression than the 851 Superbike at 10.4:1, the Strada produced a claimed 102 bhp at 9,000 rpm at the crankshaft. It also had the twin injectors per cylinder, and the same Pankl con-rods as fitted to the racing bikes. The Strada's six-speed gearbox also had more widely spaced ratios, with only first and second being the same. The

The 1988 851 Strada tricolore, *here in company with a 1989 model.*

hydraulically operated dry clutch did not get the vented clutch cover of the Superbike. Another difference between the two models was in the use of the Paso exhaust system and 16-inch Marvic composite wheels, as fitted to the 750 Montjuich and Santa Monica. The brakes were identical to the 851 Superbike, and the claimed dry weight was 185 kg (408 lb).

The Stradas were criticised for uncertain handling due to the 16-inch wheels, and had some problems with fuel vaporisation on hot days. According to *Motorrad*, in September 1988, the Strada tipped the scales wet at 215 kg (474 lb), and top speed was a disappointing 212 km/h (132 mph). Because they were very expensive, they were not a particularly successful model, and they were sold at discount prices during 1989; today the 1988 851 Strada is not particularly sought after. Their performance was not as spectacular as it was claimed to be, but it was probably the idiosyncratic handling characteristics that condemned it. However, these first available street versions of the *otto-valvole* featured many individual and hand-crafted pieces, like the rear shock absorber rocker linkage, and used high-quality components such as fully floating discs front and rear and braided steel brake lines.

1989

Marco Lucchinelli assumed the role of team manager for the World Superbike series (though he still raced at occasional rounds), with former 500 cc Grand Prix rider and 1981 World Endurance Champion Raymond Roche taking his place in the team alongside Baldassare Monti. With the 888 cc bike now having new upper outer tube Öhlins forks, Roche was immediately impressive, claiming pole position and setting fastest lap at the opening race at Donington. Electrical problems saw his retirement, however, and it was not until the fourth round, at Brainerd in the US, that Roche had a victory. Further wins at Hockenheim and Pergusa, Sicily, saw him finish third in the Championship, despite seven retirements. He still won more races than any other rider, but there was some way to go before the Ducati

was reliable enough to win the Championship. Ducati also tried a larger displacement 919 cc (95.6 x 64 mm) engine towards the end of the season, and Lockheed brake callipers instead of Brembo. However, the extra capacity somehow did not translate into faster lap times, and was at the expense of reliability.

The factory bike was now making 128 bhp, and was lighter than the previous year at 158 kg (348 lb). It proved to be the fastest of all the Superbikes at the ultimate horse-power track, Hockenheim, where Roche knocked nearly 4 seconds off the lap record, set only the previous year. Displayed at the Cologne Show in 1988, an 888 cc Lucchinelli Replica continued to be offered, unchanged, and 30 were made in 1989. In place of the 851 Superbike with its confused identity, there appeared a new model called the 851 Sport Production, designed for the Italian Sport Production racing series for street-based motorcycles.

The 851 Sport Production used a similar engine to the 1988 851 Superbike in the revised running gear of the 1989 851 Strada. With a higher compression ratio of 11.5:1, it was still 851 cc, had larger 33 mm and 29 mm valves and used the same camshafts as the 851 Superbike. It produced 122 bhp at 10,000 rpm at the crankshaft. However, it did not have the twin injectors per cylinder, or the close-ratio gearbox of the 1988 Superbike, instead having the regular Strada ratios. Fuel was now supplied at a higher pressure of 5 bar (72.5psi), and the claimed dry weight of the SP was 180 kg (397 lb).

The SP shared its frame, wheels, brakes, suspension and bodywork with the revised 851 Strada of 1989. Thus, apart from a small badge on the top triple clamp, the 1989 SP was virtually indistinguishable from the 1989 Strada, which addressed many of the criticisms of the 1988 Strada. Production of the Strada was increased to 1,500, and these greater numbers, together with a dramatic price reduction, inevitably led to some economising. While the engine remained largely unchanged from 1988, like the 851 Sport Production there was now only a single injector

per cylinder, and the compression ratio was increased to 11:1. Power was up slightly to 105 bhp at 9,000 rpm at the crankshaft. The crankshaft still used the Pankl connecting-rods, and the clutch actuation system changed to the left side of the engine with a rod passing through the gearbox main shaft. Suspension continued to be the Marzocchi 41.7 mm M1R forks and the Marzocchi Duo shock, most of the changes occurring to the frame, wheels and brakes.

The most important change to the frame (now painted white) was directly related to experience in World Superbike. To quicken the steering, the steering head angle was reduced by 3° to 24½°, with a corresponding reduction in trail to 95 mm (3.7 inches). The wheelbase was also reduced slightly to 1,430 mm (56.3 inches). Coupled with the use of new white-painted Brembo 17-inch wheels in the Superbike sizes of 3.50 x 17 and 5.50 x 17, the 1989 Strada was a considerably better-handling motorcycle than its predecessor, despite a rise in the claimed dry weight to 190 kg (419 lb). To improve weight distribution, and following racing practice, the battery was now mounted on a bracket alongside the front cylinder on the right-hand side of the engine.

While the front brake disc rotor size was increased to 320 mm, they changed from the fully floating iron to rotors in stainless steel. Brake callipers were unchanged and there was a smaller 245 mm rear disc. Now with totally red paintwork like Lucchinelli's factory bike, the 1989 Strada tested by *Motorrad* in June 1989 weighed the same as in 1988, at 215 kg (474 lb). Top speed was up to 228 km/h (142 mph). *Cycle* tested the 1989 Strada in September and found it to be the fastest two-cylinder bike they had ever tested, posting a standing quarter mile time of 11.61 seconds at 116.28 mph (187 km/h). They went on to say, 'The 851's handling is so good it's almost mystical'. The 1989 851, in either SP or Strada form, demonstrated what Ducati was learning on the track through their World Superbike racing programme and incorporating into the production line. The slightly quicker steering geometry along with the use of 17-inch rather than 16-inch wheels, absolutely transformed the 851. While it was still not an effortless machine to ride in the style of Japanese bikes, the 1989 851 was a rewarding bike in the best Ducati tradition, and it also offered comparable outright performance to Japanese 750s. If ever there was any truth in the notion that 'racing improves the breed', it was being reflected in the 851, and was even more so in 1990.

1990

Reverting to the 888 (from the larger 919), the factory bikes were sufficiently well developed for Raymond Roche to win the World Superbike Championship. With more power (130–134 bhp at 11,000 rpm) and less weight, at 147 kg (324 lb), by the end of the season it was also the improvement in reliability that clinched the Championship. Additionally, there was an improvement in tractability, with more mid-range power due to revised camshafts. Significantly, the 1990 engine made a useful 110 bhp at 8,000 rpm, which was reflected in the results, with Roche winning eight and team mate Giancarlo Falappa one, before he crashed heavily during qualifying at the Österreichring. They still suffered crankcase failures, but most of the electrical problems had been eliminated. It had been found that a faulty rpm sensor had been the cause of most of the electronic failures.

Visually, the 1990 bike was little changed from the previous year. It still used Öhlins suspension, with a revised rear linkage, and by the end of the year had more upswept exhausts with carbon-fibre mufflers. Other carbon-fibre parts appeared, such as a seat/tail section and front guard, in order to get the bike closer to the class minimum weight of 140 kg (309 lb). Starting the season at 157 kg (346 lb) with oil and water, by Monza in October the bike weighed a significant 10 kg (22 lb) less. A smaller, curved radiator raised the cooling temperature to 70–75°C because it had been found that sometimes the bikes had been running as cool as 40°C. An electronic tachometer was also used occasionally, and would appear again in 1991.

A limited number of 888 Corsa

Roche Replica (formerly Lucchinelli Replica) racers were again available to selected dealer teams. These incorporated many of the developments that had occurred during 1989, setting a pattern that was to follow in subsequent years, and meant that the privateer bikes would always be one year behind the factory. The Roche Replica of 1990 had the upper outer tube Öhlins forks, Marvic magnesium wheels, and lightweight parts such as an aluminium sub-frame and magnesium primary drive cover. As with the factory bikes, the computer was housed in a bracket off the steering head. The claimed weight was 158 kg (348 lb), and the engine used larger (34 mm and 30 mm) valves, and a new inlet camshaft. Developed from the previous racing season, this opened the inlet valve at 53° before top dead centre, closing 71° after bottom dead centre. Intake valve lift was up 1 mm to 11 mm. The exhaust camshaft was the same as before, and was shared with the Sport Production series. Compression ratio was up to 12:1. The Roche Replica also used a completely different gearbox, with different ratios.

Alongside the Roche Replica of 1990, Ducati released possibly their most significant street bike since the 750SS of 1974, and certainly the most significant new street Ducati

since the Cagiva take-over in 1985. Called the 851 Sport Production 2, this motorcycle was considerably removed from the 1989 Sport Production, and was the closest street bike to a factory racer available. In essence, it was a Roche Replica with lights and treaded tyres. Primarily aimed at the Japanese market, then Ducati's prime export destination and a market obsessed with race replicas, the SP2 was displayed at the Tokyo Show at the end of 1989.

Still called an 851, the SP2 was similar to the 1989 Sport Production but with an overbore to 94 mm to take the displacement up to 888 cc, as with the racing bikes. With the same 33 mm and 29 mm valves, and the same camshafts, power was up to 109 bhp (at the rear wheel). In the engine department there were still the Pankl con-rods, a polished and lightened crankshaft, polished rockers, oil cooler and vented dry clutch. Both the inlet and exhaust systems were considerably less restrictive, with no inlet air box and larger-diameter exhausts. The gearbox had the same ratios as the 1988 851 Superbike (lower third, fourth and fifth than the Strada), and there was a return to twin injectors per cylinder. However, while the frame was identical to that of 1989, this bike had the same suspension as the works racers, the

Raymond Roche won the 1990 World Superbike Championship on the 888 cc factory bike. (Two Wheels)

Öhlins FG9050 42 mm upside-down forks and an Öhlins DU8070 rear unit. The quality of these components alone justified the price differential between the SP and the Strada, but there were many of other differences besides the extra power. Like the 888 Corsa, the rear sub-frame was lightweight aluminium, there were fully floating iron 320 mm Brembo discs, and a carbon-fibre rear guard. The SP2 had moved further away from the Strada to become a true limited-edition race replica. Styling was very similar to the Strada, and apart from the suspension the most visible distinguishing marks were Agip and Michelin stickers on the fairing, and a numbered plaque on the top fork yoke. Dry weight was up from the SP1, largely due to the forks, at 188 kg (414.5 lb) from 180 kg (397 lb).

Performance of the SP2 dramatically eclipsed any previous street Ducati, even the 851 Strada. *Motociclismo*, in April 1990, managed an impressive top speed of 255 km/h (158 mph) from SP2 No 74. *Cycle* magazine also found the SP2 a strong performer, making 96.4 bhp at 9,000 rpm on their dyno in December 1990. *Motorcyclist*, testing the same SP2 No 50 in July 1991, powered through the standing quarter mile in an impressive 10.72 seconds at 128 mph (206 km/h). The SP2 was barely street legal in many countries, and the larger-capacity exhaust system with minimal muffling produced sounds reminiscent of the older Super Sports with their Contis, or the 750 Montjuich with its Verlicchi competition system. The racing-specification Öhlins forks transformed the handling of the 851 Strada, and the SP2 was one of the most confidence-inspiring motorcycles to ride at high speeds. *Cycle* thought it a fantastic motorcycle, claiming it to be 'perhaps the best production race bike money can buy'. To put the SP2 into perspective, they hailed it as 'one of the most desirable sporting motorcycles since the original Ducati 750SS', a statement with which I whole-heartedly agree.

In rather typical Ducati fashion, the Strada was softened slightly for 1990 with the addition of a dual seat. As the Strada and Sport Production

851 lines developed they diverged, and the performance gap between them increased. By 1990 the relationship was similar to that which existed in 1974 between the 750 Sport and 750SS, and also in 1986 between the 750F1 and 750 Montjuich. The higher-performance versions were made in more limited numbers (about 500 SP2s), and sold at a price almost 50% higher. However, in the case of the 851 series the performance difference was far more considerable between the SP and the Strada, as there was a genuine 20% power difference, and the SP had better-quality suspension, less weight, and improved weight distribution.

The 1990 Strada continued essentially unchanged in the engine department, but the Pankl con-rods were replaced by the standard Pantah style. The addition of the dual seat with a stronger sub-frame increased the weight to 506 lb (230 kg) as tested by *Cycle World* in June 1990. Performance, however, had not suffered, and their test bike posted a standing quarter mile time of 11.26 seconds at 121.29 mph (195 km/h), with a measured top speed of 150 mph (241 km/h).

1991

An indication of the outcome of the 1991 World Superbike Championship was demonstrated at an international Superbike race in Mexico in December 1990. Doug Polen and Raymond Roche were on factory 888s, and Polen won both legs. Recently having left the Yoshimura Suzuki team, Polen had only tested the Fast by Ferracci Ducati at Daytona a week before the Mexico race.

For 1991 there would still be the two factory bikes, for Raymond Roche and Giancarlo Falappa, but also support for Polen and Stéphane Mertens. Polen was racing for Eraldo Ferracci, an Italian who had spent 25 years building racing bikes in the US, and who had enjoyed moderate success with Ducati 888s in 1990 in the AMA series with rider Jamie James. In comparison to the factory effort, Ferracci operated on a much smaller budget, and Polen was contracted to Dunlop rather than

Eraldo Ferracci, tuner of Doug Polen's winning 888 in 1991.

Michelin tyres. He also teamed up with the legendary veteran Ducati tuners, Giorgio Nepoti and Rino Caracchi of NCR.

Both the factory and two supported riders had bikes close to the class minimum of 140 kg (309 lb). Through the considerable use of carbon-fibre for radiator, exhaust and fairing brackets, as well as the airbox and air ducts, rear-brake torque-arm and fuel tank, the works machines weighed 143 kg (315 lb). Other modifications such as a smaller rear disc (190 mm in carbon or steel from 216 mm in steel), smaller callipers, titanium exhausts and Termignoni carbon-fibre mufflers, also contributed to the weight reduction. An important by-product was the improvement in weight distribution, with more front weight bias. In January 1992 the Japanese magazine *Bikers Station* put the Fast by Ferracci 888 on the scales: total weight was 146.5 kg (323 lb), and weight distribution was 51/49% front to rear.

By getting close to the allowable minimum weight, Ducati were now making the most of the regulations that gave two-cylinder motorcycles a 25 kg (55 lb) advantage over their four-cylinder opposition. These regulations came in for increasing criticism from the Japanese teams, but the credit still had to be given to Ducati

Doug Polen demonstrating the style that took him to two World Superbike Championships. (Two Wheels)

for designing and developing a twin-cylinder motorcycle capable of competing with 750 cc four-cylinder bikes. When the regulations were drafted in 1987, it had appeared inconceivable that a twin could become as dominant as the Ducati did during the 1991 season. So good had the 888 racer become that Ducati won 23 World Superbike races, and they were only beaten once. Doug Polen himself was so dominant on the Fast by Ferracci Ducati that he won 17 races. He even held the outright lap record for a while at Jarama, Spain, during 1991. To emphasise the superiority of the Ducati 888, Davide Tardozzi on his Team Grottini bike won the European Superbike Championship, with four wins from six starts.

The Fast by Ferracci bike used the 888 cc engine with 36 mm and 31 mm valves, and with 11.8:1 compression produced 133 bhp at 11,500 rpm. The camshafts used by Ferracci had more lift, but less duration than even the SP, with the inlet opening 48° before top dead centre, closing 68° after bottom dead centre, and the

exhaust valve opening 68° before bottom dead centre and closing 40° after top dead centre. A new crossover exhaust system contributed to the extra 3 bhp, and more upswept

exhausts, homologated on the SP3, together with some changes to the front fairing, improved aerodynamics. Roche's bike sometimes featured different specifications, but all the

Giorgio Nepoti of NCR working on Polen's 1991 Fast by Ferracci 888. (Two Wheels)

Raymond Roche finished second on a factory 888 in the 1991 World Superbike Championship. (Two Wheels)

racing engines now used modified crankcases that solved the crankcase cracking problem of 1990. There was now more extensive webbing and ribbing around the base of the

The 1991 SP3 was similar to the SP2 but for a carbon-fibre front guard and upswept exhausts.

cylinder. Engine problems early in the season were solved by drilling an oilway up the Pankl con-rod to the gudgeon pin. Whereas the FBF bike still used the Öhlins upside-down

forks as fitted the previous year and to the 1991 Corsa and SP, Roche had a new type of Öhlins fork. Braking was usually by a combination 320 mm steel and carbon disc with Brembo callipers, and wheels a Marchesini 3.50 x 17 front, and 6.25 x 17 rear. With slightly less steering head angle, at 23.5°, the wheelbase was shortened slightly to 1,420 mm (55.9 inches).

The 50 Corsas made in 1991 included many of the modifications of the factory bikes. Using a carbon-fibre seat-tail unit together with a carbon-fibre petrol tank, the weight was down to 155 kg (342 lb). The computer was now housed in a carbon-fibre bracket incorporating the air intake and supporting the electronic tachometer. The engine was largely unchanged from 1990 (but for the stronger crankcases), and the claimed power (at the rear wheel) was 128 bhp. Wheel sizes were up to 3.75 x 17 front, and 6.00 x 17 rear. The frame, brakes and suspension were identical to 1990.

The SP3 was slightly restyled for 1991. Even though it was still called an 851, the 888 cc SP3 now had

The SP3, like the SP2, SP4, and SPS, used Öhlins upside-down forks.

upswept mufflers, carbon-fibre front mudguard and black wheels, a revised air intake system and, like the SP2, was also made in small numbers (about 500), with a numbered plaque on the top triple clamp celebrating the winning of the 1990 World Superbike Championship. With the Agip and Michelin stickers and the white racing plate on the rear seat, it was the closest replica yet and really looked like a street version of the 1991 factory racers. The claimed power of the SP3 was slightly up on the SP2, now 128 bhp at 10,500 rpm at the crankshaft, or 111 bhp at the rear wheel. All 1991 models received the stronger crankcases, and the SP3 a specially machined and polished crankshaft. While most of the engine and gearbox specifications were unchanged, one area where the SP3 was improved over the SP2 was the clutch, a notorious area of weakness; it now had eight driving plates, and could also be retrofitted to the rest of the 851 range. Still with the Öhlins FG9050 upside-down forks, the SP3 was fitted with a slightly different Öhlins DU0060 rear unit. Front brakes were the same fully floating 320 mm iron Brembo with four-piston callipers, but the front master cylinder diameter was increased from 15 mm to 16 mm. Other minor changes from the SP2 included a degasser in

the aluminium fuel tank (reducing the capacity to 17 litres from 20 litres), and remote location of the front brake and clutch reservoirs. Claimed dry weight was still 188 kg (414.5 lb) and essentially the two models were identical.

As expected, the performance of the SP3 was similar to that of the SP2. *Moto Sprint* achieved a top speed of 261.1 km/h (162.2 mph) with a 0–400-metre time of 10.78 seconds at 207.664 km/h (129 mph). *Motociclismo* managed 106.82 bhp at 10,250 rpm, at the rear wheel, so just like the SP2, the SP3 was a powerful motorcycle. Wet weight for the SP3, as measured by *Moto Sprint*, was 202.1 kg (445 lb). Being fortunate enough to have some experience of riding an SP3, I can confirm that these motorcycles were superb sporting bikes. Despite being a modern, computerised device, there was still a lot of the rawness of previous race replica Ducatis in the SP3.

The 851 Strada for 1991 gained Showa GD011 upside-down front forks, but also the Öhlins DU0060 rear unit of the SP3. Engine specifications remained unchanged but for a slightly lower compression ratio of 10.5:1, with the claimed power being 91 bhp at 9,000 rpm at the rear wheel. Dry weight went up to 199 kg (439 lb). Visually it was little changed from the dual-seat 1990 bike, and was still red with white wheels. The front brake and clutch reservoir were now remotely located, as with the SP3, and the diameter of the front brake master cylinder was also increased to 16 mm. The eccentric adjustment for the ride height was also deleted from the Strada, though it remained on the SP. The machined rear suspension rocker arm was also replaced by a forged item. As tested by *Cycle* in September 1991, the 851 covered the standing quarter mile in 11.23 seconds at 120.80 mph (194.4 km/h). *Motorcyclist*, in November 1991, weighed the 851 Strada at 220 kg (485 lb) wet, and managed a top speed of 149 mph (240 km/h).

1992

Although Ing. Bordi had talked during 1991 of a new bike with a longer-stroked engine in a Massimo

Tamburini-designed frame with a single-sided swing-arm, the 888 had proved so competitive that it continued virtually unchanged from the previous year. Whereas the street 851 and 888SP4 had a revised frame, footpeg brackets and styling, the factory racers and 888 Corsa still used the 1991 frame and bodywork.

Doug Polen was now riding for the official Ducati team, alongside Giancarlo Falappa. With sponsorship from Italian sunglasses manufacturer Police, the team was managed by another former Italian World Champion, Franco Uncini; he replaced Marco Luchinelli, who had been arrested and imprisoned for drug offences during 1991. Unfortunately, due to the bad publicity, this resulted in considerable lost sponsorship. Uncini had a long association with Ducati, having raced a 750SS during 1975 and 1976 for Bruno Spaggiari's team in the Italian Championship. Raymond Roche now found himself a privateer, electing not to become part of the Police team, but still with a factory bike, and tuned by ace tuner Rolando Simonetti. More often than not, Roche's bike was the fastest of all the Ducatis and allowed him to come from the back to win the race after one of his traditional poor starts. Other factory machines were supplied to Stéphane Mertens, Davide Tardozzi and Daniel Amatriain.

There were very few changes to the all-conquering 1991 888. With yet another new clutch and a new exhaust camshaft design, the power was up slightly to 135 bhp at 11,800 rpm. The new exhaust camshaft allowed safe revs to 12,000 rpm, and different valve sizes of 35 mm and 30 mm were tried, along with variable-length inlet tracts on Roche's bike. The biggest changes came in weight saving, not just in carbon-fibre parts, but also now within the engine. Narrower gearbox gears (6 mm to the Corsa's 10 mm), hollow camshafts and more titanium and magnesium helped to get the weight down to 142 kg (313 lb), and the shape of the Pankl con-rods was slightly altered to eliminate some of the breakages of the past. All bikes now used the new type of 42 mm Öhlins fork that Roche had used the previous year.

The type of disc rotors varied, Polen generally using US-made C-CAT carbon discs, and Roche the regular 320 mm steel Brembo type.

Due to some difficulties within the team, Doug Polen had a slow start to the season, and the Ducatis were nowhere near as dominant as they had been in 1991. Polen won nine, Roche six, and Falappa four races (out of a total of 26), but the most impressive was probably Carl Fogarty's win in the second leg at Donington on one of the production Corsas. However, Polen again won the World Championship, with Raymond Roche second, but it was obvious now that the 888 was nearing the end of its competitive life.

The weight-saving programme of the factory racers passed down to the 888 Superbike Racing (Corsa) for 1992. Still using the 1991 frame and bodywork, but with more carbon-fibre, the weight was reduced to 150 kg (330 lb). The engine now had magnesium primary drive, ignition, and camshaft covers, and, while power was still quoted at 128 bhp at 11,000 rpm, the Superbike Racer received the revised exhaust camshaft, still with 9 mm of valve lift, but with the valve opening at 71° before bottom dead centre, and closing 45° after top dead centre.

The suspension was the new type of 41 mm Öhlins forks with magnesium triple clamps, as used on the factory bikes, together with an Öhlins shock absorber as before. The 320 mm front brakes were also uprated to the latest Brembo racing type with a 19 mm PS13B master cylinder and P2105N 30 and 34 mm callipers. The rear disc was now a smaller 190 mm unit (from 210 mm). All the frame dimensions remained unchanged from 1989, but for a slight increase in trail to 98 mm (3.86 inches). The limited number of 1992 Superbike Racers made (30) were much more competitive bikes than in previous years, as witnessed by Fogarty's consistently good results on his privateer Corsa. While they were no more powerful, they were much lighter, even if there was 7 kg (15.4 lb) between the Superbike Racer and the factory bikes.

In 1992 the first signs of cost effec-

The SP4 of 1992, now an 888 desmoquattro.

tiveness became evident, even with the SP series. While the factory racers and Corsas still used the old frame with individually welded sections around the steering head, the 851 Strada and SP4 now utilised a single bent tube. Following the 1991 900SS, they also now had a flip-up steel petrol tank instead of the aluminium one. There was also an improved cooling system with a curved radiator. The fairing, tank and seat were redesigned, as were the footrest brackets that had a tendency to break on the previous model if the bike fell over. The engine of the SP4 was identical to that of the SP3, but for 1992 an even more special model was provided, the 120 bhp SPS, or Sport Production Special. The SPS had a carbon-fibre petrol tank, seat and silencers. The racing cooling radiator was fitted, without a fan, so the weight was down to 185 kg (408 lb). The engine was virtually that of the 1991 Corsa, the power being up due again to 1 mm larger valves (34 mm and 30 mm), together with a Corsa inlet cam. There were other minor engine differences between the SPS and the SP4, these being different Pankl connecting-rod bolts, and a double-roller main bearing rather than an oblique single type. As usual there was yet another clutch modification this year, with an additional driven plate.

Visually the SP4 and SPS were very similar. Now '888s', they shared the Öhlins suspension with the SP3, but had the new type of gold series Brembo P4 30/34 front brake callipers (also shared with the 851 Strada and Super Sport range). Both the SP4 and SPS also used the same series of numbered plaque on the top triple clamp. As with the SP3, these bikes were loud with their open airbox and exhausts, so for some markets (such as Germany) the SP4 came with a normal 851 airbox and clutch cover. The SP4 used the vented clutch cover of the SP2 and SP3, but the SPS had the more open Superbike Racing type.

The SPS was a strongest performing of all the 888SPs, and *Moto Sprint* achieved 268.1 km/h (166.59 mph) with a 0–400-metre time of 10.39 seconds at 212.015 km/h (131.7 mph). The SP4, with the same engine as the SP3, performed very similarly to that model. Tested by *Moto Sprint* in March 1992, SP4 No 69 was slightly slower and heavier than the SP3, managing 256.76 km/h (159.5 mph) and weighing 205 kg (452 lb). The SPS really eclipsed the SP4 with its lighter weight and higher-performing engine; it was the consummate race replica Ducati, and is still a highly desirable motorcycle. However, any of the Sport Production 888s with Öhlins forks have to be considered among the best street bikes ever produced by the factory. They were produced in limited numbers with the most expensive proprietary components, and even though they were very expensive to buy, they offered exceptional value.

The divergence of the Strada and SP lines continued further as the 851 Strada gained more weight (now 202 kg, or 445 lb) with the steel tank instead of aluminium, and lost the Öhlins rear shock absorber for a Showa GD012. The front brakes were now the same Brembo P4 30/34 callipers as the SP, but still with the 320 mm steel discs. With the new bodywork came a revised passenger seat, with flip-out grab rails. The 1992 Strada also inherited the larger SP valves (33 and 29 mm), and with 10.5:1 compression, and a redesigned cylinder head, the power was increased to 95 bhp at 9,000 rpm. It was a case of slightly increasing the power to maintain the same performance level of the earlier bikes, and to compensate for the increase in weight. The cooling system was also revised, with the curved radiator of the SP4 and the new cooling circuit.

Moto Sprint managed a top speed of 239.5 km/h (149 mph), the same as the 1991 Strada, and *Cycle World*, in August 1992, a standing quarter mile time of 11.53 seconds at 122.61 mph (197.3 km/h). These figures were on a par with the 1991 model, even though the power was measured at 90.9 bhp at 8,750 rpm, at the rear wheel. It was the increase in weight to 493 lb (223.6 kg) wet (*Cycle World*'s test) that hurt the performance.

1993

As the 888 replacement had been held over for one more year, the factory continued to race that highly developed model. Competition was now much stronger, from Kawasaki in particular, but with Honda delaying the introduction of its fuel-injected RC45 until the 1994 season, Massimo Bordi decided to do the same with the 916. The weight limit for twins was increased slightly, to 145 kg (320 lb), with the fours remaining at 165 kg (364 lb).

Following his excellent performances on a privateer bike the previous year, Carl Fogarty now took over from Doug Polen who decided to race

in the US AMA Superbike series on the Fast by Ferracci-prepared bike. Thus Fogarty was teamed with Falappa, and now managed by Raymond Roche. Other factory support went to Davide Tardozzi's Team Grottini with riders Stéphane Mertens and ex-Grand Prix and endurance rider Juan Garriga. The tuner for Grottini was Pietro Gianesin, from GPM of Vicenza, who had a long association with Ducati. Later in the season Garriga was replaced by Mauro Lucchiari.

The Roche team used Rolando Simonetti as tuner, and the bikes were a little different from the previous year. Using the 1992 production frame with the bent, rather than individually welded, tubes, and carbon-fibre footrest brackets, they also had the revised fairing and seat that had appeared on the SP4 and SPS. The extra weight of these pushed the weight above the minimum, to 147 kg. The engine was overbored 2 mm, to 96 mm, to make 926 cc, and 1 mm larger valves (37 mm and 31 mm) were used. Power was not noticeably up from the 888 (142–144 bhp at 11,500 rpm), and the engine was less responsive due to the heavier, 11.9:1, pistons. It was nicknamed *il pompone* ('big pump'), and had a second crankcase breather located next to the normal one. Other detail differences included a sprag-type anti-lock clutch, a sealed airbox, and a revised computer that allowed for the separate mapping of each cylinder. They also used an electronic quick-shifter that cut the engine between gearshifts.

Despite winning 19 races out of 26, Ducati's victories were spread between Fogarty, Falappa and privateer Andreas Meklau, so they lost the title to Scott Russell on the Kawasaki. However, in the US AMA Series, Doug Polen easily won the Championship, and Edwin Weibel won the German Superbike Championship. While the 888/926 may well have been approaching the end of its racing (and production) life, it was still a highly competent motorcycle. This was put into perspective by Carl Fogarty in 1993: at Donington during October he set a new lap record for Superbikes on his

factory 926 racer at 1 min 35.22 sec, or 152.11 km/h (94.517 mph). Only two months earlier, having a one-off ride on the Cagiva 500 cc Grand Prix bike in the British Grand Prix (where he finished fourth, and very nearly third), his fastest lap had been 1 min 35.332 sec. Not bad at all for basically a seven-year-old design.

The 888 Racing for 1993 also shared the revised frame and bodywork with the factory bikes, and through the use of more carbon-fibre (such as the footrest brackets) the claimed dry weight was down to 145 kg (320 lb). While still 888 cc, larger valve sizes of 36 mm and 31 mm, together with an increase in exhaust valve lift to 10.5 mm, raised the power to 135 bhp at 11,500 rpm at the rear wheel. There was also a completely new six-speed gearbox, with closer ratios, and an improved clutch. The Marchesini wheels, Öhlins suspension and Brembo brakes were similar to before. The 1993 Corsa also had revised mapping to optimise the individual cylinders, and the one-piece, larger-capacity airbox.

While waiting one more year for the 916, the street bikes were now all 888 cc, and there was an SP5, an SPO (for the US market), and the 888 Strada. While the Strada was developed into a better motorcycle, as had so often happened in the past, the SP5 suffered from economising. The most noticeable loss was the replacement of the expensive racing Öhlins front forks with Showa 41 mm GD061, but the Öhlins rear unit remained, now a DU8071. The SP5 did get the higher performance SPS engine (without the racing radiator), but with slightly less power at 118 bhp at 10,500 rpm. Thus it had the 34 mm and 30 mm valves, together with the Corsa inlet camshaft, still twin injectors per cylinder, and the same main bearings and con-rods as the SPS. All the 1993 bikes featured improved electronics, with reprogrammable EPROMs, and an external trimmer for adjusting the carbon monoxide level through a small hole in the rear of the seat unit. The SP5 also received the carbon-fibre mufflers of the SPS, but lost the carbon-fibre fuel tank for a regular steel item. The rear brake was also different, now with a torque-arm, initially in carbon-fibre but later in alloy because of some breakages in the carbon-fibre versions, and the clutch cover was no longer the vented type. There were no clutch modifications this year, and as before the SP5 had a smaller, lighter, 300-watt alternator than the Strada's and SPO's 350 watts. The limited number of SP5s (still about 500) also carried the plaque on the top triple clamp celebrating the winning of the 1992 World Superbike Championship. As with the 1993 900 Superlight, the Brembo wheels were now painted bronze to match the frame. Apart from the use of braided steel lines for the front brakes, these too were unchanged from the SP4 and SPS. While the claimed weight was still 188 kg (414.5 lb) dry, actual wet weight, as tested by *Cycle World* in November 1993, was 468 lb (212 kg) wet.

While not quite up to the performance level set by the SPS, *Moto Sprint* still managed an impressive top speed from their SP5 of 260.3 km/h (161.7 mph), and a 0–400-metre time of 10.57 seconds at 210.226 km/h (130.6 mph). *Cycle World*'s test bike put out 110 bhp at 10,250 rpm at the rear wheel.

For the US market a special model was produced called the SPO, or Sport Production *Omolagato*. This was an 888 Strada with the single seat, upswept exhaust pipes and Öhlins shock absorber (together with eccentric ride height adjustment) of the SP5. The engine was essentially an overbored 1992 851 Strada, and produced a claimed 100 bhp at 9,000 rpm at the rear wheel. The single fuel injector per cylinder, valve sizes and camshaft profiles were all the same as the 1992 851. Claimed weight was the same as the SP5, but when tested by *Motorcyclist* in October 1993 the

SPO weighed 482 lb (219 kg) wet, despite not having the oil-cooler of the SP5. On *Cycle World*'s dyno in July 1993 the SPO made 94.0 bhp at 8,750 rpm at the rear wheel, and turned the standing quarter mile in 11.25 seconds, at 123.45 mph (198.7 km/h).

For other markets the 888 Strada replaced the 851 Strada, and was an improved motorcycle. While still heavy, at 202 kg (445 lb) dry, the extra capacity, together with some changes to the mapping of the fuel injection, now compensated for the increase in weight. The bodywork was identical to the 1992 Strada, but for revised graphics (with the new gold Ducati logo) and the bronze-painted frame. For 1993 the Strada still had black-painted wheels. *Moto Sprint* achieved 245.9 km/h (153 mph) on their test bike, and *PS*, in March 1993, weighed their test machine at 224 kg (494 lb). While

The SP5 had Showa forks and carbon-fibre mufflers.

the weight had increased significantly since its inception in 1988, the Strada had now evolved into a thoroughly sophisticated motorcycle, and was arguably the most practical of the entire series. With the basic engine, frame, wheels and suspension unchanged since 1989, and the concept from 1987, the 888 Strada was at the pinnacle of its development as a street bike. The excellence of the original design had been well and truly vindicated, both on the street and the race track, by a system of continuous refinement over seven years.

1994

Towards the end of 1993 Ducati finally exhibited to the press a proto-type of the 888 replacement. This had actually been ready some time earlier, so by the time it was put into production the 916 was a well-developed second-generation Desmoquattro. A product of the Cagiva Research Centre headed by Massimo Tamburini (who had designed the Paso), the 916 was one of their first major designs since moving from Rimini to the nearby Republic of San Marino. It still used essentially the same engine, but in a new tubular steel frame, and was clothed in body-work inspired by the Supermono (of which more later in this chapter). The lower part of the fuel tank was designed to be incorporated into the upper part of the airbox. The basic change to the engine was to lengthen the stroke by 2 mm, to 66 mm, so that it could be homologated for the World Superbike series. Other changes were also designed to improve the potential of the bike as a racing machine. To allow for ease of removal of the rear wheel in endurance racing, a Honda-style single-sided swing-arm was used. A criticism of the 888/926, especially towards the end of its racing life, had been a lack of weight on the front wheel, so weight distribution was improved by canting the engine forward 1.5°, and shortening the bike by reducing the wheelbase to 1,410 mm (55.5 inches). The frame was made of thicker, 28 mm, tubing, with the swing-arm pivot now being supported by the frame as well as the engine cases. There was also provi-sion to alter the steering head angle from 23½° to 24½°, without altering the wheelbase. The 916 was displayed at the Milan Show in October 1993, where it caused a sensation, and was soon being developed for the 1994 World Superbike Championship.

In 1994 the 750 cc four-cylinder bikes received a weight reduction of 5 kg, to 160 kg (353 lb), so the gap between the fours and the twins was now only 15 kg (33 lb). With the prospect of increased competition from Honda's new fuel-injected RC45, the 916 was bored 2 mm to create a 955 cc version. As the racing department was limited in its ability to build a large number of these, only selected riders were to get the new 955. Virginio Ferrari (another ex-GP rider with a long association with Ducati) was now the team manager for Carl Fogarty and Giancarlo Falappa, and Fabrizio Pirovano was Davide Tardozzi's new rider. Other factory 955s went to James Whitham,

Carl Fogarty at Phillip Island, Australia, on his way to winning the World Superbike Championship in 1994. Carbon brakes were allowed this year.

riding for the British Moto Cinelli team, and occasional World Superbike rides to Troy Corser, the Australian 1993 Superbike Champion, now riding for Eraldo Ferracci in the US AMA Superbike series (on a 955 cc-engined 1994 Corsa). After Falappa injured himself badly while testing, Mauro Lucchiari replaced him in the Ferrari team.

A new type of 46 mm Öhlins upside-down fork was used, together with an Öhlins rear unit. The new airbox, with 58 mm intakes and larger valves of 37 mm and 31 mm, allowed the 955 engine to develop 150 bhp at 11,000 rpm. Titanium valves were tried, but were the cause of several engine failures throughout the season. The 955s also used titanium Pankl con-rods, and Omega 11.6:1 pistons. The weight was right on the minimum 145 kg, and 290 mm carbon front brakes were gripped by the latest type of Brembo racing calliper.

It was a lot to expect the new bike to be totally competitive immediately, and there were some initial problems in the handling department. Race results confirmed that the 955 still needed some development; winning just 12 out of the 22 World Superbike Championship races, it was nowhere near as dominant as in the past. However, some of this was probably due to injuries to Carl Fogarty and, more seriously, Giancarlo Falappa. By the end of the season most of the factory 955s had a 25 mm longer swing-arm, together with a different rear shock leverage ratio to improve rear-end traction. Fogarty received a special swing-arm, while lesser teams such as Moto Cinelli had to fabricate their own. Fogarty eventually came back from breaking his wrist at Hockenheim to win the World Superbike Championship with 10 victories. It had been an impressive debut season for the new 955.

Rather than using the new 916 as a basis, the 30 1994 Corsas owed much to the 1993 926 cc factory racer. As a thoroughly developed machine, this was still a surprisingly competitive piece of equipment, as was so ably demonstrated by Austrian rider Andreas Meklau with his two second place finishes at the Austrian round at Zeltweg. There were quite a few differences from the previous version, most noticeably the use of a 96 mm piston to give 926 cc. With a claimed 142 bhp at 11,500 rpm, the 926 used the lighter titanium Pankl con-rods, 1 mm larger inlet valve (37 mm), and new, stronger crankcases. The use of lighter Omega pistons and crankshaft assembly improved the response of the larger engine, overcoming criticisms of the past. The frame was altered too, with the steering head angle now 22½°, and the trail 102 mm (4.02 inches), and there were new Brembo P4.32-36 front brake callipers, with a 19 mm master cylinder, together with thinner discs. At the rear no torque-arm was now fitted, and other changes mirrored those of the factory 926 of 1993, including a new airbox and larger-bored exhaust, 42 mm Öhlins suspension and steering damper, a new crankcase breather and tank, and five-spoke Marchesini wheels with rim sizes of 3.50 x 17 and 6.00 x 17. The final version of the old design may have been overshadowed in 1994 by the 916 and 955, but it was still a very impressive racing motorcycle, and one that could be purchased by privateers.

When the 916 was released in early 1994, it received incredibly favourable press reports and, as in the past, a Sport Production version was made available. By 1992, with the 888/851, the Strada and SP lines had become quite diverged, but in 1993 the gap had closed again as the SP5 had not received the racing Öhlins front forks. With the 916 the gap closed even more: there was virtually no difference in weight, and while the SP made higher rpm horsepower, at the expense of the lower end, the performance differential was nowhere near as great as it had been between 1990 and 1992. The 916SP had the same higher-specification engine of the SP5, still with twin injectors per cylinder, and the same valve sizes of 34 mm and 30 mm, together with the titanium Pankl con-rods of the Corsa. With 11.2:1 compression, the claimed power was up to 131 bhp at 10,500 rpm (at the crankshaft). The titanium con-rods (still with a length of 124 mm) allowed the maximum engine rpm to be increased to an impressive 11,500. Unlike the previous SP, the 916 version used the 350-watt alternator of the Strada, and no longer had the close-ratio gearbox.

The chassis was also identical to the 916 Strada, except for the use of an Öhlins DU3420 rear shock absorber. All the bodywork, together with wheels and front suspension, was the same, and there was no carbon-fibre airbox as was initially indicated, the carbon-fibre parts being limited to the front and rear guards, chain-guard, and the Termignoni mufflers. The SP had adjustable brake and clutch levers, but the frame was identical to the Strada, down to the aluminium sub-frame, an item previously reserved for the SP series only. While the claimed dry weight was 192 kg (423 lb), the German magazine PS, in their test of August 1994, weighed their bike at 207 kg (456 lb). Their 916SP also reached 259 km/h (161 mph). As with previous SPs, the 916SP had the fully floating iron 320 mm front discs, and a white number patch on the seat.

The 916 Strada, released at the Milan Show in October 1993, was the most significant new model Ducati since the 851 (even more so than the Supermono a year earlier). While the engine was not very different from previous versions, the 916 was designed as a total package, with, for perhaps the first time at Ducati, an attempt to make the bike easy to service. The front forks were 43 mm Showa GD051, supported in a massive 80 mm steering head, with especially sturdy triple clamps. Everywhere there was the most spectacular attention to detail, from the machining of the top triple clamp with its steering damper, to the levers and controls. The wheels, shared with the SP, were three-spoke Brembo in sizes of 3.50 x 17 and 5.50 x 17, mounted with either Pirelli or Michelin tyres, the rear a larger 190/50-ZR17. Perhaps the weakest aspect in the 916 Strada specification was its Showa GD052-007-02 rear shock absorber, which was criticised for being under-damped.

In the engine department the 916 Strada was a combination of the 888

Strada and SP, having the external oil-cooler and the Pankl (non-titanium) con-rods. The clutch was the 15-plate 888 Strada type, as was the six-speed gearbox, and the camshafts were also the milder Strada, still with 33 mm and 29 mm valves. With a single injector per cylinder, claimed power was 109 bhp at 9,000 rpm (or 114 bhp depending on the source), at the crankshaft. However, in reality the 916 was a considerably faster bike than its power figures would suggest. Improved aerodynamics over the 888, and a claimed dry weight of 198 kg (436 lb), saw the 916 Strada approach the performance of the much more highly tuned 888SP models: PS, in July 1994, saw 256 km/h (159 mph). The wet weight was 211 kg (465 lb). For an engine not that different from the 888 Strada, the 916 Strada produced considerably more power, 104.3 bhp at 9,000 rpm on *Cycle World*'s dyno in July 1994. They also managed a standing quarter mile time of 10.72 seconds at 130.62 mph (210 km/h), figures approaching that of the 888 Sport Production. The 916 won every 'Bike of the Year' award in 1994, but *Motorcyclist* magazine in the US summed it up in their test of September 1994: 'The essence of the new 916 is its intoxicating blend of sound, looks, feel and the way it turns street riding into an almost religious experience.'

While most of the attention was centred on the 916, the 888 Strada also continued to be offered as a 1994 model, alongside the 888LTD for the US market. The 100 examples of the 888LTD were built in September 1993, prior to the commencement of the production of the 916, and each was fitted with an identification plaque, like the earlier Sport Production series. While they had carbon-fibre mudguards, much of the LTD was the same as the 888 Strada, including the engine, bronze-painted wheels, larger-diameter (25 mm) front axle, and black anodised foot-peg brackets and controls. The LTD retained the SPO's Öhlins rear shock absorber with eccentric ride height adjustment, and made 95.8 bhp at 9,000 rpm, at the rear wheel, on *Cycle World*'s dyno in June 1994. This was enough to propel it to a top speed of

157 mph (252.6 km/h), and through a standing quarter mile in 10.81 seconds at 128.02 mph (206 km/h). The 888LTD also convincingly won *Cycle World*'s comparison with its four-cylinder Japanese opposition.

The final 888 Strada also received the bronze wheels and larger-diameter front axle, together with braided steel front brake lines. Some testers claimed that this final version was the best of all the Stradas, but it was over-shadowed by the 916.

1995

For the 1995 season the minimum weight was increased by 2 kg (4.4 lb) to 147 kg (323 lb) for twin-cylinder and 162 kg (356 lb) for four-cylinder bikes, still maintaining the 15 kg differential. However, with more development of the 955 cc factory racers over the winter, they immediately started to dominate the 1995 World Superbike Championship, so dominant in the first three rounds that the FIM increased the weights for twins for the fourth round at Monza to 155 kg (341 lb), and reduced the fours to 160 kg (352 lb). With Carl Fogarty and Mauro Lucchiari riding for Virginio Ferrari's Ducati Corse, there was also Alfred Inzinger's Austrian Promotor Team of Troy Corser and Andreas Meklau, managed by Davide Tardozzi. Additionally there was Fabrizio

Pirovano (Taurus Ducati), and ex-GP rider Pierfrancesco Chili riding the Team Gattalone's customer 955 Corsa. In the US former World 500 cc Champion Freddie Spencer rode the Fast by Ferracci 955 in the AMA series.

One of the most significant changes for 1995 was the controversial banning of carbon discs, so all the factory bikes now used 320 mm iron front Brembo discs. Winning 13 of the 24 races, Carl Fogarty dominated in a style reminiscent of Doug Polen in 1991, and he easily won the Championship from Troy Corser with four wins.

The 955 cc engine remained virtually unchanged apart from new valves, rockers, camshafts, and the occasional use of a 996 cc engine with 98 mm pistons. With more emphasis on reliability, the horsepower, according to Virginio Ferrari, was 141–145 at the rear wheel at 12,000 rpm. There were detail modifications to the rear suspension linkages and steering head angle, but generally the increase in weight hurt the lap times compared to the previous year. Ducati's big advantage was in their use of telemetry so that they could fine the suspension very quickly.

The customer 916 Racing was essentially the 955 cc bike that Fogarty had raced the previous year, and even as they came from the

Carl Fogarty totally dominated the 1995 World Superbike Championship on the 955 of Ferrari's Ducati Corse.

The 1995 955 racer was little changed from 1994.

factory they were competitive machines. With a total of 62 constructed, they even had to take over the new 748/916 production line to be completed. They had the 96 x 66 mm 955 cc engine that now produced a claimed 155 bhp at 11,500 rpm at the crankshaft. Though still using 37 mm and 31 mm valves, a new inlet camshaft, with 12 mm of valve lift, was fitted. The timing figures were inlet opening 31° before

top dead centre, and closing 78° after bottom dead centre. Now based on the 916, the weight was up considerably from the 1994 888 Racing at 154 kg (340 lb). The Öhlins forks were now the 46 mm upside-down type as used by the works bikes in 1994, together with an Öhlins DU3360 rear shock absorber. Compared to the street bikes the swing-arm was lengthened 10 mm, to make the wheelbase 1,420 mm (55.9 inches),

only 10 mm shorter than the 888 Racing. The brakes were of similar specification to the previous year, but for a smaller (24 mm) rear brake calliper.

The 916SP was largely unchanged for 1995, but for a strengthened frame, modified wiring, steel braided brake lines, and an extended carbon-fibre chain cover. As to be expected, the performance, too, was similar to 1994, with *PS* achieving 262 km/h (163 mph) from their test bike in August 1995. Two distinct models took the place of the Strada. Following what had happened in 1990, the Strada gained a dual seat, and lost the Pankl connecting-rods for the regular forged items. This new model was called the Biposto ('twin seat'), and with a steel rear sub-frame, dry weight was up to a claimed 204 kg (450 lb). Other changes with the Biposto included a revised Showa GD052-007-02 rear shock absorber, to allow for the extra weight of a passenger. As tested by *PS* in April 1995, the 916 Biposto was faster than the 1994 Strada, at 258 km/h (160 mph), but the wet weight was up to 217 kg (478 lb).

The 916 Senna was created in memory of the great Formula 1 racing driver Ayrton Senna, tragically killed at Imola shortly after approving the new bike on 7 March 1994. Using the 1994 Strada engine with the Pankl con-rods, together with SP bodywork, Öhlins rear shock absorber, brakes and carbon-fibre mufflers and clutch cover, each of the 300 Sennas came with a plaque on the top triple clamp, and they were painted grey with red wheels. They also came with a certification document, and, like all the Desmoquattros for 1995, had a revised CPU management system, the '1.6', adapted from an automotive single-point injection system.

The new model for 1995 was the 748. The Desmoquattro had started life in 1986 at the Bol d'Or as a 748, and this same size engine was used to make a new motorcycle eligible for the 600 Supersport class, where 750 cc twins were now allowed to compete against 600 cc fours. There were two versions of the 748, an SP and a Biposto, the SP being very similar to the 916SP, and the 88 x 61.5

Waiting for the race. The unbeatable combination of Fogarty and the 955 Ducati.

A 916 Senna at the factory during 1995.

mm engine produced 104 bhp at 11,000 rpm at the crankshaft. The cylinder heads were very similar to the 888 SP2 and 3, with the same camshafts and 33 mm and 29 mm valves. The throttle size was reduced from 50 mm to 44 mm, and unlike the 916SP the 748 used the close-ratio gearbox of the 888SP. The claimed dry weight for the 748SP was 200 kg (440 lb), and in many respects it shared components with the 916SP, such as the 320 mm fully floating iron Brembo front discs, steel brake lines, Öhlins rear shock absorber, and adjustable brake and clutch levers, but there were no carbon-fibre body parts and the con-rods were the regular forged type. There was also only a single fuel injector per cylinder, the 748SP using the Weber Marelli '1.6' CPU.

Only available in yellow, kits for three stages of racing uprating were available for the 748SP, but even in standard form it was an impressive performer for its displacement. Weighing in at 210 kg (463 lb) wet, *Motorrad* tested one in April 1995 and managed a top speed of 248 km/h (154 mph). In Supersport 600, the class for which the 748SP was intended, Michael Paquay was totally dominant and easily won this World Superbike supporting series. Serafino Foti rode another 748SP to second in the Championship.

The 748 Biposto was a derivative of the 916 Biposto. The engine and gearbox were similar to the 748SP, but with the Strada camshafts, so the power was slightly less – 98 bhp at 11,000 rpm at the crankshaft. There was no oil-cooler, but because of the dual seat dry weight was up to 200 kg (440 lb), and all the frame, wheels and brakes were shared with the 916 Biposto. As tested by *PS* in July 1995,

the 748 Biposto achieved 243 km/h (151 mph).

Supermono

When Ing. Fabio Taglioni drew his sketches for the 750 V twin Ducati in 1970, he basically formed the 90° twin out of two singles on a common crankcase. The single-cylinder engine had been the basis of most Ducatis, and virtually all their production bikes, from the time he joined Ducati in 1952, and it was easier to create the twin from existing designs. What happened then was quite unexpected. The twin completely took over from the single and within four years the overhead-camshaft bevel-gear Ducati single was dead. The era of the large-capacity bike was here and, despite the oil crisis of 1974, there was no longer any demand for the economical four-stroke single.

There had been a brief flirtation

In 1995 the 916 gained a dual seat and a smaller brother, the 748.

with a belt-driven overhead-camshaft single in the late 1970s with the Utah and Rollah, both based on the Pantah twin, but it was not until 20 years after Taglioni designed the 750 twin that Ing. Massimo Bordi drew up his idea of a modern single-cylinder engine. Whereas the twin had emerged from two singles, now the single emanated from the 90° twin. In essence the new engine was a twin without one cylinder. History had come full circle.

Fabio Taglioni made his 90° twin with the crank counterweights set at 100% of reciprocating and rotating weight, giving perfect primary balance, but with a secondary vibration at right angles balanced by the other piston. This was not possible with a normal single, as the heavier crankshaft counterweights would cause an imbalance when at right angles to the cylinder axis. So, when Massimo Bordi designed his single, he used the same balancing principle as in a 90° twin. The imbalance at right angles to the cylinder axis was thus balanced by a dummy piston, as in a twin. While this effectively reduced

vibration, there was also considerable friction generated by this piston, limiting power, so in its place Bordi fitted a lever pivoting on a pin fixed in the crankcase. This lever was then attached to the small end of the second con-rod. As unique as Taglioni's desmodromic valve gear, the phrase *doppia bielletta*, 'double con-rod', was coined to describe this balance system.

In much the same way that the 750 Twin owed much to the overhead-camshaft bevel-gear singles, the Supermono was closely related to the 851/888/916 Twin. Together with water-cooling, and the double-over-head camshaft four-valve desmod-romic cylinder head, the same Weber IAW Alfa/N fuel injection system was used, with twin injectors and 'P8' CPU as in the SP and Corsas.

By late 1990 the first engine had been tested. Using the lower half of an 851, and the 95.6 mm pistons from the 919 cc racer, together with a stroke of 68 mm, the displacement was 487 cc. Later prototypes used a slightly longer, 70 mm, stroke for 502 cc. There were several departures from the 851, the most important being the use of two plain main bear-ings, rather than the four-roller type. The main journal was 45 mm in diameter, allowing a more rigid crank-shaft, and the water pump was driven off the exhaust camshaft, rather than the camshaft drive shaft. This tidied the water plumbing, allowing the cylinder to sit more deeply into the crankcase, and with only the exposed portion water-cooled. The width of the engine could now be reduced, and there was a dry 180-watt alternator, incorporating the ignition pick-ups, on the left side of the engine. The intention was to use the Supermono as a test bed for improvements that would eventually find their way into the next generation of twins.

During 1991 development of the Supermono continued under the guidance of Claudio Domenicali and Luigi Mengoli, and by mid-1992 a Sounds of Singles racing version had been tested by Davide Tardozzi at Misano. The claimed power of this 502 cc prototype was 70 bhp at 10,500 rpm, and it had bodywork similar to the 1992 SP4. However, when the Supermono was finally displayed at the Cologne Show late in September 1992, it had stunning new bodywork by designer Pierre Terblanche. He had only received the bare chassis in July, and the result was unique, and would strongly influence the 916 a year later. The Supermono was the sensation of the IFMA Cologne Show of 1992.

When it finally went into limited production during 1993, the Supermono was a Sounds of Singles racer only with an individually numbered plaque, and constructed by the racing department. Like the 888 Corsas, only the highest-quality proprietary components were used. A lightweight (6 kg) tubular steel space-frame, not dissimilar to that of the 888, was used, constructed from ALS500, not 25 CrMo4 as with the 888. The swing-arm pivoted directly on the crankcases, and operated an Öhlins DU2041 shock absorber without any rising rate linkage, to reduce weight. The Öhlins shock was adjustable for ride height via an eccentric mounted on the chassis end, and was mounted horizontally for mass centralisation. The forks were 42 mm Öhlins, with magnesium triple clamps, almost identical to the 888 Corsa, with a steering head angle of 23°, giving 92 mm (3.62 inches) of trail. The Supermono was incredibly compact with its 1,360 mm (53.5 inches) wheelbase and 760 mm (29.9 inches) seat height, the wheelbase being 20 mm less than Bordi originally anticipated. More importantly, the weight distribution placed 54.5% on the front wheel. Marchesini three-spoke magnesium wheels in sizes of 3.50 x 17 and 5.00 x 17 were fitted, together with Brembo 280 mm fully floating iron front discs, and racing P4.30-34 callipers. At the rear was a 190 mm Brembo disc with a torque-arm attached to a carbon-fibre bracket. In order to keep the weight down to 122 kg (269 lb), every body part was made of carbon-fibre, including the computer housing, located, as with other Corsas, in front of the instruments. There was no rear sub-frame, the carbon-fibre seat fulfilling this function. The Supermono was a work of art, and looked just as good with the bodywork off.

The Supermono featured the magnificent styling of Pierre Terblanche.

When it finally went into production, the engine displaced 549 cc by using a 100 mm piston, still with the 70 mm stroke. Because of the *doppia bielletta*, two Pankl con-rods needed to be used, certainly adding to the cost and making the design less attractive for later mass-production. The more compact injector body had a single 50 mm venturi tapering to 47 mm at the throttle butterfly. The valve sizes were 37 mm and 31 mm, but the camshafts had much more radical valve timing than even the 888 Corsa. With the inlet valve opening at 53° before top dead centre, and closing 71° after bottom dead centre, and the exhaust valve opening 66° before bottom dead centre and closing 48° after top dead centre, valve overlap was a massive 137°. This was reflected in the running characteristics of the engine, which was unhappy under 4,000 rpm and best above 8,000 rpm, demonstrating the advantages of the *doppia bielletta* in allowing the engine to rev to 10,500 rpm without vibration. Intake valve lift was 11 mm, and exhaust lift 10.5 mm, and with 11.8:1 compression the power was 78 bhp at 10,000 rpm at the crankshaft.

For 1995, with a 102 mm piston giving 572 cc, the power was up to 81 bhp at 10,000 rpm and there were also new suspension and brakes. With the use of plain main bearings, oil pump flow was increased on the Supermono to 3.3 litres/minute every 1,000 rpm, from 2.6 l/min/1,000 rpm

on the twin, and as with the larger Corsas the engine side covers were magnesium, and the clutch cover carbon-fibre. The six-speed gearbox was unique to the Supermono, with closer ratios than any of the twins.

Because Bordi adopted the horizontal cylinder of the V twin, making the *doppia bielletta* out of the vertical cylinder, he rediscovered the benefits of a low engine pioneered by Moto Guzzi as long ago as 1921, and developed to its ultimate fruition by Ing. Giulio Carcano with his racing single-cylinder Guzzis. The 250s and 350s in particular were incredibly successful against larger, more powerful bikes by virtue of their superior agility, lighter weight, and better weight distribution. These bikes won eight 250 and 350 cc World Championships between 1949 and 1958, demonstrating the advantages of balance and finesse over sheer horsepower.

The Supermono also confirmed these benefits convincingly. At race tracks around the world Supermonos, with more like 62 bhp at the rear wheel (as on *Cycle World*'s dyno), consistently turn in lap times similar to 100-plus bhp 600 Super Sports. They have also proven to be exceptionally reliable, with brilliant handling. *Cycle World*, testing a Supermono in September 1993, managed a standing quarter mile in 11.44 seconds at 122.11 mph (196.5 km/h) with the single-exit Termignoni exhaust. Using the

Robert Holden, here at Phillip Island, Australia, rode this Supermono to second place in the Single Cylinder TT on the Isle of Man in 1994. He won on a similar machine in 1995.

optional twin-exit with a revised EPROM as supplied with each bike would have undoubtedly produced even more performance. Fully wet, their test bike weighed 301 lb (136.5 kg), and *Sport Rider* achieved a top speed of 144 mph (232 km/h) in April 1994.

In 1995 a Supermono followed earlier Ducati singles by winning the Single Cylinder TT on the Isle of Man. After finishing a close second in 1994, New Zealander Robert Holden took his Supermono to an easy victory with a fastest lap of 111.66 mph (179.7 km/h). Set to repeat the feat in 1996 on a 572 cc 1995-spec Supermono, Holden was tragically killed during TT Formula 1 practice on a 916 Corsa. In practice for the Singles TT he had set a time 6 mph faster than his nearest competitor. Holden's death resulted in immediate abandonment of Steve Wynne's Sports Motorcycles team for which he rode, a team that had enjoyed an association with racing Ducatis for many years, including Hailwood's 1978 TT Formula 1 victory.

While the few racing bikes that were built were initially meant to

herald a range of Supermono street bikes, nothing has transpired, although Massimo Bordi has indicated to me on several occasions that he would still like to see it in production, particularly in Super Sport form. I saw prototype air-cooled four-valve cylinder heads lying around the factory in 1993, but these have now been consigned to the museum. Looking closely at the engine, it is obvious that provision was made for an electric starter, and the cases are even drilled and tapped for a clutch cable. Still, there was no provision for the mounting of a sidestand on the engine cases and these will be redesigned if the bike does go into production. It also

Air-cooled four-valve cylinder heads photographed at the factory during 1993.

seems likely that the plain main bearings will return to the previous ball type. For now, the Supermono lives only as the racing bike, leaving the handful built as rare examples of a superb and fascinating motorcycle. With production only reaching about 50 bikes by mid-1995 (although about 80 engines had been built), another series of 20 was constructed at the end of that year. These had new numbered plaques indicating that they were from the 1995 series. As a finite item, the Supermono is the rarest of all current Ducatis.

In every respect, the Supermono represents the pinnacle of the Ducati philosophy created by Ing. Taglioni with the first desmodromic singles way back in 1956. Not content with mainstream solutions to solve a problem, Ducati have continued to be different, this time with the adoption of its unique balance system. In a manner reminiscent of earlier Ducatis, superior racetrack performance is achieved, not through sheer power, but through a more balanced overall package.

There is no doubt that since its purchase by Cagiva in 1985, Ducati has not only survived, but has prospered. Without Cagiva, Ducati would

Taking over where Ing. Taglioni left off: Massimo Bordi (left) and Claudio Domenicali (right).

have disappeared entirely, swallowed up within an Italian Government conglomerate. Unfortunately, ominous signs that not all was well started to appear during 1994 and 1995. Partially constructed bikes were to be seen at the factory waiting for delivery of components from outside suppliers. By 1996 there were waiting lists for all models all around the world. Fortunately, even though

Ing. Taglioni had now retired, the management was still dominated by engineers. Massimo Bordi was General Manager of Cagiva Motorcycles, and his protégé, Claudio Domenicali, operated the racing department. These three engineers represent the past, present and future of Ducati, and it was to be the engineers that would keep the company alive through its next crisis.

14.

American Buy-Out

To anyone wishing to purchase a new Ducati during 1996 it was obvious that there were some serious production problems at Bologna. Rather than an expected increase in production, it went down from 21,000 in 1995 to 12,500 in 1996. There was no doubt that Cagiva was in financial difficulties. Suppliers were not being paid and by 1996 Ducati were finding it difficult enough to maintain, let alone increase, production. There were waiting lists for all models, particularly the Desmoquattro.

1996

Production difficulties aside, the World Superbike racing programme continued to be well supported and given high priority. Fortunately the racing team operated as if the company's financial problems were of little consequence. The cost of running a racing team, even with high riders' salaries, was still far less than that of developing a new production motorcycle, and it was important for Ducati's profile to continue at the forefront of World Superbike. Following the dominance of the 955 during 1995, the FIM again increased the minimum weights for twins to the same as fours, at 162 kg (357 lb). After Fogarty had tested a prototype 996 cc engine at the first and final rounds of 1995, Claudio Domenicali and his racing department decided to use the full capacity limit allowed by the regulations. With 98 mm pistons, all engines would displace 995.8 cc. Again there were two factory-supported teams in World Superbike, Virginio Ferrari's

Ducati Corse, and Alfred Inzinger's Promotor. With Carl Fogarty moving to Honda, former World 250 cc champion John Kocinski was signed by Ferrari as his replacement; partnering him would be GP privateer Neil Hodgson. Troy Corser again rode for Promotor, his team-mate being the American Mike Hale, and as before the team was managed by Davide Tardozzi.

The season started extraordinarily well for Kocinski and Ducati Corse with Kocinski taking a double win at Misano. Troy Corser soon matched this with a double at Donington to create some rivalry between the two factory teams. To add further spice, Pierfrancesco Chili on the Pietro di

Gianesin-tuned Gattalone 955 was often faster than the factory bikes and won two races. However, there were problems within the Ferrari team. The relationship between Ferrari and Kocinski soured and by mid-season they were barely talking to each other. Unfortunately this affected the team's results and Kocinski did not dominate the series as many had initially expected. While still taking five victories, it was Corser with seven wins who eventually took the title. As they had for every year since 1990, Ducati won the Manufacturers' Championship.

The 996 cc bike still produced similar power to the previous 955, 157 bhp at 11,800 rpm, but had about

With Fogarty deserting Ducati for Honda, former Cagiva 500 cc rider John Kocinski inherited his berth in the Virginio Ferrari team. Although the season started well, it ended on a sour note.

12 bhp more at 8,500 rpm. Valve sizes were also unchanged at 37 and 31 mm, and as always there were new camshafts with revised rocker ratios. It translated to superior track performance, but at the expense of reliability. The problem now lay with the larger cylinders, which stretched the 916 engine cases to the limit. What had started with 92 mm pistons had been progressively enlarged to accept the new 98 mm Omega pistons. Not only did the bottom of the cylinder liner have a tendency to crack then break as it was too thin (only 1 mm), the engines were prone to failure after wheel-stands because of the sudden loss of oil pressure. This was a particular problem for Troy Corser, noted for both his wheel-stands and engine failures during 1996.

The throttle bodies increased in size to 54 mm with the larger engine (up from 50 mm in 1995), together with a larger airbox and radiator, and 54 mm diameter exhaust pipes. Elsewhere, because of the 7 kg weight increase, there was less need for religious weight saving, weight distribution being more important. The engine covers were no longer magnesium, and many of the fasteners were also steel rather than magnesium. The fuel pressure was increased from 4.5 to 5.0 bar with a new regulator. There was a new primary drive ratio of 32/59 (1.84:1), creating a hunting tooth to spread the load more evenly.

On the track, so good was the 1996 factory 996 racer that it could turn in lap times comparable to those of 500 cc Grand Prix bikes, despite a weight penalty of 32 kg and considerably less horsepower. At Donington in April, Troy Corser set an outright lap record of 1 min 33.470 sec, at an average speed of 154.950 km/h (96.281 mph). Lap times on other circuits were also similar to that of the 500s, a tribute to the development and balance of the factory 996. As usual Ducati contested the AMA Championship, this time with 1992 125 cc World Champion Alessandro Gramigni on the Fast by Ferracci bike; although he won two races, he did not figure in the final AMA Championship results. Ducati achieved similar results in the *Motor Cycle News* British Superbike Championship, Terry Rymer winning two races at Brands Hatch on the Old Spice Ducati 955, and ending up third in the title. It was a different story in Germany. Now the company's premier market, Ducati took the German Pro Superbike title with the Swede Christer Lindholm.

In the World Superbike support series, Supersport World Cup, the Ducati 748 once again exhibited its superiority. With increasing participation from both Italian and Japanese manufacturers, the status of this series was elevated. There were ten races, and former Yamaha World Superbike rider Fabrizio Pirovano on the Team Alstare Corona 748SP easily won with six victories.

The 916 Racing for 1996 featured few changes. As the weight had to be

Although it went to the final round, Troy Corser won the 1996 World Superbike Championship on the 996 cc Promotor Ducati.

increased to 162kg, the suspension was re-calibrated and thicker front discs fitted. The 46 mm Öhlins forks featured a top-out spring, and the Öhlins shock absorber had an aluminium casing with fast preload adjuster; shock travel was 65 mm. There were only some detail changes to the engine, and capacity was still 955 cc. The inlet camshaft was now from the factory 1995 racing bikes, and with 12 mm of inlet valve lift the 37 mm inlet valve opened 36° before top dead centre, closing 72° after bottom dead centre. Claimed power was 153 bhp at 11,000 rpm. A free-wheel clutch was fitted, together with a new exhaust system with 52 mm exhaust headers. Other revisions included an oil pump with an enclosed relief valve, and new timing belts. Larger front Brembo brake callipers, with 32 and 36 mm pistons, featured on the 916 Racing. Externally the only way to distinguish the Corsa from the previous year was the seat unit, now without an air intake to improve the visibility of the white number plate.

Despite some inside the factory wanting to discontinue it, the 916SP was again offered, now titled the SP3. While sold at a somewhat higher price than the regular 916, the Sport Production series always had a much higher engine specification and was considerably more expensive to

manufacture. It was not only the Pankl con-rods and special main bearings that set the SP apart from the Strada; it also received Corsa-style cylinder heads. To keep the cost down, there were fewer carbon-fibre body parts for 1996; neither the clutch cover nor exhaust pipe insulating panel were carbon-fibre. As with the earlier SP888s, a numbered plaque was now fitted to the top triple clamp. It was initially also intended to produce the Senna II during 1996, also with fewer carbon-fibre parts, and with yellow wheels to distinguish it from the Senna I. However, no Sennas were manufactured in 1996, probably as a result of that year's general production problems. The Senna would make a return during 1997.

The engine of the SP3 carried over from the previous year, still using the inlet camshaft and 34 and 30 mm valves developed on Raymond Roche's World Superbike racer of 1990. Unlike the other production Desmoquattros, the SP3 used twin injectors per cylinder and thus kept with the Weber Marelli 'P8' 1.8 CPU. As before the tubular steel frames were supplied by Cagiva Telaio, and constructed in ALS450, a similar material to that used on the Supermono.

To homologate the 955 Corsa for AMA Superbike racing, 50 955SPs

were also constructed during 1996 for the United States only. Regulations required that racers and production bikes must share the same engine capacity, so these SPs came with a 955 cc engine (with 96 mm pistons) and a special numbered plaque. While essentially similar to the 916SP3, they were easily recognisable by the white front number plate and 955 fairing decals. With so few constructed it could have been a collector's item, but was soon superseded by the 996SPS.

The 916 and 748SP and Biposto were virtually identical to 1995. They received the quieter clutch with sound-absorbing clutch cover, shared with the Super Sport and Monster, and also adjustable-ratio clutch and brake master cylinders. With the total production pre-sold there was really no reason to change what had become a thoroughly well-developed product. As with the Super Sport, US 916s differed from those for the rest of the world. There was no Biposto for America, the solo-seat 916 Strada also receiving the Öhlins rear shock absorber of the SP3. Only in Australia were there problems with the unique 916 headlights; difficulties with compliance with Australian Design Rules saw all 916s and 748s fitted with exceptionally ugly square headlights. There was no easy solution to this, and these revised upper fairings were still being fitted two years later in 1998.

Other models also continued into 1996 virtually unchanged: the 600 Super Sports in 33 and 53 bhp versions, the 750 Super Sport, and the 900 Super Sport and Superlight. They all looked visually identical, although the 600 Super Sport received a stainless steel two-into-one exhaust system, the 750 sound-absorbing panels, and the 900 a sound-deadening clutch cover. The 400 Super Sport also made a return, but only for the domestic market, and 200 were manufactured. As before, the 900CR and 900SS SP were still produced for the United States, and a limited number of Superlights made. Every year there were fewer Superlights, with only 300 in 1996, considerably down on the massive 1,317 constructed during 1992.

The 916SP3 was visually identical to earlier 916SPs and offered similar performance. All came with optional carbon-fibre Termignoni mufflers.

Undoubtedly the limited edition concept had been over-used by Ducati with the Superlight; unlike the 916SP it offered no performance advantages over the standard bike and consequently was difficult to sell against the standard 900SS. The unchanged nature of the Super Sport line for 1996 indicated that it was nearing the end of its life, and total production was considerably reduced from 1995, with only 2,791 Super Sports built during 1996. Not all this decreased production was due to reduced demand, overall production being considerably reduced that year.

For 1996 the M900 finally received fully adjustable forks, now Marzocchi rather than Showa. All Monsters also had the choke mounted on the handlebar, a vacuum-operated fuel tap, rubber footrests, and the sound-deadening timing belt covers. As the M900 shared its engine with the 900SS, it also featured a sound-absorbing clutch cover. Colours were as before: red, black and yellow. The 750 Monster that had been displayed at the Milan Show at the end of 1995 was the only additional model for 1996. It was essentially a single-disc-brake 600M with non-adjustable front forks fitted with an air/oil-cooled 64 bhp 750 Super Sport engine. As with the 600, the rear wheel was an MT 4.50 x 17. Performance of the M750 was increased significantly over the 600, *Motor Cycle News* managing a top speed of 124.8 mph (201 km/h) in their test during June 1996. As the weight for the silver M750 was only increased marginally to 176 kg (388 lb), it was possibly the best balanced of all the Monsters. Though only possessing a five-speed box, the 750 cc engine was also less snatchy than the 900. The M600 continued as before in 33 and 55 bhp versions, the only changes being those that appeared on all the Monsters for 1996.

There had also been plans to produce a Special Edition Monster 900 during 1996, but production problems meant that this did not emerge. Virtually identical to the 30 'Club Italias' of 1995, the Special Edition was displayed at the Milan Show of 1995 and also featured on

Still available with a half-fairing in 1996, the 900SS was a classic design.

the 1996 Monster brochure. Special parts included fully floating cast-iron front discs and rear brake arm, leather seat, remote reservoir master cylinders, and a small fairing. Also available were a special Police M600 and M900.

Early in 1996 there were many rumours of a buy-out of Ducati. Sam Zell, a Chicago financier and enthusiast, was linked with one take-over bid through the Zell Chilmark Fund. This foundered, and eventually a new company was created through a joint venture between the Texas Pacific Group, a group of investors led by Abel Halpern, and the Castiglioni brothers. A press release of 30 September 1996 stated that 'a company called Ducati Motor S.p.A. has acquired all the assets of Ducati motorcycles from the Cagiva Group'. The final terms were that the Castiglioni brothers maintained a 49% interest in the company, TPG another 49%, with 2% held in trust in an Italian bank. Claudio Castiglioni was still chairman of the new company. What also happened was that Ducati Motor was now independent of Cagiva, and that required Ducati to set up its own commercial and research and development departments.

The transaction was facilitated by Deutsche Morgan Grenfell, who engaged Bain & Company as consultants to assess Ducati and its potential for investment. Bain then sent

Federico Minoli and a team of ten experts to study the company. Minoli was an inspired choice, as he was an Italian based in America. Hailing from Varese where Cagiva were located, he also possessed more than a passing interest in motorcycles. In his youth he had owned a Ducati Scrambler, then a Moto Guzzi before crashing it and retiring from bikes for a few years. Now he is back on an ST2 and his sister rides a 600 Monster. So impressed was he with Ducati that in April 1997 Minoli accepted the position as CEO of Ducati Motor.

Though TPG had no previous association with motorcycles, they had a strong background in rebuilding under-capitalised companies, their purchase and subsequent turnaround of the Texas-based Continental Airlines being a particular success story. With TPG's stated intention of listing Ducati Motor on the New York Stock Exchange, there was some apprehension among traditional Ducati enthusiasts. What the TPG interest initially meant was that there was an immediate increase in production as suppliers could be paid. However, it also signified a change in direction of the company, one aimed at creating a specialised niche market. The only way to make Ducati more profitable was to increase production to a projected 40,000 by the turn of the century, so to sell considerably more than the projected 1997 figure of

27,000 motorcycles an even larger market needed to be created. While many enthusiasts were initially sceptical about American involvement in a traditional Italian company, at least the company survived. More importantly, to expand the customer base TPG began to recognise the significance of racing and racing history as a marketing tool. What had always been a secret jewel for a limited number of enthusiasts worldwide was about to be unleashed on a wider market.

1997

While the company was in the middle of a managerial upheaval, the World Superbike racing programme continued largely unabated during 1997. Virginio Ferrari very enthusiastically welcomed Carl Fogarty back into his ADVF Team, still with Neil Hodgson. Ferrari no longer had outside sponsorship from Kremlyovskaya vodka, the Ducati factory now funding the team. Alfred Inzinger decided to take his Promotor team, and World Champion Troy Corser, off to the world of 500 cc Grand Prix racing, so Pierfrancesco

Chili and the Gattalone team inherited the spare factory-supported bike. Chili's tuner from the previous year, Pietro di Gianesin, had often produced embarrassingly fast bikes, so he was offered 748SPs to prepare for the World Supersport series.

In terms of racing results, 1997 was an indifferent year for Ducati. Now the stronger 996SPS crankcases had been homologated it was expected that the bikes would not only be totally reliable, but also fast. The wider SPS cylinder head studs meant thicker barrels, and 2 mm liners could now be used. The result was vastly improved reliability, but less satisfactory performance overall. For the first time in eight years Ducati failed to win the Manufacturers' Championship. Too many crashes by Fogarty also saw him lose the title to Kocinski, but he still won six races. Chili suffered some bad luck during the season, often being taken out by other riders, but managed to triumph in three races, including a brilliant ride in the wet at Misano.

The bike itself came under some particularly vocal criticism from

Fogarty, who claimed that he 'could win if he had his 1995 bike'. Unfortunately, the solution was less easy to find. The increase in weight to 162 kg had affected the weight distribution on the Ducati. New crankcases and frame were homologated with the 916SPS, and in the process the balance of the bike was altered. As Virginio Ferrari said, 'We lost the harmony between the engine and chassis.' The throttle bodies increased in size to a massive 60 mm, certainly creating a noticeable power increase but giving problems with the smoothness of the delivery. On the track it translated into lap times that were no better than in 1995, the problem being that the increase in weight had not been easy to incorporate into the 916 design.

Other changes for 1997 included a redesigned carbon-fibre fuel tank, increased in size from 23 to 24 litres, and new first and second gears; these had a slightly lower ratio than before, first at 1.88:1 and second at 1.57:1, giving the gearbox a wider spread to suit the larger engine. The 46 mm Öhlins forks had 5 mm more wheel

Back once again on the Ducati, Carl Fogarty struggled all year, eventually finishing second in the 1997 World Superbike Championship.

Though beset with handling and power delivery problems, the 1997 996 racer was still a magnificent motorcycle. The fuel tank was slightly larger, and reshaped.

travel (125 mm) with wider spacing to help cool the thicker brake discs. These were sometimes reduced in size to 290 mm, the smaller discs helping the bike to turn more quickly. Rear rim size decreased slightly from 6.00 x 17 to 5.75 x 17.

In the AMA Championship the former Cagiva 500 cc rider, Australian Matthew Mladin, rode the Fast by Ferracci 996, winning four races. However, this was not enough to win the Championship and Mladin finished third. Former champion Thomas Stevens rode for the newly formed Vance & Hines team. Again the *Motor Cycle News* British Superbike Championship was disappointing for Ducati; although taking two victories, John Reynolds on the Reve Red Bull 996 finished fourth. Ian Simpson, also on a Red Bull 996, won one race, as did Sean Emmett on the Groundwork South East Ducati. Only in the Supersport World Cup was the Desmoquattro victorious. Now with television coverage, this series continued to grow. Eleven races

were held in 1997, nine in Europe and two in Asia (Japan and Indonesia). As with World Superbike, the Ducatis were no longer as dominant, and the overall result was not decided until the final

race. This time Paolo Casoli on the Gia.Ca.Moto. 748SP, with three race wins, was triumphant by 1 point over the Yamaha-mounted Vittoriano Guareschi. So competitive was this class of racing during 1997 that these

Paolo Casoli took the Gia.Ca.Moto. 748SP to victory in the 1997 Supersport World Cup.

were the only two riders to win more than one race.

As expected, the 916 Racing for 1997 incorporated many of the improvements that had appeared on the factory racers during 1996. Within the engine there was an increase in displacement to 996, and the new crankcases with wider cylinder head studs homologated with the 916SPS. Compression with the 98 mm pistons was increased slightly from 11.8:1 to 12:1, and claimed power was also marginally higher at 155 bhp at 11,000 rpm. While the valve sizes were unchanged, as was the inlet camshaft, there was a new exhaust camshaft. The timing figures were now exhaust opening 69° before bottom dead centre and closing 47° after top dead centre; valve lift was still 10.5 mm. In line with the 1996 factory bikes there were now 54 mm exhaust pipes, and an increase in fuel pressure to 5.0 bar via a pressure regulator. The primary drive was also changed to the 32/59 of the 1996 racers.

Other changes also reflected the continual development of the factory bikes. The airbox had a greater capacity and was fed by a larger air intake in the fairing. Smaller changes were evident throughout the motorcycle: a larger oil radiator, thicker front brake discs, a new rear wheel hub assembly, and new attachments for the handlebars. While 46 mm Öhlins front forks were still used, the triple clamps now had adjustable offset. Thus while the trail was previously 97 mm, this could now be adjusted within a range of 96.6–109.2 mm. With a new Öhlins rear shock absorber, rear shock travel was increased from 65 to 74 mm, translating into 136 mm of rear wheel travel.

Perhaps the most important new model for 1997 was the 916SPS. This was intended as a very limited production motorcycle alongside the 916SP, purely to homologate the new crankcases for World Superbike and FMI Sport Production. However, there was more to the SPS than merely new crankcases and larger pistons, as 36 mm inlet valves (up from 34 mm) were used, together with new inlet and exhaust camshafts. With 10.8 mm of inlet valve lift, the valve opened 14° before top dead

centre and closed 73° after bottom dead centre. The exhaust valve now opened 57° before bottom dead centre, closing at 23° after top dead centre with 9.8 mm of valve lift. The compression ratio was marginally increased to 11.5:1 and claimed power was up to 134 bhp at 10,000 rpm. The gearbox ratios for third, fourth, fifth and sixth gears were also altered for the SPS, being shared with the 748BP and SP. The SPS also received the new primary drive gears (32/59) of the 916 Racing and the same titanium con-rods. Unlike the single-injector Desmoquattros, the SPS continued with the Weber Marelli 'P8' CPU, but the throttle bodies remained at 50 mm.

Visually similar to the 916SP, and sharing the chassis and running gear, the 916SPS had all the performance equipment associated with limited-edition Sport Production Ducatis: cast-iron fully floating 320 mm front brake discs with steel brake lines, Öhlins shock absorber, and larger-diameter exhaust pipes with carbon-fibre leg-shields. All 916SPSs came with carbon-fibre Termignoni mufflers and an alternative chip. Continuing a trend started back in 1974 with the 750 Super Sport, the 916SPS was the standard by which all sporting motorcycles were judged. It was also the fastest Ducati to date, the Italian magazine *Motociclismo* in April 1996 managing a top speed of 270.1 km/h (168 mph) in standard form, or 275.4 km/h (171 mph) with the performance kit that included the Termignoni mufflers and revised computer chip. Horsepower, too, was impressive: 122.59 bhp at 9,500 rpm, increasing to 124.35 bhp at 9,500 rpm with the performance kit. In production racing the 916SPS was immediately competitive, winning the production race at the North West 200 and coming second on the Isle of Man. Unanimously named 'Bike of the Year' by magazines around the world, it was initially intended to continue the 916SP alongside the SPS, but demand for the latter was so strong that it soon replaced the smaller bike. Rather than a proposed production series of only 200, nearly 800 916SPSs were built during 1997. With the injection of capital from

TPG, overall production was significantly increased during the year, 8,500 Hypersport 916/748s being constructed.

After a hiatus during 1996, the 916 Senna was again produced as a limited edition of 350 during 1997. As in 1995, the Senna had red wheels and steel grey bodywork, although this time a lighter colour than before. No Sennas were produced with the yellow wheels intended for the 1996 version. Although it had the Öhlins shock absorber, fully floating cast-iron brake rotors and a carbon-fibre front mudguard, the Senna retained the standard 916 engine of the Biposto and Strada. All Sennas came with a numbered plaque on the top triple clamp, but suffered in much the same way as the 900 Superlight. For a premium price they offered no performance advantage over a standard bike and too many were built for them to qualify as a very limited edition.

The 916 Strada and Biposto continued essentially unchanged – why alter something that was so successful and desirable? Even with an increase in production there were insufficient to satisfy demand. The US still received a solo-seat 916 with an Öhlins shock absorber, but it was otherwise identical to the European Biposto. There were also no changes to the 748SP and 748 Biposto. Only available in yellow, the former was manufactured in similar numbers to the 916SPS, but with fewer special parts. At the Cologne Show of 1996 a hybrid 748S was displayed. This red solo-seat 748 used the standard 748 Biposto engine (without oil-cooler) in a 748SP chassis. It never made it to the production line.

Now into its seventh year of production, the Super Sport was starting to look a little dated. For several years there had been talk of a replacement, but the financial difficulties of 1995 and 1996 had meant further delays to this project. With a new commitment to the Super Sport line, the specification was upgraded for 1997 in order to maintain sales. Overall Super Sport sales had been falling from a high of 8,545 in 1992, and while 3,741 were built in 1997 (plus 500 1998-model Final

Editions), numbers were well down on those of the Hypersport and Monster. The Superlight was no longer offered, and most of its special features made their way to the 900 Super Sport.

Although now at the end of its production run, the Super Sport for 1997 was a thoroughly developed machine. In 900 guise especially it offered a number of more appealing features over the earlier models. The engine specifications of all Super Sports were unchanged except for bimetallic inlet and exhaust valves to better suit unleaded fuel. The oil radiator on 750s and 900s was now mounted above the front cylinder, similar to that of the Monster, and a heating kit was installed on all front carburettors to minimise icing in cold weather, which had always been a problem on Mikuni-carburetted models because of their long inlet tracts.

As there was no Superlight offered for 1997, the 900 Super Sport received the fully floating rear brake and carbon-fibre front mudguard. There were also steel brake and clutch lines for Europe, and adjustable brake and clutch levers. The clutch cover was grey, and standard equipment included Michelin Hi-Sport tyres. Offered in red or yellow, the 900 Super Sport shared its

new bodywork with the 750 and 600 Super Sport; the fairing had revised graphics, with an air intake and internal sound-absorbing panels. Other improvements for 1997 were the increased steering lock to 28° either side, and a more comfortable seat. Cosmetic changes included anodised aluminium footrest plates.

With unchanged specifications, the 900 Super Sport continued to offer a balanced package with the less extreme riding position of the Hypersports 916/748, and for many it still offered enough performance. The Italian magazine *Super Wheels* of March 1997 managed 220.856 km/h (137 mph) with a standing 400 metres at 11.777 seconds at 182.426 km/h (113 mph). Significantly, however, the measured dry weight was 189.8 kg (418 lb). The gradual development of the Super Sport over a seven-year period had also seen it become a thoroughly refined sporting motorcycle, without the demands placed on the rider by the race replica Hypersports. It still appealed to those who wanted a simpler, lighter sports bike, without a racetrack orientation. Unfortunately the market also perceived the Super Sport to be old-fashioned; just as had happened with the earlier bevel-gear Super Sport, Ducati had let what was once their once most successful model run too

long and sales were suffering as a result. It was not really a case of the motorcycle being obsolete, but more the continual emphasis placed by the press on new products. Also the Super Sport was coming under increasing pressure in the marketplace from the Honda VTR1000F and Suzuki TL1000S 90° V twins. These new bikes were priced in Super Sport territory but offered more performance, albeit without the character and breeding of the Ducati model.

For the United States there was once again the 900 Super Sport SP and CR. As the regular Super Sport for Europe incorporated most of the previous Superlight features, the SP now only differed in the use of the fully floating Brembo cast-iron front brake discs, carbon-fibre rear mudguard, and numbered plaque. US bikes did not receive the steel brake lines. The 900CR continued as before, still essentially a 900 engine in a 750 Super Sport chassis. Although only 60 750 Super Sports had been manufactured during 1996, production was back to reasonable levels in 1997, and 1,146 were built. As with the 900, the oil-cooler was mounted in an upper position, and all the alterations to the steering lock, valves, carburettor heating kit, fairing, seat, and graphics also made it to the 750. The 600 Super Sport also continued, again incorporating these changes, and all Super Sports were available in yellow or red.

Of all the existing models, the M900 Monster came in for the most modifications during 1997. Previous 900 Monsters had shared engines with the Super Sport, but now the 900M received a de-tuned engine to improve low-down power, better suiting its role as a city bike. The 900 engine had always been slightly unhappy running below 3,000 rpm, so to help cure this the cylinder head received smaller valves, now 41 and 35 mm, and there were new camshafts. New and much more sophisticated computer programs that came with the TPG involvement now enabled the development department to design desmodromic camshafts much more quickly. Whereas in the past there had only been a few desmodromic camshaft

In its final year, the classic Super Sport featured some significant revisions, noticeably fairing air scoops and new graphics. Here is a 900 with a 750 behind.

profiles, 1997 saw a range of camshafts for different models. The M900 in this lower state of tune now had a camshaft that opened the inlet valve 12° before top dead centre, closing it 70° after bottom dead centre. The exhaust valve opened 56° before bottom dead centre, closing 25° after top dead centre. Valve lift was unchanged at 11.76 mm and 10.56 mm respectively. Claimed power was reduced to 77 bhp at 7,000 rpm, but more significantly the lobe centres of the camshaft were retarded for better low-down power characteristics. Other engine changes from the Super Sport were carried through to the new M900 engine: sintered steel valve seats and bimetallic inlet and exhaust valves for better compatibility with unleaded fuel, and the carburettor heating kit to prevent icing.

Complementing the lower state of tune on the M900 was a new Kokusan ignition system and revised jetting for the Mikuni 38 mm carburettors. Elsewhere the specifications were unchanged, except for the small front fairing that had featured on the projected Special Edition Monster of 1996. Colours for the M900 of 1997 were black or red. As expected, ultimate performance was reduced with the lower-tuned engine, the 1997 M900 managing a top speed of 196.3 km/h (122 mph) in a test by *Motociclismo* in April 1997; earlier M900s had achieved around 206 km/h (128 mph). *Cycle World*, when testing an M900 in November 1997, found it also to be slightly slower over a standing quarter mile at 11.98 seconds at 108.53 mph (175 km/h).

An M900 Solo with front cast-iron disc brake rotors and a single seat was also intended for 1997. Displayed at the Cologne Show in 1996, as with the Special Edition of a year earlier it was not put into production due to negative dealer response. This M900 Solo was almost identical to the M900 Police, which also had a solo seat. The silver M750 and red and yellow M600s continued as before.

To help promote the Monster in Italy, Ducati supported the 'Ducati Monster Cup 97'. Organised by Techna Racing in Rome, six races were held, with identical Gia.Ca.Moto. M900s being allocated

by lot for the series. The yellow racing Monsters had a solo seat, belly-pan, and 916-style Gianelli exhausts. Monsters had always been particularly popular in Italy, and the strength of the local market saw Monster production outstripping both the Hypersport and Super Sport, with 10,000 units in 1997.

Although it was originally intended to release it during 1996, the ST2 was also delayed due to the production difficulties experienced by the company that year. First displayed at the Cologne Show at the end of 1996, the ST2 was Ducati's first exploration of the sport-touring category since the 907IE of 1991–92. Historically this had not been the most successful area for Ducati as it meant competing directly with the Japanese. The company's past was littered with some rather dismal forays into this area, the 860GT and Paso in particular. While some other examples were excellent motorcycles, notably the 750GT, Darmah and 907IE, after initial success they never achieved the sales that were expected. Many of the earlier attempts at sport-touring motorcycles had suffered particularly from poor reliability and incomplete development. Early reports suggested that the ST2 was a finely developed machine, but still had considerable competition.

One of TPG's objectives was to expand into wider market segments, and the ST2 fitted this bill comfortably. With progress already well advanced by the time of the merger with Cagiva, it took only a short time to construct another assembly line for the ST2. Production began in April 1997, and during that year 4,300 ST2s were manufactured.

Development of the ST2 was facilitated by utilising as many existing parts as possible. Thus the basic frame was from the Monster (originally 851/888) constructed of ALS450, in concert with a swing-arm with a 916-style linkage. The 43 mm Showa front forks were also similar to the 916, but with more fork travel (130 mm), as was the new-generation Brembo front wheel. With 24° of fork rake and 102 mm of trail, steering was quicker than the earlier 907. Latest-specification Brembo brake callipers were also employed, with revised internal fluid passages and wider bolt spacing to increase rigidity. These brake callipers would find their way to other models during 1998.

Styled by Miguel Galluzzi (who was also responsible for the Monster) at Cagiva Morizone, the ST2 incorporated many features expected of sport-touring motorcycles of the late 1990s. Notable features were the aspherical

The first sport-touring Ducati since the 907IE, the ST2 was eminently equipped for two-up intercontinental touring. Standard equipment included panniers.

rear-view mirrors, and an instrument panel that incorporated a digital display for fuel consumption, fuel reserve, time, and water temperature. The entire layout of the cockpit, with the ignition key on the fuel tank and cast handlebars, gave the ST2 a look of integrated design that was new to Ducati in the sport-touring segment. Complementing its status as a long-distance machine, the ST2 came with matching panniers from Nonfango, and exhaust pipes that could be adjusted for increased ground clearance. During 1997 the ST2 came in red, silver and black.

In the engine department the ST2 took over where the 907IE had left off. The basic six-speed, two-valve, water-cooled engine was inherited from the 907, but a 2 mm bore increase to 94 mm took the displacement out to 944 cc. Compression, too, was increased on air-cooled 900s to 10.2:1. The ST2 also received new camshafts, not only with different timing, but also increased valve lift. The inlet valve opened 26° before top dead centre, closing 72° after bottom dead centre, with 11.8 mm of valve lift. The exhaust valve opened 61° before bottom dead centre, closing 34° after top dead centre, with 11.4 mm of maximum valve lift. The six-speed gearbox was carried over, but the ST2 had the revised primary gears of the Corsa and SPS (32/59). The Weber Marelli electronic fuel injection used a 40 mm throttle body and the '1.6' CPU of other single-injector Ducatis.

Although no lightweight at a claimed 212 kg (467 lb), the measured wet weight was closer to 234 kg (515 lb) as tested by *Cycle World* in December 1997. However, the ST2 was a surprisingly strong performer for this type of motorcycle. Although power was only 83 bhp at 8,500 rpm, *Cycle World* achieved a standing quarter mile in 11.81 seconds at 113.10 mph (182 km/h). Top speed was 136 mph (219 km/h). These were very similar figures to the significantly lighter 900 Super Sport, indicating that the ST2 was not only more powerful, but possessed excellent aerodynamics.

Undoubtedly a highly competent long-distance motorcycle in the best European tradition, there is still a question mark over how successful Ducati will be with this new attempt at the Sport Touring market. History tells us that it is an area where the company has always struggled. Perhaps the ST2, and the forthcoming ST4, will succeed where other models have failed.

1998

The affect of the TPG buy-out really became noticeable during 1998. The workforce increased to 714 employees, 434 in production and the remaining 280 in sales, research and administration. During 1997 the personnel had numbered 550, with 280 in production. Increased investment (30 billion lire by 1998) had seen new CNC machines installed and 30 CAD stations in the engineering department, as production moved from labour-intensive to capital-intensive. More components were sourced outside, leaving heat-treatment, finishing and engine assembly the primary processes now undertaken within the factory. While the existing motorcycles continued with only minor developments, there was a new emphasis on marketing and expanding the customer base. Thus not only were there more variations on the four themes, but TPG wanted to create a sport performance experience for Ducati owners in a manner similar to that of the Harley-Davidson lifestyle. Reflecting the increase in production was a huge increase in turnover, from 200 billion lire in 1996 to an estimated (by early 1998) 400 billion lire in 1997.

Central to TPG's plan was also a new logo and corporate identity. The previous logo had come with Cagiva in 1986 and TPG needed to create a fresh image. Ducati approached Massimo Vignelli, a leading American graphic designer responsible for corporate logos for Bloomingdales and American Airlines. Vignelli delved into the past to create a new logo that recalled the clean lines of the graphics on the 1972 Imola racers. A new symbol was also created alongside the logo; suggesting a spinning bike wheel, this came directly from the classic eagle logo of the overhead camshaft singles of the early 1960s. This interest in an association with past success would play an important role in TPG's vision for the future of Ducati.

While other great Italian marques, notably MV Agusta and Moto Guzzi, were well known for their museums and maintaining their history, Ducati itself did not have a museum, and until Cagiva bought the company in 1985 all important racing machines had either been sold or destroyed. Thus the factory had lost the racing heritage of the 1950s, '60s and '70s. Many of the most significant bikes had survived in private hands, but many more were lost. Part of TPG's plan was to create a 10,000 sq ft museum on the first floor of the factory at Borgo Panigale, but the difficulty was in reclaiming some of the earlier bikes. It was not only racing machines either – there were also few examples of street bikes from the pre-Cagiva era. Fortunately most of the prototypes that had not made the production line had not been destroyed.

Charged with creating primarily a racing museum, Marco Montemaggi worked hard at persuading collectors in Italy to lend significant racing machines to the museum for its opening in June 1998. Noted restorer Primo Forasassi was also employed to restore some of the important exhibits. The museum was eventually to be linked with the Ferrari museum at nearby Maranello, emphasising not only an underlying connection with Ferrari, but also the strong Emilia Romagna engineering tradition. Coinciding with the opening of the museum was the first World Ducati Weekend, held from 12–14 June 1998 at Misano, Rimini and Bologna.

It was obvious that TPG was now committed to raising the profile of Ducati beyond its previous boundaries. One way of doing this was by creating a special-edition silver 748L (with carbon-fibre front mudguard and chainguard) to be sold through the prestigious Neiman Marcus catalogue for men in the United States. Only 100 were available, and with a Donna Karan New York leather jacket and Dainese gloves provided, this became the first mail-order Ducati. Complementing this new marketing move was the opening of monofranchised flagship Ducati Stores, the first, along 'Gasoline Alley' in Manhattan, opening in March 1998. These 300 sq m superstores were designed by the US-based architectural studio Gensler in conjunction with Bologna architect Michele Zacchiroli. Offering accessories and an Internet site, they certainly represented a totally new direction for Ducati, and one that was not entirely welcomed by the traditional enthusiast. Other stores soon opened in various Italian cities – Bologna, Florence, Rome, Milan, Genoa, Savona, Treviso and Turin – followed by an Australian flagship store in Sydney.

One of the strongest product lines in the new Ducati Store was Ducati Performance. Formed in December 1996 as a joint venture between Gia.Ca.Moto. and Ducati Motor, it was established by September 1997. With the intention of developing new performance products with Ducati and using the same suppliers as that of original equipment, Ducati now hoped to also capture a large slice of the lucrative performance market. The Ducati Performance catalogues covered all models in the line-up, and included chassis as well as engine parts. Another new product line was that of official apparel; an agreement with the Vicenza-based Dainese company provided a range of high-quality leather racing clothing, and also available was a limited range of other lifestyle sportswear. Future developments in the accessory and performance sphere lay in specialised performance shops where customers could have their motorcycles modified with factory back-up.

Having lost the World Superbike Championship in 1997, a concerted effort was made in 1998 to win again. While out to make a profitable company, TPG realised the importance of racing, not only for product development, but also as a means of promotion. At the end of 1997 there had been some upheaval within the factory teams for World Superbike. Carl Fogarty wanted his own team and initially organised a one-rider team with a factory bike through Alstare with Corona sponsorship. In

the meantime Troy Corser was welcomed back by Ducati after a disappointing year in the 500 cc Grands Prix. After two poor seasons, Neil Hodgson lost his place in the Virginio Ferrari team, Pierfrancesco Chili inheriting that berth. When Fogarty's team failed to materialise, Ducati was left with a difficult situation. Both Corser and Fogarty were past World Champions, and to have them both in the same team would be undesirable. Another team needed to be formed for one of them. Fortunately a solution was found with the formation of Ducati Performance with Gia.Ca.Moto. Having just won the Supersport World Cup, Daniele Casolari's team was expanded to run a one-rider World Superbike factory bike alongside the Supersport 748SPS. With Davide Tardozzi as team manager, it was expected that Troy Corser would go with Gia.Ca.Moto., but surprisingly Carl Fogarty left the Virginio Ferrari camp

to a team where he was to be the sole rider.

There were some considerable changes to the factory racers for 1998. A new frame was homologated through the SPS and there were upgraded forks, brakes and rear suspension. For the engine there was a completely revised Weber Marelli engine management system developed for Formula 3 car racing. This MF3 type was reputed to operate 20 times faster than previously, with full connection to the telemetry system on the motorcycle. All the modifications were done to address the criticisms of the previous year, particularly in throttle response and handling.

As an American company, TPG was determined to win the AMA Series for 1998. Thus two teams of two riders were supplied with World Superbike-specification factory bikes. The Fast by Ferracci team fielded Mike Hale and Tom Kipp, while the West Coast-based Vance & Hines

After a disappointing season in 500 cc Grands Prix, 1998 saw Troy Corser back on a Ducati in World Superbike. This time he rode for Virginio Ferrari's Ducati Corse team.

had wild Australian Anthony Gobert joining Thomas Stevens. Future plans still called on contesting the World Endurance Championship. After winning the Supersport World Cup three years running, Ducati again supported Paolo Casoli on the Ducati Performance 748R, again managed by Stefano Caracchi.

Many of the detail improvements of the 1997 factory bikes made their way to the 916 Racing for 1998. Only 24 were built, the most significant changes being a new frame (shared with the 1998 factory bikes) and a magnesium swing-arm that lengthened the wheelbase 10 mm to 1,430 mm. The frame was TIG-welded in 25CrMo4, and while it looked identical externally, the tubes were thinner at 1.5 mm. There was also a new, lighter rear sub-frame. The front forks were similar to the 1997 factory bike and had the same axle lugs, and there was hydraulic adjustment for the preload for the rear Öhlins shock absorber. The shape of the carbon-fibre fuel tank was altered to mirror the factory racers and capacity increased by 1 litre to 24 litres. While the thicker 320 mm front brake discs were still fitted, alternative 290 mm discs of the type used on the factory racers during 1997 were also supplied.

Only detail improvements were made to the engine, primarily in the use of 60 mm throttle bodies and new intake manifolds. Lighter pistons and con-rods, a new crankshaft, and changes to the primary drive spline couplings also featured on the 916R for 1998. There was a new gearshift selector drum to smooth out the gearshift, a new crankshaft inlet oil seal, and timing belt rollers with bigger rims. Completing the alterations was a bigger water radiator and a waterproof cover for the 'P8' injection control unit. With all 916Rs allocated to various distributors, and so many new developments featured, it indicated that the factory was very serious about winning the many domestic Superbike Championships around the world. While the factory bikes had been supremely victorious on the world stage, Ducati was still waiting for those wins in England, Australia and the United States.

New for 1998 was the 748R, primarily constructed for the Supersport World Cup. The tight regulations forbade any alteration to pistons, camshafts, valve sizes or crankshaft, so most of the special parts of the 748R were confined to weight saving. Only 20 of these 170 kg 748Rs were constructed for 1998. However, other engine parts were considerably uprated. The 748R received the 916R gearbox and sintered clutch plates with stiffer springs, as well as nimonic valves and the same water and oil radiators. As with the 916R, only a 180-watt alternator was used and the wiring system located the '1.6' CPU in the front fairing. All the bodywork, sump guard, clutch cover, dashboard, chainguard, exhaust guards, mufflers and intake manifolds were in carbon-fibre. With its racing rev counter the 748R was very much a 916R with a 108 bhp engine and standard wheels, brakes and front forks. When prepared by Gio.Ca.Moto. for Paolo Casoli, power was increased to 117 bhp at the rear wheel.

So successful had the 916SPS been during 1997 that production was increased for 1998, indicated by the four-digit numbered plaque; 1,110 were planned for Europe, plus another 350 996SPs for the United States. As happened every year with the race-derived Desmoquattro, there were many more developments appearing on the 916/748 than on the Super Sport or Monster line. The 916SPS for 1998 received not only the new graphics, but the lighter frame of the Corsa (thinner tubing and no longer constructed in ALS450) and also new Showa forks to accept the revised front brake callipers. An Öhlins steering damper was fitted as well as new titanium con-rods; these were still Pankl but not the racing type that had been used on the 1997 SPS. There was also a new regulator, and a carbon-fibre airbox and heat shields. Other engine specifications remained unchanged. It was really difficult to see how the 916SPS could be improved.

There was one more series of 916 Sennas for 1998. Again with 350 constructed, there were a few changes to differentiate them from earlier versions. Though still with an Öhlins shock absorber, carbon-fibre guards, and fully floating cast-iron front discs, the Senna with its standard 916 engine was now painted black with red wheels. Other changes were a carbon-fibre airbox and heat shield. The 916 Biposto continued very much as before, except for a new regulator, braided steel brake and clutch lines and new graphics. These small changes were also shared with the Senna. For the United States the Biposto was also offered alongside the earlier solo version. 916s for the US were red or yellow.

With the small number of modifications allowed by World Supersport regulations, the 748SP was upgraded to the 748SPS for 1998. Still in yellow, it was closer to the 916SPS than the earlier SP in the use of the new 25CrMo4 frame, titanium con-rods, and new brake callipers. The rear brake and clutch lines were now braided steel, and the engine had bronze valve guides. Other alterations were to the ignition pick-ups and regulator, but general engine specifications were unchanged from the 748SP. The 748SPS still used single injectors and the '1.6' CPU. As tested by *Moto Sprint* in January 1998, the 748SPS achieved 249.4 km/h (155 mph) and produced 97.68 bhp at 10,800 rpm at the rear wheel; this was very little different from the 250.778 km/h the Italian magazine *Super Wheels* had managed from a 748SP in April 1997.

Although under the shadow of the 916, the 748 Biposto continued to account for approximately 50% of Desmoquattro production. This was not really all that surprising because the bikes looked externally identical, and engine performance on the 748 was amazingly strong given its capacity. It was only about 5 mph (8 km/h) down on top speed on a 916 Biposto, but won out with superior handling and a smaller price-tag. The only changes for 1998 were the generic ones of new graphics, new regulator, and no battery charge light on the dashboard. For the United States the 748 came in both Biposto and solo-seat versions, either yellow or red. With one production line designated to producing Hypersports, output was limited by the number of engines that could be built, and total production of 916s and 748s for 1998 was similar to that of the previous year, at 8,744.

To celebrate the end of the distinguished production run of one of the classic modern Ducatis, the 900 Super Sport, a limited Final Edition was produced, 500 for Europe and 300 for the United States. More a continuation of the Superlight concept, the Final Edition was designed to appeal to collectors, or those with strong memories of the earlier classic silver 900 Super Sports of 1975–78. Just like the earlier bikes, the 900SS FE had silver bodywork, but with new graphics, accentuated by black wheels. As with the Superlight, there was only a single seat, upswept Termignoni exhausts, cast-iron floating front brake discs, and carbon-fibre mudguards. Carbon-fibre extended to the chainguard and simplified dashboard (without a battery warning light). The two versions differed slightly in specification: the European FEs used 1997 engines with silver engine covers and Mondial pistons and cylinders with external cylinder oil lines, and also had a carbon-fibre clutch cover and steel brake lines, while the US 900 FEs were produced later, in January 1998, and used 1998-specification engines with grey engine covers and clutch cover. The new Tecnol cylinders were neater

looking as the oil lines were now incorporated internally. As usual for the United States, these bikes had rubber brake lines. The FE would be the last Super Sport with carburettors and was a fitting end to the line that had started back in 1990 for the 1991 season – a line that cemented the position of the Super Sport alongside the Desmoquattro as the Ducati for traditionalists, with emphasis on the street rather than the racetrack.

In late 1997 and early 1998, a final run of 900CRs was manufactured, these (together with the US-spec Final Edition) being the last bikes of this Super Sport series. Still with the earlier Cagiva graphics, 200 red and 200 yellow of these final 900CRs were produced, and they were unusual in that, unlike other 750s and 900s, the oil cooler was still mounted underneath the front cylinder. The 1998-specification 900 engine was also used, with Asso pistons and Tecnol cylinders, and without external oil lines.

The delayed production of the ST2 during 1997 saw it continue into 1998 with only a few changes. Following criticism, a longer gearshift lever was fitted and there was easier access to the spring preload adjuster on the rear shock absorber. In line with all models, it received new graphics. Always envisaged as a companion to the ST2, the ST4 was

an easy amalgamation of the 916 Desmoquattro engine in the ST2 chassis. Although production was delayed until July 1998, this was purely done to enable the new Super Sport to be established. The ST4 was actually ready to go into production earlier than the SS, and was visually similar to the ST2. The engines provided quite different characteristics, however, the smaller, more powerful ST4 having a stronger top-end at the expense of the mid-range.

Where the TPG influence became most noticeable was in the Monster line-up. No longer being available in a limited range of three capacities, the basic Monster was now offered in a variety of options, with three 900s and two 600s alongside the 750 and a 400 for the Italian market. While the Monster M900 continued as before in red, black or yellow, with limited alterations, more interest now lay in the two new Monsters, the 900S and 900 Cromo.

For 1997 the M900 had a number of modifications, notably the addition of a small fairing, and a de-tuned engine. Splitting the 1997 900 Monster idea in two resulted in the M900S and M900. The M900S used the more highly tuned Super Sport engine and featured the handlebar fairing, and the M900 came without a fairing but retained the lower-tuned engine. Both 900s received fully adjustable 41 mm GD 021 Showa forks (the same as the 900SS Final Edition) rather than Marzocchi. Other features shared with the SS were the remote reservoir brake and clutch master cylinders, and the braided steel brake and clutch lines.

Unlike the European 900SS FE, however, the engine of the M900S was full 1998 specification, with Asso pistons and Tecnol cylinders. These engines also used the 520-watt alternator of the ST2. In other respects the M900S was very much like the limited-edition Super Sport. Wheels were black and the front brakes fully floating cast iron, with a rear brake torque-arm. Mudguards, side panels and exhaust heat protector were carbon-fibre, and there was also a lower rear mudguard under the swing-arm. The black continued through to the frame, fuel tank and seat cover.

Resting on the Futa Pass between Bologna and Florence in winter, the 900SS Final Edition was the Superlight concept at its zenith. Although not as efficient as its replacement, it was still an excellent sporting motorcycle.

The expansion of the Monster line-up was exemplified by the M900 Cromo, with a chrome fuel tank. This is a pre-production example at the factory in early 1998.

Undoubtedly the M900S was the most appealing Monster since its first appearance in 1993 and showed that by broadening the concept there was still life left in the now ageing design.

Other 900 Monsters for 1998 fitted below the M900S in specification. The 900 Cromo, so called because of the chrome-plated tank, took the basic M900 with its 71 bhp engine but added the black frame and wheels, and carbon-fibre mudguards and side panels of the 900S. With its carbon-fibre seat cover, the Cromo certainly expanded the Monster idea to new boundaries. Whether factory customising in such a way would be successful for a performance-oriented company like Ducati remained to be seen.

Because of the two new special 900 Monsters, the basic Monster 900 was downgraded slightly. It did receive the Showa forks, remote reservoir master cylinders and braided steel brake and clutch lines, but lost its exhaust heat shield and now had plastic side panels. This led to a converging of the basic 900 and 750 Monsters. The M750 now had dual front disc brakes and came in a choice of silver, red or yellow. In terms of equipment there was little to separate the 750 and 900 except for steel brake lines, remote reservoir master cylinders, a narrower rear wheel, and non-adjustable 40 mm Marzocchi forks.

Even performance was quite similar, the lower power of the 750 engine being balanced by the lighter weight.

For the first time since 1991 the five-speed small crankcase 750 (and 600) engine came in for a small redesign. There was a new wet clutch with the actuation moved to the left side as with all the large-crankcase engines. This meant that the clutch could be disassembled without the need to bleed the hydraulic system. The camshaft belt covers were also like those on the 900, being split to allow for easier belt tension adjustment. The same changes were made to the 600 engine, but only the 750 received an oil-cooler.

Despite the release of the new Super Sport, perhaps the most significant new model for 1998 was the Monster Dark. As an entry level Ducati sold at an extremely competitive price worldwide (but not in the United States), it was designed to attract younger buyers to the marque. Functionally identical to the regular 600 Monster with its single front disc brake, the slightly lower-priced Dark came in three colour combinations, all with a flat black fuel tank: bronze frame and rear shock U-bolt with black wheels; black frame and shock U-bolt with black wheels; and yellow frame, U-bolt and wheels. The Dark also came with an unpainted front mudguard, no footpeg rubbers, and no

seat cover. The new engine provided slightly more sprightly performance than earlier 600 Monsters. *In Moto*, testing a Dark in February 1998, managed a top speed of 182.7 km/h (113.5 mph) with a standing 400 metres in 13.1 seconds at 158 km/h (98 mph). Early reports suggested that the Dark was a bold marketing move, proving particularly successful in Italy. As a long-term strategy, models like the Dark would prove to be important for the company to sell the proposed 40,000 motorcycles a year.

With the demise of the 400 Super Sport, there was an even more basic specification Monster for 1998. However, unlike the 400 Super Sport that had a six-speed gearbox, the M400 used the five-speed 1997 600 engine as a basis, but with smaller pistons and shorter stroke. The clutch modifications that had appeared on the 600 and 750 Monsters did not make it to the 400, this now being the only Ducati with the clutch actuation on the right-hand side of the engine.

The big news at the 1997 Milan Show was the long-awaited 900 Super Sport replacement. It was a tribute to the excellence of the design that the current Super Sport had lasted so long, having existed largely unchanged since 1991. However, the style was now becoming dated, and the suspension and brakes were an older generation to that fitted to the ST2. Also continual noise and emission requirements would eventually see the end of all carburetted engines, and the new Super Sport was the first of the traditional models to incorporate fuel injection. It would also be the first new model conceived after the TPG buy-out.

On 15 December 1996 Massimo Bordi had approached Pierre Terblanche and asked him to co-ordinate the design of the new Super Sport. Terblanche, responsible for the Supermono, was at that stage working in nearby San Marino at the Cagiva Research Centre with Massimo Tamburini. He immediately resigned from CRC to concentrate fully on this project.

Terblanche's brief was quite specific, and much of the existing motorcycle needed to be carried over. This was not only to minimise cost, but also to maintain links with the Super Sport concept because the SS customer was considered very traditional. Thus water-cooling was eschewed, the engine remaining at 904 cc as with the previous version. This was primarily because the extra heat generated from the larger capacity made the cooling marginal for the rear cylinder with an air/oil cooling system. Later plans may call for a larger engine with water-cooling, but in the meantime the venerable Pantah engine continued.

Another carry-over part was the frame, although with a new rear section and a steering head angle 1° steeper at 24°. To facilitate easier development and early production, many components were shared with other models in the range. The instruments and footpegs came from

A symbol of the future: the new 1998 900 Super Sport in front of the huge mural of the ST2 on a factory wall at Borgo Panigale.

the 916, and the front forks and brakes from the ST2. The 43 mm Showa forks were new generation, as were the Brembo brakes. The calliper mounts were wider apart to improve rigidity, and the brake callipers had increased internal fluid capacity. Both the clutch and front brake master cylinders were also a new generation, with revised lever ratios. The Brembo front wheel was from the 916, and the rear from the ST2. A by-product of the heavier forks and bigger silencers was a slight increase in dry weight to 188 kg (414 lb).

The new Super Sport was the first Ducati designed in-house, and the first to use three-dimensional computers and mathematical surfaces. As Ducati had no design studio in Bologna, Terblanche initially went to Futura Design in Birmingham, England, to produce the clay mock-ups. For a Ducati it all happened very quickly, and only 15 months separated the first drawings and the eventual production motorcycle.

There were a number of significant alterations to the engine, notably the use of Weber Marelli electronic fuel injection. To complement the injection there were also new camshafts, with new valve timing. The inlet valve opened 25° before top dead centre, closing 75° after bottom dead centre, and the exhaust valve opened 66° before bottom dead centre, closing 28° after top dead centre. Valve lift was slightly different, and the same as the ST2, the inlet opening 11.8 mm and the exhaust 11.4 mm. While peak power was only marginally increased to 80 bhp at 7,500 rpm, the engine ran more cleanly, particularly at under 3,000 rpm. The new camshafts and injection system meant that there was no need for a high inertia flywheel and a lighter flywheel could be used. The Weber Marelli fuel injection ECU, the '1.5', was the third generation to be used by Ducati, and the first Marelli processor designed specifically for a motorcycle application. Not only was it cheaper and smaller than earlier units, but it could also be adapted for multi-point systems and would eventually be used on those models with twin injectors. Incorporating the absolute air pressure sensor inside the

ECU, it also promised better reliability. With the injection system came a new 10-litre airbox.

Other engine changes for 1998 were new cylinders (Tecnol), pistons (Asso), and piston rings (NPR). There were also new intake manifolds and the ST2 520-watt alternator. Finally the troublesome 31/62 primary drive became the 32/59 (1.84:1) of the ST2 and 916SPS.

Many observers were surprised to see the new Supersport retain a similar frame and the cantilever swing-arm of the earlier bike. However, factory testers believed that for 90% of road use the cantilever rear suspension was a good compromise. It was lighter and simpler than linkage suspension, which was not seen as so critical on a sports bike that would see its use on the street rather than the track. The stroke on the Showa GD132-007-00 shock absorber was increased to 71 mm (up from 65 mm). Also, by retaining the cantilever swing-arm the historical link with the TT2 was retained.

Although his design came in for some criticism, Pierre Terblanche had tried to incorporate many of the features that had made the Supermono an outstanding design in 1992. As he said to me in early 1998, 'It is much more difficult designing a Supersport than a Hypersport because there are many compromises in the style. It cannot be a total racing look with a low front and high rear. A Supersport is by definition a less extreme motorcycle than a 916, more like a Honda CBR600. Though I found this a challenging project I am very pleased with it.'

One of the problems faced by the new Supersport in the marketplace was the typical reaction to something different, and with the Supersport customer being traditional and conservative, this effect was exaggerated. There was a similar reaction to the new logo at the end of 1997. However, with the new bike offering undoubted advantages in the areas of power delivery and handling, it was certain to gain acceptance over time. The new Supersport had no seat cover, but a single-seat version was planned for a later date using a redesigned seat unit. Beginning in

March, production was scheduled for 4,585 units during 1998.

Following on from the success of the 'Ducati Monster Cup' held during 1997, the 1998 Supersport took to the Italian circuits in the 'Supersport Cup'. As with the Monsters, these were prepared by Techna Racing in Rome, the solo-seat Supersports being allocated by lot over a six-race series.

Although Pierre Terblanche was now Ducati Chief of Design, during 1997 a five-year contract was signed with 916-designer Massimo Tamburini to work on a special project. While the 916 was still successful, thought had to be given to its replacement. By 1998 Ducati was still working on the layout, but the trademark desmodromic 90° V twin in a tubular steel frame would undoubtedly be retained. The intention was to develop the engine and frame together to create a unified structure. Other plans looked at combining Massimo Bordi's 1975-thesis four-valve desmodromic cylinder head rocker layout with fuel injection to narrow the included valve angle. Certainly the engine would have horizontally split crankcases for the first time with plain bearings throughout, and would be tilted back in the frame to move it further forward.

Other plans called for a Monster replacement, but in the short-term, 900 Monsters would become fuel injected. As had been the case since 1993, the biggest question mark was over the future of the Supermono. It had always been the intention to produce this as a street bike, but somehow it always got put aside in favour of other projects. Massimo Bordi has consistently been a strong advocate for the street Supermono, and still the idea has not been shelved. By 1998 the engine tooling had been finalised and there would be new crankcases. Even though the original had been designed to accept an electric starter, there was no provision for a sidestand so the crankcases needed to be deeper. It also looked as if the plain main bearings would revert to the regular ball type to maintain uniformity with the other Desmoquattros. The production engine would be larger

than the few racing types, at 595 cc, with a 103 mm bore and 71.5 mm stroke, which was the maximum that the design allowed. Although there had been some air-cooled prototypes, this idea was discarded and the Supermono, if it makes the production line, will undoubtedly be water-cooled with fuel injection. As with all production motorcycles it will be the cost of development and the ultimate price to the consumer that will determine the viability of the Supermono. One plan to reduce costs was the use of a 900 Supersport chassis, but this would not be a recipe for success; a street Supermono needs to replicate the magnificent racer, and no single-cylinder four-stroke will ever produce large amounts of horsepower, so the bike needs to be light. Just as it was always Taglioni's dream to see a production bike with desmodromic valve gear, Bordi's was to see a Supermono street bike. Taglioni's dream was fulfilled in 1969, 13 years after his first desmo, and 21 years after he designed it. Time will tell whether Bordi's fantasy will come to fruition, but it is unlikely that he will have to wait as long as Taglioni.

On 31 July 1998, the Texas Pacific Group and Deutsche Morgan Grenfell announced that they had purchased the remaining 49% of Ducati Motor S.p.A. from Claudio and Gianfranco Castiglioni. This was also the most successful year to date for the company, with net sales of 465.1 billion lire and production up to 28,011 motorcycles. This success would pave the way for a global public offering of shares in March 1999.

1999

In 1998, Ducati triumphed again in World Superbike with Carl Fogarty taking his third World Superbike crown. Ducati also won the Constructors' Championship again, with ten race victories (Chili five; Fogarty three; and Corser two). During the season there had been some problems with Virginio Ferrari, and after five years his contract was not renewed.

So for 1999 there was only one officially supported factory team, that of Ducati Performance, managed by

For 1999 the 996SPS incorporated new decals, black Marchesini wheels, and new front brake discs. The class-leading engine and chassis were unchanged.

Davide Tardozzi. The racing department was reorganised with the formation of a separate company, Ducati Corse, headed by Claudio Domenicali, supplying teams for four different championships: World Superbike, AMA, Supersport, and the Italian Championship. The two riders for World Superbike were Fogarty and Corser, and the 996 racer was little changed from the previous year. Thus it incorporated the revised injection system with three injectors, and the new frame and airbox that had been introduced at Kyalami midway through the 1998 season. There were a few changes to the brakes and suspension, most notably the use of smaller diameter (42 mm) Öhlins front forks and grand prix-style radial brake calipers.

To the surprise of many observers, the 1999 World Superbike 996 and Carl Fogarty were even more dominant than they had been in 1998. The 996 in the hands of Fogarty and Corser won the first five races in the championship and throughout the season Fogarty was so dominant that it was almost a repeat of 1995. He ended up with 11 victories and had the championship sown up before the final round in Japan. Not only was this a tribute to Fogarty's undoubted skill, but the excellence of the continually developed 996 was evidence of the brilliance of the Ducati Corse engineering department. Ducati again convincingly won the Constructors' Championship for the eighth time since 1991.

After finishing fourth in the World Supersport Championship of 1998, Paolo Casoli again rode the Ducati Performance 748SPS. Casoli was also the chief development and test rider for Ducati Corse in the five-round Italian Superbike Championship. Here, new developments were tested on an *Evoluzione* 996 before they made their way to the World Superbike machines. Unfortunately, in World Supersport, Casoli struggled and a crash in Yugoslavia in July saw

him sidelined for much of the season. His best finish was a second at San Marino. He did however, take the Italian Superbike Championship, winning every race.

Though dominant in World Superbike, Ducati still failed to win any important national championships during 1998. Thus for 1999 factory support was extended, particularly in the US. For the AMA Superbike Championship two teams received factory 996s. Anthony Gobert and Ben Bostrom for the Vance & Hines team, and Matt Wait for Fast by Ferracci. Additionally, several teams received support with the new customer 996 Racing Special. These included Lucio Pedercini and Doriano Romboni in World Superbike, and Neil Hodgson and Troy Bayliss for the GSE Racing team in British Superbike. Other 996RSs went to Sean Emmett and John Reynolds of the Reve Red Bull team for the British Championship, Craig Connell and Steve Martin for the Australian Superbike Championship, and Andreas Meklau in the German Superbike Championship. Though Ducati still failed to take the AMA Championship, Steve Martin was finally victorious in Australia and Troy Bayliss won the British Superbike Championship.

The 996SPS continued as for 1998 but for minor changes. These included a three-phase 520-watt alternator, five-spoke black Marchesini wheels, and 320 x 5 mm semi-floating stainless steel front discs on aluminium carriers. As with 1998, production was about 1,500 units. To homologate the revised mid-season frame for World Superbike, 200 Fogarty-Replica 996SPSs were manufactured in July 1998. While essentially standard 996SPSs, these were intended for the UK market and came complete with a full set of racing decals.

There were more changes to the 916. Now nearly five years old, this was updated for 1999 by growing to 996 cc, the stronger crankcases and 98 mm pistons shared with the SPS. The 996 now featured twin injectors, although still with the Marelli 1.6 CPU. Thus the two injectors operated simultaneously and not sequentially as with the P8 system of the 996SPS. The 996 also featured the 36 and 30 mm valves of the SPS, but retained the 916 camshafts. For the 996 the exhaust system was a larger diameter (45 mm), with a 120 x 420 mm silencer. Other features shared with the 996SPS were the three-phase alternator, 32/59-tooth primary drive gears, revised brake calipers with wider lug spacing, and the new front discs. The wheels of the 996 were as before, but were now lighter, being constructed of a higher silicon alloy (GA/Si7). Many of these features were shared with the 748 for 1999, although the front discs were 320 x 4 mm and the 31/62-tooth primary gears were retained. The 748SPS became more of a homologation model for World Supersport racing, being the only model to retain the lighter 350-watt alternator.

Released in October 1998, the ST4 was the most significant new model for 1999. Basically the 916 engine of before was installed in an ST2 rolling

Expanding the Sport Touring line-up for 1999 was the ST4 with a 916 engine. This is the author testing an ST4 at the press launch near Bologna in October 1998.

chassis, creating one of the best performing sport touring motorcycles available. To retain the same weight distribution as the ST2, the cylinder heads were shorter, with the exhaust camshaft moved 10 mm closer to the centre of the engine. Other improvements were shared with the ST2, noticeably the revised sidestand, and 34 mm rear brake caliper. Both models now had lighter wheels, and the three-phase alternator.

As the main new model of 1998, the 900 Supersport continued unchanged, but was joined by a 750 and half-faired varieties. The 750 Supersport used the five-speed 750 Monster engine, but with Weber Marelli electronic fuel injection with a 1.5 CPU. If anything characterised 1999, it was the proliferation of Monsters. This included the expansion of the highly successful 600 Dark to 750 and 900 cc, along with the creation of the City. As before there were two types of 900 engine, both with Mikuni 38 mm carburettors. The Monster 900, 900 Dark, 900S, 900 Cromo, and 900 California received

the 74 bhp version, while the Monster 900 City and 900 City Dark used the small valve 71 bhp engine. The 900S was the highest specification Monster, with an Öhlins shock absorber, steering damper, and numerous carbon fibre parts. The Dark represented the austere Monster with its black frame and matt black tank and guards. In between were the Cromo with a chrome-plated fuel tank, and the City with its windshield, more comfortable seat, higher handlebars and Mandarina Duck bags. Along the lines of the 900 was the Monster 750 Dark, 750 City, and 750 City Dark. These were also supplemented by the Monster 600 City and 600 City Dark. Along with the regular 600 and 750 Monster there were now 15 Monsters in the line-up.

Future production Ducatis could well follow the pattern set by Pierre Terblanche's Mike Hailwood Evoluzione, first shown at the Munich Intermot in September 1998. Terblanche went to AKA design in Hitchin, north of London, where he

Pierre Terblanche with his Mike Hailwood Evoluzione of 1998. This stylistic exercise harked back to the magnificent NCR racers of the late 1970s that Terblanche remembered so well.

developed this project in a mere 11 weeks working with a three-dimensional computer model. Terblanche always had an affinity for the NCR Ducatis of the late 1970s. He admired their elemental simplicity. Thus he used an air-cooled 904 cc two-valve fuel injected 900 Supersport engine as the basis. 'I have a horror for all those ugly wires and tubes everywhere,' says Terblanche, 'that's why I have created sump covers to hide the oil cooler and lines, and placed the ignition coils on the camshaft bearing supports on the cylinder heads. It was my intention to visually clean up the engine.' Special components abounded on the bike including the lightweight diaphragm clutch, 305 mm Selcom (carbon-silesium) front disc, nylon polymer integrated fairing and fuel tank, 80 mm Valeo headlight, television rear view mirror and voice recognition locking system. The frame was specially constructed by the Dutch company

Consistent development of the factory 996 racers again saw them dominant in the World Superbike Championship of 1999. There were smaller diameter front forks and new radial Brembo brake calipers but the engine was largely unchanged from the previous year.

Troll, placing the engine as far forward in the frame as possible, with a 23½° steering head angle, and 1,420 mm wheelbase. The next development will be the establishment of a Ducati Design centre within the factory at Borgo Panigale. This will embrace new technology, with 3-axis and 5-axis computers capable of creating models from design data. These will also be linked to state-of-the-art machining facilities, independent of the manufacturing plant.

On 4 March 1999, an initial public offering of 90,200,000 shares of common stock was issued in the form of shares or American Depository Shares, each representing ten shares. The initial price was 2.90 Euros or US$31.67 per ADS, with the public ownership expected to be 66.1%. There were 900,000 shares reserved

The 996 Corsa was a tribute to the developmental skills of the Ducati Corse team. Although the design was now six years old it was still a most competitive superbike.

Carl Fogarty showed that he was the class act of World Superbike when he easily won his fourth World Championship in 1999. As the most successful rider ever in the series he seems to get better with age.

Following the release of the new fuel-injected 900 Supersport in 1998 came the fuel-injected 750 Supersport for 1999. This (and the 900) was also available with a half fairing as an alternative to the full fairing.

for Ducati employees. This public offering coincided with an overall increase in production and sales, with motorcycle production up 11.7% (to 8,110 units) during the first quarter of 1999. Through until the end of June, 19 new Ducati stores were opened, bringing the total to 39 stores worldwide, including 23 in Italy.

By September, figures were released showing net income for the six months ending June 1999 at an all time high of 11.8 billion lire (US$6.3 million) with total sales of 330.9 billion lire (US$143.4 million). The increased success and profitability of the company was reflected in the increase in production to 19,006 motorcycles to 30 June 1999. This compared with 14,270 for the same period in 1998. These sales also saw an increase in the range of official accessories available.

2000

After such a successful 1999 season, Carl Fogarty again signed with the Ducati Performance team to contest

the World Superbike Championship. Troy Corser's contract wasn't renewed, his place in the team now being taken by Ben Bostrom who had finished second in the AMA Superbike Championship in 1999.

Although there was much speculation in the press regarding a replacement for the 996, it was always obvious that while the machine was still so dominant on the racetrack it was not necessary to replace it. So for the 2000 Model Year there were few surprises when the range was released at the Milan Show in September.

While the 996 and 748 continued largely unchanged, there was a new name for the range, Superbike replacing Hypersport, and an expansion into five separate models. Comprising 29% of sales, the Superbike range, although the most expensive, was also pivotal in maintaining the performance image of the company. As before, the top production model was the 996SPS, this becoming even higher specification for 2000.

While the engine of the 996SPS

was unchanged, chassis improvements included 43 mm Öhlins forks with titanium-coated forklegs, racing-style subframe and lighter Marchesini wheels. The wheels and frame were now painted 'gun-metal' and weight saving measures included a sealed-for-life battery. The dry weight was now only 197 kg (412 lb). On all Superbike models the clutch master cylinder too was the smaller PSC 12 mm, reducing lever effort by providing an increased hydraulic ratio.

Largely unchanged too was the 996, now with 'gun-metal' five-spoke Marchesini wheels, and titanium-coated 43 mm Showa forks. There were more changes to the 748. Available in three versions, the basic 748 was now offered as an entry level Superbike with chrome-plated 43 mm Showa forks, Sach-Boge shock absorber, frame with non-adjustable rake, and gold-painted frame and Brembo wheels. The previous 748 Strada evolved into the 748S with the same engine as the 748 but 'gun-metal' frame and Marchesini wheels, titanium-coated Showa forks and Showa shock absorber. The most exciting new model though was the 748R, replacing the 748SPS. Released in response to the disappointing World Supersport results, the 748R featured the chassis of the 748S (but with the 996SPS Fogarty-Replica frame) and a higher specification engine. With regulations strictly limiting modifications to the camshafts and cylinder head, the 748R featured NC precision machined combustion chambers, 36 and 30 mm valves, and camshafts modelled on those of the 996 racers. These provided inlet and exhaust valve lift of 12.5 and 10.5 mm. The inlet opened 20° before top dead centre, closing 60° after bottom dead centre, and the exhaust opened 62° before bottom dead centre, closing 38° after top dead centre.

Although the 1.6 CPU was retained with single injectors, there were now 54 mm throttle bodies, matching length intakes, and a larger volume airbox. The lower end of the engine was the same as the 748SPS, including the same close-ratio gearbox, 31/62-tooth primary drive and titanium con-rods. However, the 748R received a new water and oil pump. The power was 106 bhp at 11,000 rpm, and a racing upgrade kit was available that increased power to 112 bhp. Soon after the release of the 748R Ducati Corse announced that an official two-man team would contest the 2000 Supersport World Championship. Joining Paolo Casoli was 21-year old Spanish rider Ruben Xaus.

While the ST range, comprising 10% of total sales, was also basically as for 1999, there were a few refinements. Along with revised decals there were new front disc rotors, these being 320 x 4mm on the ST2 with semi-floating aluminum carriers. The ST4 had thicker, 320 x 5 mm front discs and both models featured the new PSC 16 master cylinder and PSC 12 clutch master cylinder. The PSC 16 used technology developed from racing radial master cylinders. To differentiate the ST4 from the ST2, ST4 had 'gun-metal' wheels and frame and the 996 Corse-style electronic instrument panel. There was also a larger, 180/55-17 rear tyre for the ST4. Other features on both STs included a specially made Kryptonite anti-theft padlock housed in a recess under the seat. To fully cater its role as a Sport Tourer, there was now an electrical power output point to supply accessories or a special battery charger that reversed the current flow.

There were few changes to the Supersport for 2000, these being confined mainly to decals, brakes and riding position. With Supersports making up 18% of the Ducati market, the 900 engine was largely unchanged, now incorporating oil jets to spray the underside of the piston crowns. Unlike the 900 Monster for 2000, the Supersport continued with the air/oil-cooled cylinders and still produced 80 bhp at 7,500 rpm. The chassis too continued as before, but the frame and wheels were dark metallic grey and the windscreen was higher. In response to criticism of the rather sporting riding position and to improve comfort, the handlebars were raised by 12 mm, and the neoprene tank protection made thinner. As with others in the range, the clutch master cylinder was reduced to a PSC 12 and the brakes upgraded, the braking system being identical to that of the 1999 748. The 750 Supersport shared all the small cosmetic and ergonomic revisions with the 900. Unlike the 900 though, the 750 retained the PSC 13 clutch master cylinder and gold-painted wheels and frame. The engine and chassis were unchanged except for a Sachs-Boge shock absorber similar to that of the 2000 Monster and 748. As before, both full and half-faired versions were available.

New models for the Year 2000 included the 748R (left) and fuel-injected 900 Monster Special (centre right). These were joined by the ST4 (centre left) and 900 Supersport (right).

For the 2000 Model Year the Monster received its first stylistic revisions since its inception. As the range comprised 43% of Ducati sales these were significant alterations. Pierre Terblanche set about tidying up the styling. This involved a new rear number plate, taillight assembly, and front mudguard. The Cromo was no longer available but instead there was now a Monster Metallic. Derived from the Dark and inspired by the metalflake fashion of the 1960s and 1970s, as evidenced by the desmo 'silver shotgun' and Imola racers, these had metalflake black, blue, red, silver or fuchsia fuel tanks.

All 900 Monsters for 2000 used an engine based on that of the post-1998 900 Supersport. The camshafts were the same but unlike the Supersport the cooling system was now entirely by air, with no oil circulation of the cylinders. Jets directed oil underneath the piston crowns and there was a larger oil cooler to cope with the increased temperatures. The electronic fuel injection system was the same Marelli 1.5 CPU as the 900 Supersport, with 45 mm throttle bodies and new single injectors operating at a pressure of 3 bar. Shared with the Supersport was the 32/59-tooth primary drive. The six-speed gearbox however was different, this being the close ratio unit from the 748 Superbike. New, larger silencers saw the power slightly less than the Supersport at 78 bhp at 8,250 rpm.

While the basic frame was unchanged, 43 mm Showa upside-down front forks replaced the earlier 41 mm units. However, these were now the non-adjustable type and similar to those of the 750 Supersport. There was a steel swingarm and the Sachs-Boge rear unit of before featured on all 900 Monsters except the 900S. In line with the rest of the range the front discs were now 320 x 4 mm with aluminum carriers and the Brembo brake calipers the P4 30-34 with wider bolt spacing. The front

brake master cylinder was the new PSC 16 and the clutch master cylinder a smaller PSC 12mm. Along with the new forks and swingarm came Brembo 17-inch wheels, similar to the ST2.

Terblanche's redesign of the bodywork was notable for the emphasis on ergonomics, long a Terblanche strong point. To enable a more comfortable riding position the fuel tank was narrowed and reshaped where it met the more thickly padded seat. The handlebars too were raised by 10 mm. Cosmetic restyling included a small fairing that incorporated a complete instrument panel including a tachometer. The restyling continued to the rear number plate and taillight assembly. It had taken a few years to get there but the 2000 Monster 900 was undoubtedly the best yet and also the most coherent in terms of styling uniformity. With more power and the same weight as before (187 kg, 412 lb) improved performance in standard form was also promised.

Sensing an expanding market for modified and custom Monsters, Ducati released their version of the ultimate Monster for 2000, the M900S. Although sharing its 78 bhp engine with the regular 900 Monster, the M900S had considerably upgraded suspension. The 43 mm Showa forks were fully adjustable and there was an aluminum swingarm and Öhlins shock absorber. This model also featured a small handlebar fairing, integrated instruments, and carbon fibre mudguards, heat guards and side panels. In line with other range leaders, the M900S was distinguished by the gun-metal-painted wheels and frame.

As before, the 750 Monster was available in Standard, Dark, and City varieties, with the addition of the Metallic for 2000. General styling revisions were shared with the 900 Monster. The 62 bhp engine was unchanged, but unlike the 750 Supersport, still retained the Mikuni

BSDT 38 carburettors. These now featured electrical heaters in the float bowls that were automatically activated at temperatures lower than 3° Celsius. The forks were the same as the regular 900 Monster, these being non-adjustable 43 mm Showa. Braking was still by twin discs, with revised brake calipers and 320 mm discs with aluminum carriers and a new PSC 16 master cylinder. Wheels too were the new lighter three-spoke Brembo, the rear still being 4.50 x 17-inches.

The general alterations to the 600 Monster followed those of the 750 and 900 Monsters. Even the 600, sold as the most basic Ducati, received the 43 mm Showa forks and new Brembo wheels. The braking system too was upgraded, although the 600 still only featured a single 320 mm disc with an aluminum carrier. The Mikuni carburetted 51 bhp engine was identical to the 1999 version but for automatic electric carburettor float bowl heaters and lighter clutch springs to aid city use. Still offered as the Dark and City, these were joined by the Metallic.

As for the future of Ducati, much has changed since the TPG buy out. Most of the management was replaced almost immediately, and there was considerable expansion of the marketing and communications divisions. Worldwide marketing was co-ordinated through joint venture distribution in major markets, particularly Germany, France and Japan. No longer will Ducati be only for the cognoscenti, and more investment and increased profitability will only add to the quality and competitiveness of the product. With exciting developments on the horizon, Ducati should be able to stay at the forefront of motorcycle technological supremacy. After four changes of ownership since 1926, and several more managerial upheavals, this new era for the company offers an exciting scenario for the next millennium.

Appendix – Ducati Motorcycles 1952–2000

Model	Years	Engine	Bore (mm)	Stroke (mm)	Displ (cc)	Comp ratio	Cooling system	Fuel System	Trans	Front Susp.	Rear Susp.	Front tyre	Rear tyre	Wheel base	Weight (kg)
65N, T, S TL, TS	1952-57	1 Cyl, OHV	44	43	65	8:1	Air	Weber carburettor	3 speeds	Hydraulic fork	Twin shock swing-arm				55
98N, T, TS TL, Sport Bronco	1952-62	1 Cyl, OHV	49	52	98	7:1	Air	Dell'Orto carburettor 16mm	4 speeds	Hydraulic fork	Twin shock swing-arm	2.50 X17	2.75 X17	1,245	87
55/R/E	1954-56	1 Cyl, OHV	39	40	48	6.7:1	Air	Weber carburettor	2 speeds	Leading link	Twin shock swing-arm	2.00 X18	2.00 X18	1,092	45
125TV, TS, Aurea	1956-66	1 Cyl, OHV	55.2	52	124	6.8:1	Air	Dell'Orto carburettor 18mm	4 speeds	Hydraulic fork	Twin shock swing-arm	2.50 X17	2.75 X17	1,285	90
Bronco 85T, S	1957-61	1 Cyl, OHV	45.5	52	85	9:1	Air	Dell'Orto carburettor 16mm	4 speeds	Hydraulic fork	Twin shock swing-arm	2.50 X17	2.75 X17	1,245	79
175T	1957	1 Cyl, SOHC	62	57.8	175	7:1	Air	Dell'Orto carburettor 22mm	4 speeds	Hydraulic fork	Twin shock swing-arm	3.00 X17	3.00 X17	1,320	103
175 Sport	1957-60	1 Cyl, SOHC	62	57.8	175	8:1	Air	Dell'Orto carburettor 22.5mm	4 speeds	Hydraulic fork	Twin shock swing-arm	2.50 X18	2.75 X18	1,320	106
48 Sport	1958-65	1 Cyl, 2-stroke	38	42	48	9.5:1	Air	Dell'Orto carburettor 15mm	3 speeds	Hydraulic fork	Twin shock swing-arm	2.25 X18	2.25 X18	1,180	54
100S	1958	1 Cyl, SOHC	49	52	98	9:1	Air	Dell'Orto carburettor 18mm	4 speeds	Hydraulic fork	Twin shock swing-arm	2.50 X17	2.75 X17	1,320	89
125S/T/TS	1958-65	1 Cyl, SOHC	55.2	52	124	8:1	Air	Dell'Orto carburettor 20mm	4 speeds	Hydraulic fork	Twin shock swing-arm	2.50 X17	2.75 X17	1,320	100
175TS Americano	1958-60	1 Cyl, SOHC	62	57.8	175	7:1	Air	Dell'Orto carburettor 22mm	4 speeds	Hydraulic fork	Twin shock swing-arm	2.50 X18	2.75 X18	1,320	108 (118)
200 Elite Americano TS	1959-65	1 Cyl, SOHC	67	57.8	204	8.5:1	Air	Dell'Orto carburettor 24mm	4 speeds	Hydraulic fork	Twin shock swing-arm	2.75 X18	3.00 X18	1,320	111
200 Motocross	1959-60	1 Cyl, SOHC	67	57.8	204	8.5:1	Air	Dell'Orto carburettor 27mm	4 speeds	Hydraulic fork	Twin shock swing-arm	2.75 X21	3.00 X19	1,380	124
250 Monza	1961-68	1 Cyl, SOHC	74	57.8	249	8:1	Air	Dell'Orto carburettor 24mm	4/5 speeds	Hydraulic fork	Twin shock swing-arm	2.75 X18	3.00 X18	1,320	125
250 Diana/ Daytona	1961-64	1 Cyl, SOHC	74	57.8	249	8:1	Air	Dell'Orto carburettor 24mm	4 speeds	Hydraulic fork	Twin shock swing-arm	2.75 X18	3.00 X18	1,320	120

Model	Years	Engine	Bore (mm)	Stroke (mm)	Displ (cc)	Comp ratio	Cooling system	Fuel System	Trans	Front Susp.	Rear Susp.	Front tyre	Rear tyre	Wheel base	Weight (kg)
250 Scrambler	1961-67	1 Cyl, SOHC	74	57.8	249	9.2:1	Air	Dell'Orto carburettor 27mm	4/5 speeds	Hydraulic fork	Twin shock swing-arm	3.00 X19	3.50 (4.00) X19(18)	1,350	109 (120)
48 Brisk Piuma	1962-67	1 Cyl, 2 stroke	38	42	48	6.3:1	Air	Dell'Orto carburettor 12mm	1 speed 3 speeds	Hydraulic fork	Twin shock swing-arm	2.00 X18 (X19)	2.00 X18 (X19)	1,160 (1,170)	45 (52)
80 Setter	1962-64	1 Cyl, 2 stroke	47	46	80	7.1:1	Air	Dell'Orto carburettor 15mm	3 speeds	Hydraulic fork	Twin shock swing-arm	2.25 X18	2.50 X17		62
48, 50 Piuma Sport	1962-66	1 Cyl 2 stroke	38	42	48	6.3:1	Air/fan	Dell'Orto carburettor 15mm	3 speeds	Hydraulic fork	Twin shock swing-arm	2.25 X18	2.25 X18	1,160	49
250 Mark 3	1963-67	1 Cyl SOHC	74	57.8	249	10:1	Air	Dell'Orto carburettor 27/29mm	4/5 speeds	Hydraulic fork	Twin shock swing-arm	2.50 X18	2.75 X18	1,320 (1,350)	110 (112)
48/100 Brio	1964-68	1 Cyl, 2 stroke	38/51	42/46	48/94	7/10:1	Air/fan	Dell'Orto carburettor 12/16mm	3 speeds	Leading link fork	Twin shock swing-arm	2.75x9 3.50x8	2.75x9 3.50x8		63.5/ 80
48/50 SL1/2	1964-69	1 Cyl, 2 stroke	38 (38.8)	42	48/50	7/11:1	Air/fan	Dell'Orto carburettor 15/18mm	3/4 speeds	Hydraulic fork	Twin shock swing-arm	2.25 X19	2.25 X19	1,150	58/61
100 Cadet, Falcon	1964-68	1 Cyl, 2 stroke	51(52)	46	94/98	10:1	Air/fan	Dell'Orto carburettor 18(24)mm	3/4 speeds	Hydraulic fork	Twin shock swing-arm	2.25 X18	2.50 X18	1,160	66
100 Mountaineer	1964-68	1 Cyl, 2 stroke	51(52)	46	94/98	10:1	Air/fan	Dell'Orto carburettor 18(24)mm	3/4 speeds	Hydraulic fork	Twin shock swing-arm	2.50 X16	3.50 X16	1,170	68
250GT	1964-66	1 Cyl, SOHC	74	57.8	249	8:1	Air	Dell'Orto carburettor 24mm	5 speeds	Hydraulic fork	Twin shock swing-arm	2.75 X18	3.00 X18	1,320	125
250 Mach 1	1964-66	1 Cyl, SOHC	74	57.8	249	10:1	Air	Dell'Orto carburettor 29mm	5 speeds	Hydraulic fork	Twin shock swing-arm	2.50 X18	2.75 X18	1,350	116
160 Monza Junior	1964-67	1 Cyl, SOHC	61	52	156	8.2:1	Air	Dell'Orto carburettor 22mm	4 speeds	Hydraulic fork	Twin shock swing-arm	2.75 X16	3.25 X16	1,330	106 (108)
350 Sebring	1965-67	1 Cyl, SOHC	76	75	340	8.5:1	Air	Dell'Orto carburettor 24mm	5 speeds	Hydraulic fork	Twin shock swing-arm	2.75 X18	3.00 X18	1,330	123
125 Cadet, 4 Lusso Scrambler	1967	1 Cyl, OHV	53	55	121	8.4:1	Air	Dell'Orto carburettor 18mm	4 speeds	Hydraulic fork	Twin shock swing-arm	2.50 (2.75) X18	2.75 (3.25) X18(16)	1,160	72 (75)
50 Rolly	1968	1 Cyl, 2 stroke	38	42	48	7:1	Air	Dell'Orto carburettor 12mm	1 speed	Hydraulic fork	Solid	2.00 X18	2.00 X18		42

Model	Years	Engine	Bore (mm)	Stroke (mm)	Displ (cc)	Comp ratio	Cooling system	Fuel System	Trans	Front Susp.	Rear Susp.	Front tyre	Rear tyre	Wheel base	Weight (kg)
250 Scrambler (wide-case)	1968-74	1 Cyl, SOHC	74	57.8	249	9:1	Air	Dell'Orto carburettor 27(26)mm	5 speeds	Hydraulic fork	Twin shock swing-arm	3.50 X19	4.00 X18	1,380	132
250 Mark 3, (wide-case)	1968-74	1 Cyl, Desmo	74	57.8	249	10:1	Air	Dell'Orto carburettor 29mm	5 speeds	Hydraulic fork	Twin shock swing-arm	2.75 X18 (X19)	3.00 (3.50) X18	1,360	127
250 Mark 3D, Desmo	1968-74	1 Cyl, Desmo, SOHC	74	57.8	249	10:1 (9.7:1)	Air	Dell'Orto carburettor 29mm	5 speeds	Hydraulic fork	Twin shock swing-arm	2.75 (3.25) X18	3.00 (3.50) X18	1,360	127
350 Scrambler	1968-74	1 Cyl, SOHC	76	75	436	9.5:1	Air	Dell'Orto carburettor 29mm	5 speeds	Hydraulic fork	Twin shock swing-arm	3.50 X19	4.00 X18	1,380	133
350 Mark 3	1968-74	1 Cyl, SOHC	76	75	340	10:1	Air	Dell'Orto carburettor 29mm	5 speeds	Hydraulic fork	Twin shock swing-arm	2.75 X18 (X19)	3.00 (3.50) X18	1,360	128 (127)
350 Mark 3D Desmo	1968-74	1 Cyl, Desmo, SOHC	76	75	340	10:1	Air	Dell'Orto carburettor 29mm	5 speeds	Hydraulic fork	Twin shock swing-arm	2.75 (3.25) X18	3.00 (3.50) X18	1,360	127
50/100 Scrambler	1969-70	1 Cyl, 2 stroke	38.78/52	42/46	50/98	10.5/11.2	Air	Dell'Orto carburettor 18/24mm	4 speeds	Hydraulic fork	Twin shock swing-arm	2.75 (2.50) X18	3.50x16 2.50x17	1,150/1,180	59/67
450 Scrambler	1969-74	1 Cyl, SOHC	86	75	436	9.3:1	Air	Dell'Orto carburettor 29mm	5 speeds	Hydraulic fork	Twin shock swing-arm	3.50 X19	4.00 X18	1,380	133
450 Mark 3	1969-74	1 Cyl, SOHC	86	75	436	9.3:1	Air	Dell'Orto carburettor 29mm	5 speeds	Hydraulic fork	Twin shock swing-arm	2.75 X18 (X19)	3.00 (3.50) (X18)	1,360	130 (127)
450 Mark 3D, Desmo	1969-74	1 Cyl, Desmo, SOHC	86	75	436	9.3:1	Air	Dell'Orto carburettor 20mm	5 speeds	Hydraulic fork	Twin shock swing-arm	2.75 (3.25) X18	3.50 X18	1,360	130 (127)
125 Scrambler	1971	1 Cyl, SOHC	55.2	52	124	8.5:1	Air	Amal carburettor 20mm	5 speeds	Hydraulic fork	Twin shock swing-arm	2.50 X19	3.50 X18	1,340	105
450R/T	1971-73	1 Cyl, Desmo, SOHC	86	75	436	9.3:1	Air	Dell'Orto carburettor 29mm	5 speeds	Marzocchi fork 35mm	Twin shock swing-arm	3.00 X21	4.00 X18	1,450	128
750GT	1971-74	2 Cyl, SOHC	80	74.4	748	8.5:1	Air	2 carburettors 30mm	5 speeds	Hydraulic fork 38mm	Twin shock swing-arm	3.25 X19	3.50 X18	1,530	185
750 Sport	1972-74	2 Cyl, SOHC	80	74.4	748	9.3:1	Air	2 Dell'Orto carburettors 32mm	5 speeds	Hydraulic fork 38mm	Twin shock swing-arm	3.25 X19	3.50 X18	1,530	185
750 Super Sport	1974-79	2 Cyl, Desmo, SOHC	80	74.4	748	9.65:1	Air	2 Dell'Orto carburettors 40mm	5 speeds	Marzocchi fork 38mm	Twin shock, swing-arm	3.50 X18	3.50 120/90 X18	1,530 (1,500)	180 (189)

Model	Years	Engine	Bore (mm)	Stroke (mm)	Displ (cc)	Comp ratio	Cooling system	Fuel System	Trans	Front Susp.	Rear Susp.	Front tyre	Rear tyre	Wheel base	Weight (kg)
860GT, GTE	1974-76	2 Cyl, SOHC	86	74.4	864	9:1	Air	2 Dell'Orto carburettors 32mm	5 speeds	Ceriani fork 38mm	Twin shock swing-arm	3.50 X18	4.00 X18	1,520	206 (217)
125 Six Days	1975-77	1 Cyl, 2 Stroke	54	54	124	10.5:1 14.5:1	Air	30/32 mm carburettor	6 speeds	Hydraulic fork 35 mm	Twin shock swing-arm	3.00 X21	3.75/ 4.00 X18	1,420 (1,430)	108 (97)
900 Super Sport	1975-82	2 Cyl, Desmo, SOHC	86	74.4	864	9.3:1	Air	2 Dell'Orto carburettors 40 or 32mm	5 speeds	Marzocchi fork 38mm	Twin shock, swing-arm	100/90 (3.50) X18	110/18 (3.50) X18	1,500	205 (190)
860/900 GTS	1976-79	2 Cyl, SOHC	86	74.4	864	9.8:1	Air	2 Dell'Orto carburettors 32mm	5 speeds	Hydraulic fork 38mm	Twin shock, swing-arm	3.50 X18	120/90 X18	1,520	217
350GTL	1976-78	2 Cyl, SOHC	71.8	43.2	350	9.6:1	Air	2 Dell'Orto carburettors 26mm	5 speeds	Marzocchi fork 35mm	Twin shock, swing-arm	3.25 X19	3.50 X18	1,400	170
500GTL	1976-78	2 Cyl, SOHC	78	52	497	9.6:1	Air	2 Dell'Orto carburettors 30mm	5 speeds	Marzocchi fork 35mm	Twin shock, swing-arm	3.25 X18	3.50 X18	1,400	170
350 Sport Desmo	1977-80	2 Cyl, Desmo, SOHC	71.8	43.2	350	9.6:1	Air	2 Dell'Orto carburettors 26mm	5 speeds	Paioli fork 35mm	Twin shock, swing-arm	3.25 X18	3.50 X18	1,400	181
500 Sport Desmo	1977-80	2 Cyl, Desmo, SOHC	78	52	497	9.6:1	Air	2 Dell'Orto carburettorts 30mm	5 speeds	Paioli fork 35mm	Twin shock, swing-arm	3.25 X18	3.50 X18	1,400	185
350GTV	1978-80	2 Cyl, SOHC	71.8	43.2	350	9.6:1	Air	2 Dell'Orto carburettors 26mm	5 speeds	Paioli fork 35mm	Twin shock, swing-arm	3.25 X18	3.50 X18	1,400	183
500GTV	1978-80	2 Cyl, SOHC	78	52	497	9.6:1	Air	2 Dell'Orto carburettors 30mm	5 speeds	Paioli fork 35mm	Twin shock, swing-arm	3.25 X18	3.50 X18	1,400	181
900 Darmah	1978-1984	2 Cyl, Desmo, SOHC	86	74.4	864	9.3:1	Air	2 Dell'Orto carburettors 32mm	5 speeds	Hydraulic fork 38mm	Twin shock, swing-arm	3.50 X18	120/90 X18	1,550	216
900 Mike Hailwood Replica	1979-84	2 Cyl, Desmo, SOHC	86	74.4	864	9.3:1	Air	2 Dell'Orto carburettors 40mm	5 speeds	Marzocchi fork 38mm	Twin shock, swing-arm	100/90 X18	110/90 X18	1,500	210.5
900SS Darmah	1979-80	2 Cyl, Desmo, SOHC	86	74.4	864	9.5:1	Air	2 Dell'Orto carburettors 32mm	5 speeds	Marzocchi fork 38mm	Twin shock, swing-arm	3.50 X18	120/90 X18	1,550	216
500SL	1980-84	2 Cyl, Desmo, SOHC	74	58	499	9.5:1	Air	2 Dell'Orto carburettors 36mm	5 speeds	Hydraulic fork 35mm	Twin shock, swing-arm	3.25 X18	3.50 X18	1,450	180
600SL	1982-84	2 Cyl, Desmo, SOHC	80	58	583	10.4:1	Air	2 Dell'Orto carburettors 36mm	5 speeds	Hydraulic fork 35mm	Twin shock, swing-arm	3.25 X18	4.00 X18	1,450	187

Model	Years	Engine	Bore (mm)	Stroke (mm)	Displ (cc)	Comp ratio	Cooling system	Fuel System	Trans	Front Susp.	Rear Susp.	Front tyre	Rear tyre	Wheel base	Weight (kg)
350XL	1982-84	2 Cyl, Desmo, SOHC	66	51	349	10.3:1	Air	2 Dell'Orto carburettors 30mm	5 speeds	Hydraulic fork 35mm	Twin shock, swing-arm	3.00 X18	3.50 X18	1,450	177
600TL	1982-84	2 Cyl, Desmo, SOHC	80	58	583	10.4:1	Air	2 Dell'Orto carburettors 36mm	5 speeds	Hydraulic fork 35mm	Twin shock, swing-arm	100/90 X18	110/90 X18	1,450	177
900S2	1982-84	2 Cyl, Desmo, SOHC	86	74.4	864	9.5:1	Air	2 Dell'Orto carburettors 40mm	5 speeds	Marzocchi fork 38mm	Twin shock, swing-arm	100/90 X18	110/90 X18	1,500	190
650SL	1984-86	2 Cyl, Desmo, SOHC	82	61.5	650	10:1	Air	2 Dell'Orto carburettors 36mm	5 speeds	Marzocchi fork 35mm	Twin shock, swing-arm	100/90 X18	110/90 X18	1,450	187
Mille MHR, S2	1984-85	2 Cyl, Desmo, SOHC	88	80	973	9.3:1	Air	2 Dell'Orto carburettors 40mm	5 speeds	Marzocchi fork 38mm	Twin shock, swing-arm	100/90 X18	130/80 X18	1,500	198 (193)
750F1	1985-88	2 Cyl, Desmo, SOHC	88	61.5	748	9.3:1 (10:1)	Air and oil	2 Dell'Orto carburettors 36mm	5 speeds	Hydraulic fork 38 (40)mm	Adjustable single shock	120/80 X16	130/80 X18	1,400	175
350F3	1986-88	2 Cyl, Desmo, SOHC	66	51	349	10:1	Air	2 Dell'Orto carburettors 30mm	5 speeds	Marzocchi fork 35mm	Adjustable single shock	100/90 X16	120/80 X18	1,400	165
400F3	1986-89	2 Cyl, Desmo, SOHC	70.5	51	398	10.4:1	Air	2 Dell'Orto carburettors 30mm	6 speeds	Marzocchi fork 35mm	Adjustable single shock	100/90 X16	120/80 X18	1,400	165
Montjuich Lag. Seca S. Monica	1986-88	2 Cyl, Desmo, SOHC	88	61.5	748	10:1	Air and oil	2 Dell'Orto carburettors 40mm	5 speeds	Forc. Italia fork 40mm	Adjustable single shock	12/60 X16	18/67 X16	1,400	155
750 Paso	1986-90	2 Cyl, Desmo, SOHC	88	61.5	748	10:1	Air and oil	Weber twin choke carburettor	5 speeds	Marzocchi M1R 42mm	Single shock, rising rate	130/60 X16	160/60 X16	1,450	195
Indiana 750/650 350	1986-90	2 Cyl, Desmo, SOHC	88 (82) (66)	61.5 (51)	748 (650) (349)	10:1	Air	2 Carburettors 36mm (30mm)	5 speeds	Hydraulic fork 40mm	Twin shock, swing-arm	110/90 X18	140/90 X15	1,530	180
750 Sport	1988-90	2 Cyl, Desmo, SOHC	88	61.5	748	9.5:1	Air and oil	Weber twin choke carburettor	5 speeds	Marzocchi 40mm	Adjustable single shock	130/60 X16	160/60 X16	1,450	180
851 Strada	1988	2 Cyl, Desmo, DOHC	92	64	851	10.4:1	Liquid	Marelli electronic fuel injection	6 speeds	Marzocchi M1R 42mm	Single shock, rising rate	130/60 X16	160/60 X16	1,460	185
851 Strada	1989-90	2 Cyl, Desmo, DOHC	92	64	851	11:1	Liquid	Marelli electronic fuel injection	6 speeds	Marzocchi M1R 42mm	Single shock, rising rate	120/70 X17	180/55 X17	1,430	190 (192)
888 Racing	1989-93	2 Cyl, Desmo, DOHC	94	64	888	12:1	Liquid	Marelli electronic fuel injection	6 speeds	Upside down fork 42mm	Single shock, rising rate	S1016	S1423	1,430	155 (150) (145)

Model	Years	Engine	Bore (mm)	Stroke (mm)	Displ (cc)	Comp ratio	Cooling system	Fuel System	Trans	Front Susp.	Rear Susp.	Front tyre	Rear tyre	Wheel base	Weight (kg)
900 Super Sport	1989-90	2 Cyl, Desmo, SOHC	92	68	904	9.2:1	Air and oil	Weber twin choke carburettor	6 speeds	Marzocchi 40mm	Adjustable single shock	130/60 X17	170/60 X17	1,450	180
906	1989-90	2 Cyl, Desmo, SOHC	92	68	904	9.2:1	Liquid	Weber twin choke carburettor	6 speeds	Marzocchi M1R 42mm	Single shock, rising rate	130/60 X16	160/60 X16	1,450	205
851(888) Sport Production	1990-93	2 Cyl, Desmo, DOHC	94	64	888	11:1	Liquid	Marelli electronic fuel injection	6 speeds	Upside down fork 42mm	Single shock, rising rate	120/70 X17	180/55 X17	1,430	188
350 Super Sport	1991-93	2 Cyl, Desmo, SOHC	66	51	341	10.7:1	Air	2 Mikuni carburettors 38mm	5 speeds	Upside down fork 41mm	Adjustable single shock	120/60 X17	160/60 X17	1,410	173
400 Super Sport	1991-97	2 Cyl, Desmo, SOHC	70.5	51	398	10:1	Air	2 Mikuni carburettors 38mm	5 speeds	Upside down fork 41mm	Adjustable single shock	120/60 X17	160/60 X17	1,410	172
750 Super Sport	1991-97	2 Cyl, Desmo, SOHC	88	61.5	748	9:1	Air and oil	2 Mikuni carburettors 38mm	5 speeds	Upside down fork 41mm	Adjustable single, rising rate	120/60 X17	160/60 X17	1,410	173 (176)
851 Strada	1991-92	2 Cyl, Desmo, DOHC	92	64	851	10.5:1	Liquid	Marelli electronic fuel injection	6 speeds	Upside down fork 41mm	Single shock, rising rate	120/70 X17	180/55 X17	1,430	199 (202)
900 Super Sport	1991-97	2 Cyl, Desmo, SOHC	92	68	904	9.2:1	Air and oil	2 Mikuni carburettors 38mm	6 speeds	Upside down fork 41mm	Adjustable single shock	120/70 X17	170/60 X17	1,410	183 (186)
907IE	1991-92	2 Cyl, Desmo, SOHC	92	68	904	9.2:1	Liquid	Marelli electronic fuel injection	6 speeds	Marzocchi M1R 42mm	Single shock, rising rate	120/70 X17	170/60 X17	1,490	215
900 Superlight FE	1992-98	2 Cyl, Desmo, SOHC	92	68	904	9.2:1	Air and oil	2 Mikuni carburettors 38mm	6 speeds	Upside down fork 41mm	Adjustable single shock	120/70 X17	170/60 X17	1,415	176 (179) (182)
Supermono	1993-95	1 Cyl, Desmo, DOHC	100 (102)	70	550 (572)	11.8:1	Liquid	Marelli electronic fuel injection	6 speeds	Upside down fork 42mm	Adjustable single shock	310/480 R17	155/60 R17	1,360	122
888 Strada	1993-94	2 Cyl, Desmo, DOHC	94	64	888	11:1	Liquid	Marelli electronic fuel injection	6 speeds	Upside down fork 41mm	Single shock, rising rate	120/70 X17	180/55 X17	1,430	202
900M Monster	1993-	2 Cyl, Desmo, SOHC	92	68	904	9.2:1	Air and oil	2 Mikuni carburettors 38mm	6 speeds	Upside down fork 41mm	Single shock, rising rate	120/60 X17	170/60 X17	1,430	185
600M Monster	1994-	2 Cyl, Desmo, SOHC	80	58	583	10.7:1	Air	2 Mikuni carburettors 38mm	5 speeds	Upside down fork 41mm	Single shock, rising rate	120/60 X17	160/60 X17	1,430	174

Model	Years	Engine	Bore (mm)	Stroke (mm)	Displ (cc)	Comp ratio	Cooling system	Fuel System	Trans	Front Susp.	Rear Susp.	Front tyre	Rear tyre	Wheel base	Weight (kg)
600 Super Sport	1994-	2 Cyl, Desmo SOHC	80	58	583	10.7:1	Air	2 Mikuni carburettors 38mm	5 speeds	Upside down fork 41mm	Adjustable single shock	120/60 X17	160/60 X17	1,410	172
888 Racing	1994	2 Cyl, Desmo DOHC	96	64	926	12:1	Liquid	Marelli electronic fuel injection	6 speeds	Upside down fork 42mm	Single shock, rising rate	12/60 X17	18/67 X17	1,430	145
916 Strada	1994	2 Cyl, Desmo DOHC	94	66	916	11:1	Liquid	Marelli electronic fuel injection	6 speeds	Upside down fork 43mm	Single arm rising rate	120/70 X17	190/50 X17	1,410	195
916 Sport Production	1994-96	2 Cyl, Desmo DOHC	94	66	916	11.2:1	Liquid	Marelli electronic fuel injection	6 speeds	Upside down fork 43mm	Single arm rising rate	120/70 X17	190/55 X17	1,410	195
748 Biposto	1995-	2 Cyl, Desmo DOHC	88	61.5	748	11.5:1	Liquid	Marelli electronic fuel injection	6 speeds	Upside down fork 43mm	Single arm rising rate	120/70 X17	180/55 X17	1,410	202
748 SP/SPS 748R	1995-	2 Cyl, Desmo DOHC	88	61.5	748	11.6:1	Liquid	Marelli electronic fuel injection	6 speeds	Upside down fork 43mm	Single arm rising rate	120/70 X17	180/55 X17	1,410	200 (192)
916 Biposto	1995-	2 Cyl, Desmo DOHC	94	66	916	11:1	Liquid	Marelli electronic fuel injection	6 speeds	Upside down fork 43mm	Single arm rising rate	120/70 X17	190/50 X17	1,410	204
916 Senna	1995-98	2 Cyl, Desmo DOHC	94	66	916	11:1	Liquid	Marelli electronic fuel injection	6 speeds	Upside down 43mm	Single arm rising rate	120/70 X17	190/50 X17	1,410	201
916 Racing	1995-96	2 Cyl, Desmo DOHC	96	66	955	12:1	Liquid	Marelli electronic fuel injection	6 speeds	Upside down fork 46mm	Single arm rising rate	12/60 17SC	18/76 17SC	1,420	154
750M Monster	1996-	2 Cyl, Desmo SOHC	88	61.5	748	9:1	Air and oil	2 Mikuni carburettors 38mm	5 speeds	Upside down fork 41mm	Single shock, rising rate	120/60 X17	160/60 X17	1,430	178
916 Racing	1997-	2 Cyl, Desmo DOHC	98	66	996	12:1	Liquid	Marelli electronic fuel injection	6 speeds	Upside down fork 46mm	Single arm rising rate	12/60 17SC	18/60 17SC	1,430	162
996 SPS 996	1997-	2 Cyl, Desmo DOHC	98	66	996	11.5:1	Liquid	Marelli electronic fuel injection	6 speeds	Upside down fork 43mm	Single arm rising rate	120/70 X17	190/50 X17	1,410	190 (198)
ST2	1997-	2 Cyl, Desmo SOHC	94	68	944	10.2:1	Liquid	Marelli electronic fuel injection	6 speeds	Upside down fork 43mm	Single shock, rising rate	120/70 X17	170/60 X17	1,430	212
900 Super Sport	1998-	2 Cyl, Desmo SOHC	92	68	904	9.2:1	Air/oil	Marelli electronic fuel injection	6 speeds	Upside down fork 43mm	Single shock	120/70 X17	170/60 X17	1,410	188
400M Monster	1998-	2 Cyl, Desmo SOHC	70.5	51	398	10:1	Air and oil	2 Mikuni carburettors 38mm	5 speeds	Upside down fork 40mm	Single shock, rising rate	120/60 X17	160/60 X17	1,430	174

Model	Years	Engine	Bore (mm)	Stroke (mm)	Displ (cc)	Comp ratio	Cooling system	Fuel System	Trans	Front Susp.	Rear Susp.	Front tyre	Rear tyre	Wheel base	Weight (kg)
ST4	1998-	2 Cyl, Desmo, DOHC	94	66	916	11:1	Liquid	Marelli electronic fuel injection	6 speeds	Upside down fork 43mm	Single shock, rising rate	120/70 X17	180/55 X17	1,430	215
750 Supersport	1999-	2 Cyl, Desmo, SOHC	88	61.5	748	9:1	Air and Oil	Marelli electronic fuel injection	5 speeds	Upside down fork 43mm	Single shock	120/60 X17	160/60 X17	1,405	183
900M Monster	2000-	2 Cyl, Desmo, SOHC	92	68	904	9.2:1	Air	Marelli electronic fuel injection	5 speeds	Upside down fork 43mm	Single shock, rising rate	120/70 X17	170/60 X17	1,430	185

Index

Pictures are indicated by bold type and colour pictures by the letter 'C'.

Adamo, Jimmy 90, 104, 106
ADAC Eight Hour race 104
Aermacchi 114
Aero Caproni 10
Agostini, Giacomo 46, 56-7, 59
AKA design 169
Alboreto, Michele 128
Alfa Romeo 69, 99
Allied Naval Intelligence 9
Alstare 162
AMA Superbike series 88, 90, 135, 140, 143-4, 168-9, 172
Amaroo Park 85
Amatriain, Daniel 138
American Airlines 161
AMF Harley-Davidson 83, 114
Angel, Ron 57, 63
Antoni, Gianni Degli 13, **14,** 17-18
Armaroli 94-5
Assen 84, 104
Australian Design Rules 154
Australian Superbike Championship 168
Autodromo Dino Ferrari 56
Autodromo Santa Monica 106
Bain & Company 155
Balboni, Amedco 24
Baldwin, Mike 90
Barcelona 24 hour race 15, 24, 26, 63, 69, 106
Bathurst 63, **64**
Battle of the Twins 90, 104, 107, 112, 130
Bayliss, Troy 168-9
Benelli 36-7
Berliner, Joe 34
Berliner 25, 29, 34-5, 37, 41, 50
Bertone 69
Bike magazine 43
Bikers Station 135
Bimota 93, 104, 114-5, 131
Blake, Kenny 57, 63, **64-6**
Bloomingdales 161
BMW 34, 56, 88
Bol d'Or 81, 106, 129-30, 146-7
Bologna 9, 13, 38-9, 85, 94, 99, **100,** 117, **169**
Bologna Motor Show 39, 68, 73, 75, 123
Bologna University 13
Bordi, Massimo 79, 92, 116, 122-3, 126, **129,** 138, 140, 148, 149, **151,** 165, 167
Borgo Panigale 9, **10,** 11, 13, 78, 94, **122,** 171
Bostrom, Ben 168, 172

Brainerd 133
Branch, Jerry 88
Brands Hatch 153
British Superbike Championship 153, 157, 168-9
Broccoli, Massimo 104
Brown, Bob 107
BSA 27, 56
Bultaco 63
Cagiva 93, 99, 108, 112, 114-5, 117, 151, 152, 155, 157, 160-1, 167
Cagiva Morizone 160
Cagiva Research Centre 142, 165
Camp, Vic 37, 56
Canellas, Salvador 63, 81, 83, **84,** 102
Caracchi, Stefano 163
Carcano, Giulio 149
Cardus, Carlos 84, 106
Carini, Mario **15**
Carrachi, Rino 81-2, **83,** 85, 87, 135
Casolari, Danielle 162
Casoli, Paolo **157,** 163, 168, 173
Castiglioni brothers 118, 128-9, 155
Castiglioni, Claudio 114, 155, 167
Castiglioni, Gianfranco 114
Castrol Six Hour race 63, **66,** 67, **84,** 85-6
Cavazzi, Piero 81-2
Cere 36
Cesenatico 36
Chadwick, Dave 18
Chili, Pierfrancesco 144, 167
Ciceri, Sandro **15**
'Club Italia' 128, 155
Cobas, Antonio 107
Coca Cola Eight Hour race 86, **87**
Cologne Show 36, 96, 119-20, 123, 127, 133, 149, 160
Connell, Craig 168
Continental Airlines 155
Cooley, Wes 90
Cooper, John 56
Corser, Troy 143-4, 152, **153,** 156, 162, 167-8, 172, **C**
Costin, Mike 129
Cosworth 129
Coupe d'Endurance 36, 82, 84, 88
Cowan, Errol 57
Cowie, John 86
Cussigh, Walter 104, 106
Cycle 39, 49, 53, 67, 74, 88, 109-10, 115, 117-8, 120-1, 123, 133, 135, 138

Cycle World 27, 71, 77, 111, 119-20, 124, 126, 132, 135, 139-41, 144, 149, 160-1
CZ 39
Daspa 82, 85
Daytona 24, 36, 55-7, 59, 61, 88, 90, 104, 106, 129-30, 135
Daytona Show 35
Del Piano, Guido 102
De Portago 15
Deutsche Morgan Grenfell 155, 167
DKW 17
Domenicali, Claudio 147, 149, **151,** 152, 168
Domiracer 35
Donington 86, 131, 133, 138, 140, 152, 153
Donna Karan 161
Drusiani, Alfonso 13
Ducati, Adriano **9**
Ducati, Antonio 13
Ducati, Bruno **9**
Ducati Concessionaires 19
Ducati Corse 168, **171,** 173
Ducati Elettrotecnica 13, 46, 65
Ducati, Marcello **9**
Ducati Meccanica 13
Ducati Monster Cup 160, 167
Duckworth, Keith 129
Dunscombe, Alan 56
Dunstall Norton 45
Eccher de 57
EFIM Group 81, 87, 94
Emde, Don 56
Emilia Romagna 161
Emmett, Sean 157, 168
Estrosi, Christian 82
European Superbike Championship 136
Falappa, Giancarlo, 134-5, 138, 140, 143
Fargas, Ricardo 26, 84
Farinelli, Aldo 10
Farnè, Franco 18, 24, 28, 36, 81, 87, 102, 104, 106, **107**
Ferla, Osca la 106
Ferracci, Eraldo **135,** 136, 140, 143-4
Ferracci, Fast by 153, 157, 162, 168
Ferrari 15, 161
Ferrari, Piero 128
Ferrari, Virginio 81, 106, **107,** 130, 142-4, 152, 156, 162, 167, **C**
Ferri, Romolo 18
FIAT 10

FIM 36, 46, 61, 144, 147, 152
Fiorio, Giovanni 11, 13
Florence **108,** 162
FMI Sport Production 158
Fogarty, Carl 87, 138, 140, **142,** 143, **144, 146,** 147, **152, 156,** 162, 167-9, **171,** 172, **C**
Fogarty, George 87
Fondo Industrie Meccaniche 9
Forasassi, Primo **107,** 161
Formula 750 55, 57, 63
Foti, Serafino 147
France 174
Francini, Wanes 88, **89,** 102
Frasers 50
Futura Design 166
Gallina, Roberto 36, 56, 114
Galluzzi, Miguel 127, 160
Gandossi, Alberto 14-15, 18-19
Gardner, Wayne 86, **87**
Garriga, Juan 106-7, 130, 140
Gattalone 156
Genoa 162
Gensler 162
German Pro Superbike 153
German Superbike championship 140, 168
German TüV 79
Germany 174
Gia.Ca.Moto 157, 160, 162-3
Gianesin, Pietro di 140, 152, 156
Gilera 17-18, 44
Giro d'Italia 13-15, 20, 22
Giovanardi 36
Giugiaro, Giorgetto 30, 33, 63, 69, 72, 76, 79, 108
Gobert, Anthony 163, 168
Giuliano, Ermanno 45, 56, 82
Gramigni, Alessandro 153
Grands Prix
Belgium 18
Britain 140
Canada 57
Greece 57
Isle of Man 18
Italy 18, **20,** 21, 24, 36
Nazione 46
San Remo 46
Sweden 17-19
Ulster 19
US 35
Granie, Marc 104
Grant, Mick 59-60
Grant, Ron 56
Grasetti, Silvio
Grau, Benjamin 63, 81-3, **84,** 104, 106, 110

Graziano 15
Groundwork South East Ducati 157
GSE Racing team 168
Guareschi, Vittoriano 157
Guichon, Philippe 104
Hailwood, Mike 19, 21, 46, 55, 82-3, **84-9**, 91, 150
Hailwood, Stan 19, 21
Hale, Mike 152, 162
Halpern, Abel 155
Hannah, Bill 28
Harley-Davidson 34, 88, 161
Hill, Damon 127
Hitchin 169
Hockenheim 133, 143
Hodgson, Neil 152, 156, 162, 168
Holden, Robert 107, **150,** 151
Honda 45, 49, 51, 56, 63, 81-4, 86, 107, 140, 147, 152, 159, 167
Huguet 81
Husqvarna 114
Imola 17, 21, 46, 49, 51, 55-6, **57-60,** 62-3, 67-8, 70, 76, 81-2, 85-6, 88, 146
In Moto 165
International Six Days Trial 39
Inzinger, Alfred 144, 152, 156
Isle of Man 18, 21, 28, 37, 46, 83-5, 88, 90, 103-4, 150, 158
Istituto di Riconstruzione Industriale 9
Italian Championships 19, 45, 60, 88, 102, 104-6, 138, 168
Italian Carabinieri 35
Italian FMI 14
Italian Trophy team 39
Italjet 42, 72, 77
James, Jamie 135
Japan 174
Jarama 136
Jawa 39
Jeffries, Tony 56
Jerez Eight Hour race 106
Juan, Enrique de 84, 104, 110
Kavanagh, Ken 20-1
Kawasaki 51, 56, 63, 67, 82, 86, 88, 104, 140
Kelly, Terry 67
Kipp, Tom 162
Kneubüller, Bruno 59-60
Kocinski, John 147, **152,** 156
Korhonen, Pentti 82
Kyalami 168
Laguna Seca 106, 112
La Moto 112
Laverda 14, 49, 56, 61
Lega, Mario 84
Le Mans 81, 83, 147
Leoni, Reno 90, 104
Liège 24 Hours 104
Linto 37
L'Istituto Mobiliare Italiano 9
Loigo, Claudio 59
London 169
London Show 90
Lucchiari, Mauro 140, 143-4
Lucchinelli, Marco 83, 106, 112, 114, **130-1,** 132-3, 138
Magee, Kevin 107
Mallol, Jose 82, 84
Mallory Park 86
Mandolini 15, 26
Manhattan 162
Maoggi, Giuliano 14
Maranello 161
Maranghi 15
Marconi, Guglielmo 9
Mariannini, Giovanni 82-3
Martin, Steve 168-9
Matchless 45
McGregor, Graeme 104, 106

Meklau, Andreas 140, 143-4, 168
Menchini, Paolo 102
Mengoli, Luigi 116, 148
Mercedes-Benz 17
Merkel, Fred 132
Mertens, Stéphane 135, 138, 140
Milan 10, 12, 114, 155, 162
Milan Show 10, 12, 20, 22, 61, 63, 69, 77, 88, 95-6, 98-9, 110, 114, 128-9, 142-3, 155, 165, 172
Milano-Taranto 13-15, 22
Mille Miglia 15
Miller, Sammy 18
Milvio, Arnaldo 45, 51, 57
Minoli, Federico 155
Misano 81-3, 87, 102, 106-7, 112, 148, 152, 156, 161
Mladin, Matthew 157
Modena 13, 36-7, 56, 58-60
MO magazine 125
Mondial 13, 17-18
Montano, Dr Giuseppe 12
Montemaggi, Marco 161
Montessa 17
Monti, Baldassare 133
Montjuich Park 26, 63, 81-4, 104-7, 110
Monza 10, 18-19, 21, 46, 106, 115, 134, 144
Morri, Giuseppe 114
Mortimer, Charles 37
Mosport 57
Motociclismo 42, 61, 99, 113, 115, 123, 128, 136, 138, 158, 160
Moto Guzzi 18, 35, 44-5, 49, 56, 77, 150, 161
Moto Morini 39, 114
Moto Sprint 163
Motor Cycle 55, 95
Motor Cycle Mechanic 85
Motor Cycle News 75, 92, 98, 119, 153, 155, 157
Motor Cycle Weekly 79, 90, 96
Motor Cycling 26
Motorcycling Monthly 74
Motorcyclist 112, 115, 118, 124, 128, 136, 138, 141, 144
Motorcyclist Illustrated 54
Motorrad 61, 77, 93, 109, 111, 117, 126, 149
Moto Sprint 111-2, 120, 124, 138-9, 141-2
Mototrans 21-2, 26, 38
Mugello 81-2, 104
Munich Intermot 169
Mussolini 9
MV Agusta 17-19, 37, 44, 46-7, 49, 51, 56, 59-60, 161
Nation, Trevor 104
NCR 59, 81, **82,** 83-8, 90, 93, 135, 170
Neilson, Cook 61, 85, 88, **90**
Neiman, Marcus 161
Nepoti, Giorgio 81, **82,** 135, **136**
Nero, Nani 87
New York Stock Exchange 155
Nicholls, Roger 84-5
Nieto, Angel 102
Norton 49, 56
North West 200 158
Noyes, Dennis 95
Nürburgring 84-5, 104
Olympia Show 45
Oran Park 86
Österreichring 104, 134
Oulton Park **85,** 87
Palomo, Victor 83-4
Paris–Dakar race 118
Parlotti, Gilberto 36
Parquay, Michael 147
Pasolini, Renzo 36, 56, 115

Paton 37
Paul Ricard 130
Pazzaglia, Sauro 83, 102
Pedercini, Lucio 168
Pedretti, Giuliano **107, 131**
Performance Bikes 119
Pergusa 133
Perugini, Carlo 81, 83, 88
Pickrell, Ray 56
Pirovano, Fabrizio 153
Pirovano, Maurizio 144
Pocono 90
Polen, Doug 135, **136,** 138, 140, 144
PS magazine 126, 142, 143, 146-7
Provini, Tarquino 18
Read, Phil 21, 45-6, 56, 84, 86
Recchia, Mario 81-2
Rechtenbach, Dieter 106
Regazzoni, Clay 128
Reiss, Wolfgang **85**
Reve Red Bull 157, 168
Revs magazine 68
Reyes, Luis 104, 110
Reynolds, John 157, 168
Ricardo 46
Ricci, Mauro 88
Riccione 37
Rimini 36-7, 114, 142, 161
Rippa, Enzo 26
Ritter, Paul 90
Roberts, Kenny 107
Roche, Raymond 133, **134,** 135, **137,** 138, 140, 154
Rogers, Alistair 28
Romboni, Doriano 168
Rome 162
Ruiz 81
Russell, Scott 140
Rutter, Tony 103-4, **105-6,** 107
Rymer, Terry 153
Saarinen, Jarno 56, 59-60
Saltarelli, Carlo 82
San Marino 142, 165, 168
Savona 162
Scaysbrook, Jim 85-6
Schilling, Phil 24, 61, 88, **89**
Schlachter, Richard 90
Scuderia Speedy Gonzales 36
Sebring 12 Hour race 28
Sears Point 90
Seeley, Colin 45-6, 49, 55
Senna, Ayrton 146
Sheene, Barry 56, **60,** 127
Siata 10
Silverstone 46, 55, 86
Simonetti, Rolando 138, 140
Simpson, Ian 157
Slight, Aaron 107
Slinn, Pat **87,** 103
Smart, Paul 46, 56, **57-8,** 59, **60**
Società Scientifica Radio Brevetti Ducati, 9
Spa 18
Spaggiari, Bruno 15, 18-19, 36-7, 39, 45-6, 56-7, **58-60,** 95, 138
Spairani, Fredmano 45-6, 51, 55-6, 60
Spanish Endurance Championship 84
Spencer, Freddie 90, 144
Sport Rider 150
Sports Motor Cycles 84-5, 87
Sprayson, Ken 21
Stevens, Thomas 157, 163
Studio Italdesign 69
'Supersport Cup' 167
Supersport World Cup 153, 156-7, 162-3
Super Wheels 159, 163

Surfers Paradise race **66**
Surtees, John 21, **C**
Suzuki 56-7, 87, 104-5, 107, 159
Sydney 162
Sydney Motorcycle Exhibition 108
Taglioni, Fabio 13-14, **15-17,** 18, 20-2, 25, 29-30, 32, 34-6, 38, 44-6, 49, 51, 55-8, 61, 63, 76, 79, 81, 88, 92, 94-6, 102-4, 106, 114, 118, 129, 147, 148, 151, 167
Taglioni, Narina **15**
Tait, Percy 56-7
Tamarozzi, Ugo 10
Tamburini, Massimo 93, 114, 121, 142, 165, 167
Tardozzi, Davide 131, 136, 138, 140, 144, 148, 149, 152, 162, 167
Tartarini, Leopoldo 20, 42, 69, 72, 77, **C**
Taveri, Luigi 18-19
Techna Racing 160, 167
Tejedo, Alejandro 82, 84
Terblanche, Pierre 149, 165-7, 169, **170,** 174
Texas Pacific Group 167, 174
Thruxton 81
Tonkin, Steve 84
Tokyo Show 122, 134
Treviso 162
Triumph (motorcycles) 49, 56
Triumph (cars) 29
Troll 171
Tumidei, Ing. 76
Turin 162
Two Wheels magazine 39, 42, 53
Ubbiali, Carlo 18-19
Uncini, Franco 60, 114, 138
Vance & Hines 157, 162
Varese 101, 114, 117
Velocette 27
Venanzi, Arturo 82
Verlicchi 82
Vignelli, Massimo 161
Vila Real 104-5
Villa, Franco 18, **20,** 21, 24-5
Villa, Walter 56, 83, 104-5, **106**
VM Group 78, 94, 114
Vuillemin, Didier 104
Warrian, John **66,** 67
Webster, Marvin 88
Weibel, Edwin 140
Whitham, James 143
Williams, Ron 103
World Championships (races)
  Endurance 63, 81-2, 84, 101, 104-6, 130, 163
  Formula 1 (TT1) 81-4, 106, 86-7, 101, 112
  Formula 2 (TT2) 103-4, 118
  Formula 750 83
  Superbike 81, 84, 120, 122, 127, 129, 131, 134-8, 141-4, 151-2, 156-8, 162, 167-8, **169-70,** 172
  Supersport 157, 168-9, 172-3
World Ducati Weekend 161
Wynne, Steve 84-5, 87, **89,** 102-3, 150
Xaus, Ruben 173
Yamaha 57, 59, 63, 86, 88, 104, 115, 153, 157
Yoshimura Suzuki 90, 135
Zacchiroli, Michele 162
Zell, Sam 155
Zell Chilmark Fund 155
Zeltweg 131, 143
Zitelli, Glauco 10